THE MYSTERY OF HUMAN SEXUALITY

THE MYSTERY OF HUMAN SEXUALITY

By

John Abbam Nyarko

Box 400

Cape Coast, Central Region

+233203667766/+233577318998

Publisher: Golden Power Inc.

Cover Design: Kennedy K. Amponsa

Copyright ©2021 by John Abbam Nyarko.

All rights reserved. Except permitted under the Ghana Copyright Act of 2005 (Act 690), this book is sold subject to the condition that it shall not, by way of trade or otherwise, be lent, resold, hired out, or otherwise circulated without the publisher's prior consent in any form of binding or cover other than that in which it is published.

First Edition: November, 2021.

First eBook Edition: December, 2021.

ISBN-13:978-1-257-90629-1

> If you purchased this book without a cover, you should be aware that this book is stolen property. It was reported as "unsold and destroyed" to the publisher, and neither the author nor the publisher has received any payment for this "stripped book".

To all those who encouraged me while writing this book, especially Kennedy Kwame Amponsa, who designed the cover of the book and all those who yearn to understand the complexities of human behaviors and sexualities.

Table of Contents

PREFACE vi

ABOUT THE AUTHOR x

ACKNOWLEDGEMENT xii

INTRODUCTION xiii

CHAPTER I 1

CHAPTER II 28

CHAPTER III 63

CHAPTER IV 113

CHAPTER V 144

CHAPTER VI 215

CHAPTER VII 243

CHAPTER VIII 276

CHAPTER IX 329

CHAPTER X 391

BIBLIOGRAPHY 413

PREFACE

The issue of sexuality raises some levels of hostilities amongst people for various reasons. Some of these reasons can be attributed to discomfort the issues stir in others consciously or unconsciously as well as religious and sociocultural influences. As a result, there have been diverse reasons propagated in the defense for why one thinks a specific sexuality is supposed to be the normative for which everyone irrespective of your gender should promote.

The subtle hostilities have forced many to murder others or reject families, relatives and friends in the name of cleansing the abominations brought or being sought to bring by these "alien" sexual beings. Others have broken the thriving and fruitful relationships they once had with others, and have developed enmity towards them as a result of sexuality difference either in practice or in opinions.

There are many different stories witnessed in our everyday societies in relation with people's sexuality. For example, there is an incident of a father murdering his 14-year-old son for his indifference of the socially accepted sexuality; there is also the classic case of parental hate for their children who are not 'normal' like them—that is, their sexualities don't subscribe to heterosexuality. There was an incidence where a mother who has three sons with two heterosexuals and one homosexual; found the homosexual son disdainful, thus subjecting the homosexual son to police-military brutalities where this homosexual son was being battered with wantons by these security personnel, forced to arm press under duress and electrocuted with their electrocautery.

Finally, there are incidents where people have been subjected to mob justice especially in Africa for being sexually different without the states in Africa taking up the matter to bring the perpetrators to justice. These deafening silences by the masses and the harm and its related threats caused onto those sexually different from the larger society needs actions and remedies if we are to build inclusive, thriving and fostering societies irrespective of our social constructions.

To better unravel the mysteries behind sexuality, there ought to be the need to avoid all forms of prejudices and the deception of oneself that we can know, understand and explain humanity and its choices completely with either religion or psychology without flaws or some inconsistencies that deviates from the majority. The belief that man is a master to fully and perfectly understand what informs his/her own psychological makeup and nature is what creates bridle and needless animosity towards one another especially when they don't share in our values, beliefs and systems either as a larger society or as a cult. We must understand that we are all unique and complex in our own makeup, but the complexities shouldn't cause chaos and hatred towards one another especially when the actions and inactions of the other doesn't affect us directly or to a higher degree.

To adequately comprehend the mystery of the human sexuality, man should understand that s/he isn't a god or goddess but a fallible being who is still in the learning processes to understand who s/he is exactly especially in the areas of sex and its related desires for which form part of the human existence. It is an undeniable fact, that human beings are sexual species just like animals except their have the ability to alter their environment. Humanity cannot determine the course of life with precision.

It is this specificity of thinking, that humanity ought to show empathy to people who are different from the masses. Humanity should come to a stage where they can say that we are still learning how the different species of the human race act, behave, perceive, see and feel things. Even the gods cannot comprehensively understand humanity to the extent of determining the course of life without challenges.

We must continue to search on how to better understand others different from the broader masses without judging them or thinking we are better than them in terms of thoughts, perceptions or self-esteems. We are all humans first and diversified in categorization of social constructions such as gender, morality, sexuality, religion, race, languages, intelligence, status etc., yet we are all going to one-day return to wherever we came from. This must and ought to be the guiding principle for humanity to live harmoniously with one another irrespective of whatever visible differences.

As perfect as we may deem ourselves to be, we are unable to fully explain our inactions and actions, yet we tend not to feel the same way for those we perceive to be different from us in all social construction categorizations. It is a fact that every living specie exhibits an affinity for others of similarity irrespective of the comparisons of any categorization. To understand sexuality affinity of each specie, humanity developed imagination, fortitude, and creative abilities which could be lacking in them at other times of human evolution.

Sexuality and its desires cannot be suppressed for it could be likened to a river, which even though damned, causing the flowing water's force to be channeled into the penstock of a giant dynamo. If it does not find a useful outlet, it will eventually break through the restraining walls and cause destructions. Matters of sexuality offers humanity the opportunity to appreciate and tolerate their differences just as man has tolerated differences in terms of race, status, age and gender and still lives and coexists peacefully with one another. It directly and indirectly informs humanity of how diverse the nature of humanity is and that the human nature isn't fixated or unidirectional or binary, therefore the need to appreciate the different shades of nature itself.

This book seeks to inform readers on the complexities of sexuality, and how best humanity can understand and appreciate human sexuality in its diverse forms and avoid foisting a social normativity of sexuality on all irrespective of their makeups which are complex. The differences existing amongst humans in the field of sexuality, do not interpret as others are superior to others nor others are "normal" humans than others nor are others psychologically deficit for which the larger society ought to help them or force them to change to fit into the social normativity.

ABOUT THE AUTHOR

John Abbam Nyarko is a Ghanaian author who is a graduate of the Kwame Nkrumah University of Science and Technology (KNUST) with a degree in Political Science. He is an alumnus of the prestigious college, Prempeh College and of the X-Culture Academy where he serves as an Academic Coach.

He is a Columnist and a Humanitarian. John currently works with the Centre for National Culture, (CNC), Cape Coast, a department of the National Commission on Culture, NCC as a Marketing Researcher.

Other books by John Abbam Nyarko

Central Region: Origins & Culture

The Mythical Pandora of Africa

Corruption and Good Governance Deficits—Ghana's Developmental Challenges

The Law and the Politics of the State: Politics, Law and Policies of the State

ACKNOWLEDGEMENT

The ideas in this book are the results of my thoughts, readings and understanding over the many years since I become very conscious of my personality, temperament, immediate surroundings and to think on my own. I am very appreciative of all former teachers, colleagues, and friends both casual and intimate I have known and been in contact with over the years. I have benefitted enormously from the encouragements of my former lecturers especially Dr. George Meyeri Bob-Milliar of the Kwame Nkrumah University of Science and Technology, KNUST for exposing me to my writing and critical thinking abilities while I was a student.

I am also grateful to my editors for their continued encouragement for this book, support and comments.

I would also like to thank all my beta-readers who either read the entire manuscript or portions of it and their comments.

INTRODUCTION

Sexuality is a topic that often sparks controversies as for a long time, societies have perceived sexuality to have one form only—heterosexuality. Any sexuality that diverts from the sexuality of heterosexuality is met with harshness and disgust from the conservatives and those called naturalists or essentialists. Many at times, families feel betrayed and disappointed when their members whether close or distant open up to them that their sexuality diverts from the normative sexuality of heterosexuality. Parents have disowned their once loving kids; others have murdered or contributed to the depression of those whose sexuality diverts from the normative principle of sexuality sometimes leading to suicides of these people. Interestingly, for some countries, the issue of sexuality has forced them to enact draconian laws or seeking to enact legislations that touches on the basic right of pursuit of happiness of humanity even when the chase of this pursuit of happiness doesn't endanger the very fabric of society and its security.

The Mystery of Human Sexuality is a book designed to unravel the different perceptions surrounding the sexuality of humanity and to inform society that the divergence of sexuality need not warrant battles of superiority in order to determine those who are psychologically deranged or amoral as well as being consciously dead. Nobody can claim superiority over another because of sexuality for even the race of humanity isn't in one form nor does humanity come in one shape or form even in the body. The concept of morality is subjective and relative just as the concept of conscience, thus it is erroneous for one to think s/he could determine the manner in which a person ought to experience sexual desires for which they ought to be whipped in line.

The book is based on extensive research of academic journals, books and research papers from diverse fields. The focus is mostly on rationality using science and the realities from human experiences. It is the belief and conviction of the author that the various reasons and explanations espoused would go a long to break down the needless impregnable walls built consciously around us when examining sexuality which could be blamed on the propagation of one concept from many centuries and entrenched through education and laws spanning over millennial. The author further hopes that the book helps to throw away all surrounding myths on sexuality when it doesn't bother on heterosexuality and to show humanity how to be empathetic and gracious to those whose sexual desires deviates from what had been termed as the "normal" sexuality for centuries.

The book delves into the areas of religion, socio-historical, law, psychology, sociology and science to demystify the concept of all forms of sexuality as being "normal" just like heterosexuality. The book has 10 chapters which explores all the relevant areas that seek to explain the controversial subject matter: sexuality. Chapter 1, 'Sexuality and Gender' discusses the controversies surrounding the duo terms as well as the theories of these terms while looking at the historical periods and their attached meanings by various scholars.

Chapter 2, 'Religion and Sexuality' examines the relationship between the two as well as the independence of both terminologies. It further explains why sexuality is very important in the arena of religion for which religious fanatics and groups become very intrigued and emotional when there are discussions on the matter of sexuality.

Chapter 3 examines the foundations and perceptions of psychoanalysts when examining sexuality. The chapter looks at the arguments made by the earliest proponents of sexuality as well as those that have sought to explain the concept in relation to contemporary times. There is an examination of the Freudian School of Sexuality and the anti-Freudian School of Sexuality.

Chapter 4 looks at the scientific evidences espoused in explaining the mystery surrounding sexual orientation. The chapter focuses on biological explanations and findings of geneticists and other scientists in trying to help humanity understand the complexities of the human sexual orientation.

Chapter 5 examines the legal reasons for regulating sexuality and the reason why all legal related regulations and policies are focused on homosexuality. The chapter delves into the history of homosexuality criminalization and why there is the perceived hostility for people who advocate for the recognition of non-heterosexuals as well as offer protection for them under national, regional and international laws. Finally, the chapter examines why certain laws by states are dangerous and draconian, thus infringes on the human rights of these minorities.

Chapter 6 focuses on the sociological explanations ascribed to sexuality. The chapter examines the role society plays in matters of sexuality and the impacts of such social roles. The chapter further focuses on the discrimination meted out to non-heterosexuals by examining the underlining rationales as well as the ordeals that women in general experience as 'less' citizens with equal powers and authority as their male counterparts.

Chapter 7 discusses issues of intersex and how society should be encouraged and educated on the need to support such people as well as respect them for their differences.

Chapter 8 examines the commonest sexually transmitted diseases and sexually transmitted infections. This section looks at the various causes of the commonest sexually transmitted diseases and focuses more on HIV as well as on Herpes and Chlamydia.

Chapter 9 explores some successful non-heterosexuals from the civilization of societies who have helped shape and make life very comfortable for humanity. The chapter looks at these non-heterosexuals spanning from philosophy to science to literature to business.

Finally, chapter 10 focuses on how both heterosexuals and non-heterosexual humans can live harmoniously together without the majority putting the lives of the minority at risk just because of sexuality differences.

CHAPTER I

SEXUALITY & GENDER

"If repression has indeed been the fundamental link between power, knowledge, and sexuality since the classical age, it stands to reason that we will not be able to free ourselves from it except at a considerable cost"—
Michel Foucault

Humans are sexual beings and therefore, a person cannot be understood without considering the individual's sexuality and gender. The issue of sexuality and gender has been ravaging amongst scholars and the general public for centuries. While others consider identification of a person visibly by using the gender ascribed, others have espoused the need to ask the person how s/he desires to be addressed. Sex is a word that defines the biological differences between male and female—the visible difference in genitalia, the related difference in procreative functions. Gender, on the other hand is a matter of culture; it refers to the social classification into "masculine" and "feminine".

Sexuality and gender are separate organizing features of social relations but intersects by mutually constituting, reinforcing, and naturalizing each other. Gender relations include how masculinity and femininity are mapped onto identities and how gender is displayed, enacted, and understood—naturalize, reinforce and support sexuality, which includes the display, enactment and meanings of sexual desire and sexual identities. Likewise, sexuality simultaneously naturalizes, reinforces and support gender. There is a dissonance between how people talk about sexuality and how they enact sexual desires. While people tend to think of sexualities in terms of stable homosexual and heterosexual identities, their everyday experience of sexuality, at least to some degree emerged at the end of the nineteenth century.

ORIGIN OF THE CONCEPT 'SEXUALITY'

The term 'sexuality' is first recorded in the English lexica at the end of the eighteenth century based on the noun, sex and adjective, sexual. Sex as a word came into the English language in the fourteenth century as a borrowing partly from French and partly from Latin. Its primary default meaning has been *'either into the two main categories (male and female) into which humans and many other living things are divided on the basis of their reproductive functions'*.

The earliest use of the adjective, sexual (another borrowing from Latin) in the seventeenth century also referred to characteristics peculiar to the feminine. The earliest time sexuality is used in reference to humans is in 1833 and defined as '*sexual nature, instinct, or feelings; the possession or expression of these*'.

Therefore, sexuality is something usually assumed to be inherent in all normally functioning human beings although usage differ considerably according to the user's standpoint on a number of sociocultural issues. The second major sense of sexuality as applied to human beings was in 1897 and defined as '*a person's sexual identity in relation to the gender to which he or she is typically attracted, the fact of being heterosexual, homosexual, or bisexual; sexual orientation*'.

Nonetheless, the word is employed and interpreted by people with a wide variety of different social, political, moral and religious standpoints which affect how different people conceptualize human sexuality.

The term labels a concept that is at the center of an important battlefield in modern sociocultural debates. In addition, the mapping between word and concept is different and relatively uncomplicated—what is at issue is how various persons define or conceptualize 'sexual nature, instinct, or feelings', as well as crucially what people understand to be 'normal', 'natural' or part of the expected or accepted spectrum of human feelings and behaviors.

Whenever sexuality is given a possessive pronoun, the construction typically refers to a particular sexual identity to which a person is (usually if not uncontroversially) taken to belong categorically; uses typically refers to recognition, suppression, repression, or acceptance of one's sexuality. Surprisingly, the usage of sexuality has been referred to homosexuality; if a person is described as 'hiding his/her sexuality', this nearly always means that the person is hiding the fact that s/he is homosexual (however this is construed) not that s/he is hiding hers/his heterosexuality. Such uses are often, but not always from contexts with clear echoes of psychoanalytical discourse.

Hence, individuals are conceptualized as possessing a sexuality in two distinct yet overlapping meanings: one is a matter of group membership (heterosexual, homosexual, bisexual); the other, a question of sexual urges or instincts and how these affect behaviors.

Sexuality is a comprehensive term that translates into the sum total of a person's wellbeing and humanity. An understanding of a person's sexuality is an all-encompassing process. Therefore, sexuality education is important. Sexuality education is a lifelong process of acquiring information and forming attitudes, beliefs and values about identity, relationships and intimacy. It encompasses sexual development, reproductive health, interpersonal relationships, affection, body language and gender roles. Sexuality education addresses the biological, sociocultural, psychological and spiritual dimensions of sexuality.

Sexuality as a word was coined during the Victorian period. From the 1880s, sexologists such as Richard von Kraft-Ebing and Havelock Ellis pioneered as well as studied and categorized sexual preferences; they created terms including heterosexuality, homosexuality and nymphomaniac. Significantly, this began a new opposition of homo- and heterosexuality, categories which did not simply denote sexual behavior but were perceived as central to each person's identity. A look to the history of these terms will show that there is rather a social construction than naturality when emphasis is placed on sexual identity.

Sexuality can be defined as the emotional embodiment of a person which influences who s/he behaves and interacts with others sexually as well as in terms of sexual attraction. Sexuality isn't a matter of sexual preference nor a definition of a person sexually based on who the individual engages in any erotic affairs with. Sexuality and its response is a complex matter which can only be understood based on the interaction of psycho-social factors as well as other factors such as interpersonal, cultural, physiological and gender-influenced processes. Gender is a product of sexuality and not the definite mold in which men and women learn different sexualities.

Both males and females show similar central nervous system pathways of activation, deactivation and similar neurotransmitter activities when it comes to sexual desires. Changes of sexual responses are similar in both traditional gender and these changes are reinforced by behavior, experiences and neuroplasticity. As humans, we must understand that there is no normative standard for engaging one's sexual activities. There is nothing like sexual dysfunction when it comes to differences in patterns of sexual experiences and activities irrespective of it is different from what may be satisfying to other people or what is considered normative in a given culture or subculture.

Furthermore, having unrealistic expectations of one's sexual experiences and desires, or inadequate sexual stimulation does not warrant a person labeled as sexually dysfunctional. However, people who show lack of knowledge (e.g. about a person's own body, sexual functioning and sexual responses), psychological or behavioral differences (e.g. negative attitudes towards sexual activities, adverse past sexual experiences, poor sleep hygiene, overwork) are those who suffer some sexual dysfunctions. The origin and maintenance of sexual dysfunction involves both physical and psychological factors.

Many people experience gender incongruence and these incongruences take the forms of: (a) a strong desire to be, or an insistence that the person is of different gender; (b) a strong dislike of a person's own sexual anatomy or anticipated secondary sex characteristics, or a strong desire to have the sexual anatomy or anticipated secondary sex characteristics of the desired gender; and (c) make believe or fantasy plays, toys, games, or activities and playmates that are typical of the experienced gender rather than the assigned sex.

These three factors must go-in-hand since the presence of the third and the nonappearance of the other two is merely a description of gender variant behavior. People with gender incongruence are at an increased risk for psychological distress, psychiatric symptoms, social isolation, school dropout, loss of employment, homelessness, disrupted interpersonal relationships, physical injurious, social rejections, stigmatization, victimization and violence.

Before the second half of the 20th century, understanding of the relationship between gender and sexuality was an expression of an underlying natural universal order: a natural order that relies on notions of sexual and gender dualism/binaries (male/female); heterosexual/homosexual; masculine/feminine, and based on complementary polarity. This way of understanding is based on the naturalist approach or the principle of consistency. This paradigm assumes that sex-gender-sexuality relate in a hierarchical, congruent and coherent manner, and that a *"disruption in expectations to one element presumably carries consequences for all the other elements"*.

These approaches see sexuality as a product of gender, i.e. gender is pregiven and located in the gendered/sexed body. However, by the 1960s and 1970s, sociological works on sexuality and gender emerged which critiqued the "essentialist" modes of thinking and signaled a shift away from biologically based accounts of the relationship between gender and sexuality to social analysis. This period opened up the analysis of the relationship between the two. It achieved this through contesting and pluralizing the associated meanings to the two terminologies, therefore depicting that these are social rather than pregiven, natural categories and associated with denaturalizing understanding of their relationship in certain important respects.

Others have argued that gender is the central organizing principle in the process of constructing sexual selves and scripts. In order words, gender is constitutive of sexuality and sexuality can be seen as expressive of gender simultaneously. This is evidential when males frequently express and gratify their desires to appear "masculine" through certain forms of sexual conduct as well as majority of feminine stewing their relationships as one of the critical mechanisms by which gender inequalities are constituted and maintained.

At this juncture, gender is a social product, the result of a hierarchy where men have systematic and institutionalized power and privilege over women as a form of social classes. Gender under this paradigm with its associated categories would not exist if social divisions did not exist and that the binary divide between heterosexuality and homosexuality are derived from gender. Furthermore, some scholars have also argued that gender is an effect of sexuality. This thinking is grounded in psychoanalysis following Freud. Sexual desires and sexual object choices are seen as pivotal, the driving force to the formation of gendered subjectivity through Oedipal processes.

From this perspective, to become "properly gendered" is to become heterosexual; and one of the key proponents of this perspective was MacKinnon who argued that sexuality constitutes both gendered subjectivities and the gendered power inequalities in society:

"sexuality is that social process which creates, organizes, expresses and directs desire, creating the social beings we know as women and men, as their relations create society...Women and men are divided by gender, made into the sexes as we know them, by the social requirements of heterosexuality, which institutionalizes male sexual dominance and female sexual submission. If this is true, sexuality is the linchpin of gender inequality."

All these perspectives are concerned with the articulation of gender's relationship to sexuality yet it is heterosexuality that these perspectives are focusing on as the form of sexuality. These views are based on institutionalization of heterosexuality gender. The dominance of separation of sexuality and gender emerged in the 1990s when the assumption that gender and sexuality have to be examined together was challenged. This period saw the emergence of queer theories which called for a 'radical separation' of gender and sexuality; and one of such influential proponents of this perspective was Rubin who postulated that sexuality cannot be adequately theorized through gender and that there ought to be separation between the two concepts on the premises that they are domains of independence from each other.

Rubin argued that "*gender affects the operation of the sexual system, and the sexual system has had gender-specific manifestations. But although sex and gender are related, they are not the same thing, and they form the basis of two distinct arenas of social practice*". This perspective allows the possibility to think about sexualities without genders where sexual desires, practices and identities do not depend on a person's gender for their meaning. Under this view, the opposition of homosexuality and heterosexuality is understood and solved.

The final perspective is that gender and sexuality conflate. There is the assumption that gender intersects with sexuality so fundamentally as to negate the possibilities of abstracting either one. All these perspectives espoused to explain gender and sexuality all have flaws and it is time for new perspectives to be propounded where such theories address how gender's links to sexuality is not determinate or unidirectional, but complex, dynamic, contigent, fluid and unstable.

Such propounding of perspectives/ frameworks must allow for more complex analyses of the dynamics, historically and socially specific relationships between sexuality and gender as well as the gendered and sexualized specificity of their interconnections. This is necessary as it would avoid the tendencies of the past which presumed western frameworks and therefore acknowledge also non-western localized understanding of gender's relationship to sexuality that shows the complexities and variability involved.

Gender and sexuality intersect at four various levels of social construction: at the level of social structures through institutions such as the law, education, the state and the media; at the level of social and cultural meaning; at the level of everyday interactions and routine practices; and at the level of the individual subjectivities. These intersecting levels may be different due to the differences in aspects of social constructions and even variations within each levels.

Without gender categorization, sexual desires and identities cannot be categorized; nonetheless sexuality is intelligible to us outside of a gendered discourse and we can think of gender without invoking sexuality. History has shown that in the early 20th century, men could have sex with other men and still be thought of as "normal" (heterosexual) by virtue of their masculinity. 'Real' or 'authentic' homosexuals were 'fairies', who were thought to be 'like-women', and therefore desired sex with 'normal men'. Therefore, during this period, gender conformity was taken as a sign of 'real' homosexuality. In this historical period, it was difficult to imagine gay macho or lesbian femininity.

The label "homosexuality" had been classified as mental disorder until the last 50 years when various national and regional classifications removed diagnostic categories which defined homosexuality as a mental disorder. This shift in scope can be attributed to emerging human rights standards and the recognition that homosexual behavior is a widely common aspect of the human behavior as well as the lack of empirical evidence to support pathologization and medicalization of various variations in sexual orientation expressions. Same-sex orientation isn't a social deviance or a disease since there is currently no empirical evidence from international studies to demonstrate that the condition has demonstrable public health and clinical utility effects as seen in a disease label.

There is also the issue of sexual maturation disorder. This disorder is defined as: (a) uncertainty about one's gender identity or sexual orientation and (b) distress about the uncertainty rather than about the particular gender identity or sexual orientation. With people facing this order, empirical evidence has consistently shown that, there emerges same-sex orientation with time with the process usually beginning in late childhood or early adolescence. Nonetheless, evidence shows that often there is a substantial level of anti-homosexual stigma and ostracizing in the environment of such people causing stress for them.

Lesbians when compared to gay men tend to recognize and act upon their same sex attractions at a later age. Majority of lesbians have had heterosexual sex and marry heterosexually. However, gay men who marry their fellow gay men tend to stay married longer and happier in marriages. Lesbians greatly marry heterosexually as a result of reflecting a history of accommodation to males in a sexual context or of conformity to social expectations.

This phenomenon may reflect men's relatively higher rates of all kinds of sexual activities coupled with women's relative lack of personal freedom to live as they choose. Sexual orientation is beyond the choices of gender of a romantic or sexual partner. In some people, sexual attraction is not immutably determined from birth. Some lesbians are motivated at least by their desires to escape the limited social roles available to women as well as the social meanings attached to gender role plays.

Another reason for the presence of visible lesbians is the growth of lesbians-feminist cultures of the 1970s. During that period, many women seemed to come to the consciousness of their same-sex attraction through the vehicle of the women's movement. Lesbians don't think being a lesbian is about sexuality but rather defines lesbianism as the entire sense of self as a woman. Lesbianism is not sexism as sexism is not the sole determinant of amorous relationship. The expression of sexual identity encapsulates sex, personal, interpersonal, and family dynamics, biological or innate predisposition.

Same-sex erotic attraction is probably necessary but not sufficient condition for homosexual identity or behavior. Most women tend to be bisexuals in behavior and/or experience bisexual fantasies and attractions. Women who often identify as lesbians and live a lesbian lifestyle do so for reasons more complex than merely strength of erotic attraction. Erotic attraction in bisexuals (i.e. women) in marriages are more fluid and variable. These evidences of research cast doubt upon the widely held belief in the inflexibility of sexual orientation and attraction over time, as well as the assumption that homosexual attractions are developed and "fixed" in early childhood or adolescence.

The implication is that lesbianism is a multifaceted lifestyle, and not merely the expression of a biological imperative or of some intransient orientation fixed early in childhood. Lesbians are similar to heterosexual women when it comes to relationship i.e. about 82% of lesbians tend to live with their partners and show enormous commitment in relationships as they see commitment as the most important value in their lives.

Again, lesbians are socialized like most women to value relationships more highly than careers or other life goals. Nonetheless, they tend not to be more successful in relationship than heterosexual women or gay or heterosexual men. Single lesbians tend to have less frequent sex and fewer different partners compared to gay men. However, until the advent of AIDS, gay men were probably more sexually active than any sexuality groups. When compared to heterosexual women, lesbians tend to be more sexually responsive and more satisfied with sex they do have.

Lesbians satisfaction to sex is speculated to be caused by their sexual techniques which tend to be sensuous, less genitally and orgasm focused, and less oriented to vaginal penetration. Lesbians do not seem to have pervasive sexual problems as against heterosexual women except they do seem to have strikingly low rates of sex within long-term committed relationships. Research available suggest that a third of lesbians in relationships of 2 years or more tend to have sex once a week or more with close to half of lesbians in relationships of over 5 years having once a month or less.

This is in contrast to heterosexual couple, where two-thirds of couples together for more than 5 years have sex once a week or more, and only 15% had sex once a month or less. Furthermore, gay men tend to have slightly less sex in their primary relationships than do heterosexual couples; however gay males tend to have the highest rate of extramarital sex. Lesbians tend to prefer bugging, cuddling and other nongenital physical contact to genital sex as compared to heterosexual women. Lesbians couples mostly prefer oral sex as against manual stimulation and tribadism and tend to have extramarital episodes as do heterosexuals. Both lesbians and gay men tend to have sex in the context of "open" relationship in contrast to the secretive sexual encounters common amongst heterosexuals.

Lesbians tend to have higher terminations of relationships because of dissatisfaction and low sexual frequency. This absence or decrease in sex tend to cause partners to leave the relationship or seek an outside lover and eventually leaving her partner for that lover. Women naturally tend to value committed relationships highly at the expense of individual differentiation and development of personal autonomy and emotional self-sufficiency. They tend also to fuse sex and love together to express their sexuality in the context of emotional pair-bond. Also, lesbians tend to interpret sexual attraction as love and move in with partners within days or weeks denying them the chance to explore the practical feasibility of the relationship. These reasons account for the higher endings of relationships among lesbians.

Masculinity is defined and affirmed through heterosexual display and getting women. This is the normative society and this explains why the larger society see homosexuals and their allies as sexual aliens. For heterosexuals, what affirms masculinity is being sexually active while affirmation of femininity is being sexually attracted to men. It is why heterosexual marriages are considered important venues since they shore up the notions of the self as an appropriately gendered person.

There are more than 5 million gay marriages globally with more than one-eighth of humanity being homosexuals. Due to societies inability to recognize homosexuals, homosexuals are forced to engage in heterosexual marriages or willingly engage in heterosexual marriages and relationships to cover up and secretly engage in their sexual orientations. Such homosexuals are eventually caught in some form of homosexual activity or because they need to relieve the psychological stress of the situation. The battle of sexuality is based on the quest for sexuality supremacy.

Heterosexuals in their quest to lord their sexuality over homosexuals and transvestites, directly position those whose lifestyle or sexual orientation don't conform to the heteronormativity as impure, deviant or even evil; or through what is known as "normalizing logic" in which homosexuals who approximate heterosexual ideals are tolerated and granted some level of social inclusion/privilege precisely due to this action of upholding heterosexual ideals. Homosexuals who enter into heterosexual relationships do so as a result of a desire to have children, to have a "normal" life, to avoid rejection by family and friends, to deny a homosexual identity, and/or to potentially "cure" homosexuality.

Such reasons emanate from a set of social conditions that connect heterosexuality, gender, reproduction and marriage to normalcy. Heterosexual relationships stabilities thrive on males' responses-desires and commitment-which become a testament to how well a woman is doing femininity. This implies that such stability and satisfaction are linked to the sustained performance of women as objects of male pleasures. A lot of homosexuals are trying to marry because of social constructs such as trying to avoid being labelled as a social misfit, and the assertion by heterosexuals that being homosexual is "too risky and embarrassing" as well as the fallacy of to be right and normal and build a successful and fulfilling life, you ought to be heterosexual. Heterosexual males think women do not like sex and postulate that having sex with a man as a woman is a duty to obey, hence they fail to pay attention to whether heterosexual women enjoy it or not. Heterosexual women think they ought to look attractive and good to men hence doing everything to get that attention which sometimes lead to depression.

Homosexuality is an immutable part of a person, however, the presence of a homosexual desire does not erase the possibility of heterosexual physical intimacy. Therefore, both sexual desires can coexist without taking on second-class status. The expression of love cannot be in one form nor can it be an either/or scenario. Love is beyond binary projections of gender. Understanding sexuality entails developing a more fluid understanding of love and sexuality, recognizing that people and relationships are not an either/or equation. The battle and supremacy consciousness of one's sexuality over another is based on ideologies that make only certain courses of action seem appropriate and that provide criteria for self-evaluation.

These ideologies are thus a kind of roadmap for interaction, creating modalities for what a good person should be and do. The difference between heterosexual and homosexual relationship is clear. While heterosexuals look for commitment, stability and love of value, homosexuals look for passion and nothing concrete. Until the homosexuals begin to understand this, society isn't ready for them. History has proven that parents are sometimes to blame for the sexuality of kids especially before they reach the age of 6 years.

This evidence is found in the concept of sworn virgins. A sworn virgin is a village girl raised as a male because the family has no male children. This is similar to the concept of transvestites and transgender. While transsexuals are seen as people going against societal norms to perform their desired identities, in the case of sworn virgins, it is the patriarchal society that forces the women to live as males. Historically, sworn virgins have lived and still live in the mountainous regions of Northern Albania and neighboring Kosovo, Serbia and Montenegro. These virgins swear an oath of celibacy and adopt male dresses and roles in society. Some are made so by their parents in childhood, usually because there is no male child to inherit and rule the patriarchal household; others choose to become sworn virgins themselves to avoid marriages to undesirable husbands.

The evidence of sworn virgins provides a perfect case of "gender as a culturally constructed concept". Therefore, gender could be described as "a set of repeated acts within a highly rigid regulatory frame that congeal over time to produce the appearance of substance, of a natural sort of being". These sworn virgins may not marry due to their oath of celibacy, and some flirt with women and challenge anyone who impugns their masculinity with violence. These sworn virgins function to reinforce the patriarchal structure. It is as if one of the regulatory rules of hegemonic culture—that a man must be born with a male sex body—were trumped by another—that a household must have a man as its head.

During 19th century, as homosexuals and crossdressers increasingly moved to large urban centers, physicians were called upon by police for guidance on how to deal with these "sexual deviants". This proliferation of "perverse sexualities" was met with a corresponding rise in the social control of sexuality which was increasingly medical and psychiatric. Hence, it is usually asserted that the medical community developed the nomenclature for the classification of sexual "perversities". The medical community set out the standards by which to assess sexual behaviors, but these classifications probably influenced people's behavior as they conformed to medical expectations or refused them.

Homosexuality became conceptualized due to the feminist challenges to Victorian sexual ideology, changing social conditions, and emerging "homosexual consciousness". Victorian sexual ideology saw men as sexually "active" and women as sexually "passive" and anyone who transgressed this rule was considered a "sexual invert". Homosexual relations therefore were seen as pathological since it disrupted the Victorian sex roles. The Victorian period which is in the 19th century saw the enjoyment of sex as an exclusively male prerogative.

Also, the term, lesbian before 1900 was used both as an adjective and a noun to describe women who desired and pleasured each other more than a century and half before the OED's first entry of meaning. Later researchers and theorists began to confront this sex/gender system by either conceptualizing sexual inversion in purely sexual terms such as transvestism which was largely believed as a heterosexual phenomenon or by differentiating sexual objects from aims.

Confusion of sexualities began in the late 1800s and continued to early 1950s. During these times, medical discourse did not simply adjudicate the difference between homosexuals, heterosexuals' transvestites. It is a misconception of most people who believe in the separation of sexes into male and female or the dualism of the sexes. It is erroneous if an individual perceives that both are fully separate entities, one from the other. However, the constantly present merging of both into one is the core for the genesis and substance of a person's personality. Thus, everyone is bisexual in the sense of personality since we have both male and female qualities; and that all of us to a greater or lesser degree work towards the blending of these two dimensions of experience.

While human race is acknowledged to be man and woman, it can be distinguished by the sexual organs, physical characteristics, sex drive, and emotional characteristics; there are also "mixed forms" labelled "sexual intermediaries". These mixed forms are due to variations in sexual organs (such as hermaphrodite), physical characters (such as gynecomastia), sex desires (as in passive heterosexual men) and emotional characteristics.

In conclusion, gender and sexual categories must be seen not as binary logic of which understanding of gender and sexuality are fixed, coherent and stable but rather should be seen as plural, provisional and situated. This shift is crucial. The issue of sexuality is puzzled and to comprehensively appreciate and understand the scope of sexuality, we can learn about socialization, as well as the possible contributions of biology, including genetic and prenatal influences.

CHAPTER II

RELIGION & SEXUALITY

"The lust of the flesh directs those desires [of personal union], however, to satisfaction of the body, often at the cost of a real and full communion of persons"—Pope John Paul II

In order to understand reality, and eventually have to change circumstances, we must be prepared to abandon certainties and to accept tempolabile pain of an increased uncertainty about the world. Having the courage to confront the unknown is a precondition for imagination, and the capacity to imagine another world is an important element in social progression of our humanity. Sexual behavior regulations for many religious groups have been a critical concern at various periods of civilization and in cultural settings.

Religion is a complex and multidimensional concept, and capturing its essence within a single definition can prove challenging. Religion of recent has been viewed as a political arena as well as mobilizing fear, misunderstanding and unrest about the role of religion in the lives of humanity. Therefore, religion is an essential tool in unravelling and appreciating the complexities of sexuality not only due to the gruesome violence being perpetuated on people in the name of or against religion, but also due to the sizeable portion of societies having actively to participate in religious activities as well as possessing strong religious inclinations and identifications.

The desire for life's meaning and purpose and interest in love, relationships and fulfillments associates sexuality knowledge and education with the domain of the religious. Religion has indeed proven to be not truly public, democratic and inclusive when it comes to understanding sexuality since a significant group feels its values and views are simply ignored. Religion's understanding of sexuality should be based on critical thinking. Critical thinking here involves, not just breadth, but it requires logical rigor and the reasoned assessment of evidence and arguments. Should religion go beyond mere preaching and indoctrination, its converts and adherents must have critical orb and leverage on what they learn. They must be open to and informed about alternative ways of making sense of the world and lives of all.

The etymology of religion today comes from the Latin word 'religionem' translating as *'respect for what is sacred, reverence for the gods, sense of right, moral obligation, sanctity',* obligations, the bond between man and the gods'. However, in classic antiquity, religion comes from the word 'religio' believed to be the ultimate origin, and signifies conscientiousness, sense of right, moral obligation or duty to anything. In the antiquate and medieval worlds, the etymological Latin root, 'religio' was understood as an individual virtue of worship in mundane understanding and never as doctrine, practice or an actual source of knowledge.

In general, religio meant broad social obligations to the family, neighbors, rulers, and even towards God. The Romans used religio not in the context of a relation towards but as a range of general emotions such as hesitation, caution, anxiety, fear, feelings of being bound, restricted, inhibited; which came out of heightened attention in anything mundane. By the 13th century, the term 'religio' came into the English lexicons as religion meant *'life bound by monastic vows or orders'*. However, it was not until the 16th century that religious things were separated from worldly things when compartmentalizing the concept of religion. In the

1500s, the concept of religion for the first time was used to distinguish the sphere of the Church and the sphere of civil authorities.

Contemporary concept of religion as an abstraction entailing distinct sets of beliefs or doctrines is a current invention in the English language dating from the 17th century as a result of events such as the splitting of Christendom during the Reformation of Protestants and globalization in the age of exploration which involved contacts with different foreign cultures with non-European languages such as the Japanese and Hindu cultures. The concept of religion was formed in the 16th and 17th centuries yet ancient sacred texts like the Christian Bible, the Islamic Qur'an (Koran) and others did not have a word or a concept of religion in the original languages and neither did the people or cultures in which these sacred texts were written.

For example, amongst the Hebrews, Judaism as a religion today was not having a clear distinction in terms of interpreting it as a religion; it meant a religious, national, racial and ethnic identity. One of its central concept is 'halakha' translating as law guiding religious practices and beliefs and many aspects of daily life. Jews saw Judaism or Jewish identity as being about an ethnic or national identity, and did not entail a compulsory belief system or regulated rituals. It was in the 19th century that Jews began to see their ancestral culture as a religion, analogous to Christianity. In the Qur'an, the Arabic word 'din' is often translated as religion in modern translation, nonetheless until the 1600s, it was expressed as law.

The role of religion in sexuality understanding gives opportunities to critically think about one's own and others' understanding, perspectives and explanations of sex and sexuality. This is crucial because of cultural diversities of societies, hence it is not easy to circumscribe a concept of sex and sexuality that is shared by all. The opportunities to engage in comparative perspectives of sexuality can begin the process of disrupting dominant discourses of sexual identities such as heterosexuality as identity presented as the 'normal' sexuality. Religion must understand that conversation and frames about sexuality cannot be based on just religion but must also be based on scientific and medical paradigms. This positions the specific and varied meanings of sexuality among different individuals central to sexual identity formation.

This framing can allow societies to project a privilege status for themselves, model a more incisive examination of particular sexualities and sexual identities and learn new forms of sexual knowledge. Christians who profess to know God must be guided also that they are not the deciders of one's sexuality and should resort to 1 Samuel 2:3 'Talk no more so exceedingly proudly; let not arrogancy come out of your mouth: for the LORD is a God of knowledge, and by him actions are weighed' as well as 2 Chronicles 1:10 'Give me now wisdom and knowledge, that I may go out and come in before this people: for who can judge this thy people, that is so great?'

One such approach is to facilitate ideology-critique. Ideology-critique is the invitation of a commitment on the part of the thinker to reflect critically on personal beliefs, listen respectively to any oppositional beliefs and to then engage in cultural negotiation where the aim is respect, inclusion and knowledge gain as depicted by JESUS CHRIST in John 8:1-11.

Religion sees sexuality that deviates from heterosexuality as a source of problem and causer of diseases. People who employ religion as challenging dominant, hegemonic sexual ideology see the subject as their way of confirming how sexuality should be as a way to demonstrate the relations of power and knowledge, and to exert control. When hegemonic factors are at play in sexuality education, and people are not exposed to counter hegemonic meanings to sexuality, dynamics of subordination, subjection and binary oppositions become engrained in the minds of impressionable youth and adults which become the logical way of thinking and passing 'common sense'.

Humanity has an innate drive towards deviance that can be restrained by bonds to social groups. It is believed that whenever people are bonded to a social organization with conservative norms regarding sexual behavior which contemporary religion seeks to effect, they would or should be motivated to delay sexual behaviors. Religion tends to act as a social control as it provides consequences for deviances such as guilt, shame, public embarrassment, and thrust or expectation of divine punishment. Knowledge and fear of such consequences provide motivation for conformity to religious doctrines.

Nonetheless, the deviation of the religious norms is thought to cause a person to experience these repercussions and the associated psychological distress, a type of 'cognitive dissonance'—a mental state that arises when there is a contradiction between when an individual believes and how s/he behaves. Consequently, for a person to decrease the strain of cognitive dissonance, s/he typically changes either the behaviors or cognitions that are in opposition.

It is important to understand that cognitive dissonance is not automatic when a person holds opposing beliefs. However, they must have an awareness of the inconsistency to feel discomfort. Not everyone experiences cognitive dissonance to the same degree. Other factors that affect the degree of cognitive dissonance include the types of beliefs, the values of the beliefs and the size of the disparity.

The degree of such regulations by any religious sect depends on either the group concerned is sectarian and consequently world-rejecting in its response to the prevalent societal values or whether it has become established and has become world-affirming. In addition, the perceived goals of a religious group and the manner it wants to achieve such latent goals also influences how the group will control sexual expressions amongst its members. The issues that determine sexual behavior regulation of most religious bodies are to test members' 'fidelity' to religious doctrines and practices, verifying the depth of spiritual maturity of their members, specifying the manner of interpersonal relationships particularly across the gender division, and as a means of subordinating members to the leaders.

Religious groups believe they ought to regulate sexuality due to the notion that modern evilness in the society is associated partly with sexual perversion which if left to proceed unchecked and unchallenged could cause the destabilization of the society. The sexual revolution that characterized the second part of the 20th century did challenge the restraint on sex, and thereafter, moral puritanism about sex, except in the case of pedophilia, ceased to be a public matter but was rather transferred into the domain of an individual's privacy.

For example, the Mormons practiced a form of polygamy that encouraged mating to populate the world with godly children. Likewise, in Nigeria, the College of Regeneration founded by Emmanuel Odamosu possessed sexual privileges and authority over any female member or the wives of his members in the 1960s and 1970s. Women submitted themselves to Odamosu and even had children for him and considered it as part of their religious obligations to the sect. The Anglican Church in the West have ordained homosexuals as priests to promote a liberal view of human sexuality that coincides with contemporary sexual freedom.

Stoic, Musonius Rufus (who taught at Rome circa 80 A.D. and again was not influenced by Jewish or Christian thought). He rejects all homosexual conduct as shameful. Sexual conduct is decent and acceptable only within marriage. The point of marriage includes not only procreation and the raising of children, but also, integrally and essentially, a complete community of life and mutual care and affection between husband and wife.

Despite these cases, orthodoxy Christianity has generally sought to regulate and control sexual expressions amongst their congregants along what has been perceived as biblical standards. For example, the Shakers, a religious group in the 19th century North America outlawed marriage and sexual expression. Marriage was deemed as the source of evil; therefore, the Shakers separated sexes into 'communal family' and encouraged celibacy and communal child rearing.

Surprisingly however, the Pentecostals believe lesbianism, homosexuality, sexual pleasures for its sake, and oral sex, all of which are part of the sexual revolution as having satanic origination. Hence, unbridled sex and its sexual desires assumed a religious significance from the belief that it is rooted in satanic control, therefore attracted the opposition of the Church.

Similarly, certain sectarian groups in the second half of the 12th century legislated strictly on the sexual behaviors of their members. Examples included the choice of marriage partner, the date of wedding, the manner of the wedding ceremony, the manner of expressing sexual intimacy ceased to be an individual's choice but became the decision of certain marriage committees or the pronouncements of leaders and pastors.

These regulations by the religious bodies raises the question of the extent to which these groups recognize members' sexual rights and freedom of choice in pursuance of healthy and pleasurable sexuality. It is this ongoing concern about individual choices, reproductive rights, the quest for sexual freedom and pleasure and generally, the debates to extend human rights to the sexual and reproductive spheres. The control of sexual behavior by religious groups is an institutional way and the most ubiquitous modalities through which religious sects demonstrate power and exercise social control over their members. Those who affirm themselves as members of specified religious groupings are presumed to have submitted their whole being including their sexuality to be influenced by the norms and teachings of the groups.

The central idea in understanding the Christian perspective of sexuality is chastity; thus, the abstinence from premarital sex, around which healthy relationship is what entails opposite sex attraction, around which sexual rights can be expressed. To the Christian fanatics, sexuality is actually a secret and must not be portrayed as a vehicle to self-knowledge, love and pleasure and that sexuality and its related sexual desires can only be expressive within the contexts of heterosexual relationships and marriages; for which anything divergent of this standard is regarded as sinful and opprobrious.

The voices of religious groups are loudest when it comes to the opposition of equality rights for sexual minorities. Religion and sexuality evoke strong responses because both are usually understood as core elements of identification, categories through which humanity identifies. Consequently, any social discourse where religion and sexuality are invoked elicit emotional engagements from members.

Religious groups have witnessed internal confrontations and alterations regarding sexual diversity and religious ideologies in relation to homosexual marriages, the sexual accountability of clergies, and violence against women and sexual minorities. In some circumstances, the discourses of sexuality have divided religious groups dramatically enough to cause schisms. The regulation of sexuality is strongly influenced and controlled by religious groups and philosophies. Religion is recognized as building resilience for mental wellbeing and significant in the sexual health decisions of youngsters especially the females.

To some youth who identify as religious, religion is a significant ideological domain where the learning of sexuality occurs. Thus, to view religious knowledge as significant to sexuality learning, there ought to be an approach that is based on critical ideas. It will instead promote critical thinking, counter hegemonic ideological structures and initiate changes in social attitudes and behaviors.

Traditional Christian theology affirms that sexuality is part of the creation and that, it is fundamental to the human experience and Christian identity. To the traditional Christian, Genesis 1:26 introduces gender distinction, biological differences and the responsibility of procreation and productivity. To them, procreation rather pleasure is the aim of any sexual intercourse. Moreover, following the Apostle Paul's injunction in 1 Corinthians 7:1-11, the position of every Christian on sexual matters is one of a personal responsibility to chastity and to maintain the sanctity of human sexuality within a controlled space from the understanding that the body is the 'temple of the HOLY SPIRIT'.

Therefore, there is little room for personal choice in sexual expression that departs from the biblical standards. The available choice is then that of conformity, not of unlimited freedoms. For Christians, the sexual morality of secular society is too accommodating and unhelpful to the Christian; to the Pentecostal Christians, sex is allowable only in marriage since sex before marriage spoils courtship because that part of life tends to shoulder the aspect of being the most important. Also to the converts of Deeper Life converts, touching is a wonderful sense, but it can lead to "trouble" if indulged in too freely and can arouse passions which may be difficult to control.

Christians believe that unauthorized sexual activity is part of Satan's tool to target Christians and lead them astray from God. Illicit sex therefore becomes the entry point for attacks and demonic possessions. The opposition of any sexuality form aside heterosexuality by Christians is based on the notion of protecting marriage and the home. The foci on marriage and the home have forced some church leaders to try and regulate the types of wedding dresses brides can wear into the church for the solemnization ceremonies.

As a result, many publications have emanated from the sects of Christendom such as marriage is a God-ordained institution and that all humans must marry; that in the choice of future partners, one must insist on biblical standard of marrying Christians within the Church; interfaith marriages are not allowed, while some discourage interchurch marriages; that only monogamous relationships are allowed and as such polygamy is condemned; that the wife should be obedient and must submit completely to the husband, while the husband must love the wife as the Bible commands; that sexual relationship should be confined within marriage to the exclusion of others, and that each should not deny the other any sexual intimacy unless for important reasons such as health and spiritual discipline of fasting and prayers; that marriage is a lifetime covenant and divorce is not allowed.

Abusive relationships are dealt with through counselling by the pastors. Separation and divorces are considered ungodly choices; parenting is within heterosexual marriage, and single parenthood is regarded partly the result of a sinful lifestyle, and

Christians must distance themselves from this practice in whatever disguise. Christians perceive homosexuals as 'worse than animals in the forest'.

Homosexual behaviors are seen as devilish and satanic, and that it comes directly from the pit of hell. They believe it is an idea sponsored by Satan himself and being executed by his followers and adherents. Christians' opposition of homosexuality comes from the account narrated in the Bible and found in Genesis 18 and 19 as well as under Deuteronomy 23: 17. However, the reference made in Deuteronomy 23:17 where Moses instructed that "There shall be no whore of the daughters of Israel, nor a sodomite in the sons of Israel", the translation of sodomite is in Hebrew. (שרק). The transliteration is qâdêsh (Latin) which means a sacred person that is a male devotee (by prostitution) to licentious idolatry.

This definition of the word sodomite is rehashed in 1 Kings 14:24; 15:12; 22:46 and 2 Kings 23:7. Therefore, this quotation by Christians is flawed. However, it is very interesting how both major and minor prophets of the Bible consistently compare the biblical nation of Israel with the cities of Sodom and Gomorrha especially in reference to

Genesis 19, Jeremiah 23:14, Lamentations 4:6; Ezekiel 16:46/16:48-49,53,55-56; Amos 4:11; Zephaniah 2:9 all compare the Israel nation to Sodom and Gomorrah. Furthermore, the man whom Christians believe in and ascribe to his teaching, JESUS CHRIST, also made references to the two cities of Sodom and Gomorrah in relation to rejection of the Gospel and these can be found in Matthew 10:15/11:23-24; Mark 6:11; Luke 10:12/17:29.

The Apostles Peter and Jude in 2 Peter 2:6 and Jude 1:7 respectively are quite clear also that anyone who lives ungodly should remember the cities of Sodom and Gomorrha and their neighboring cities as an ensample. Apostle Jude was quite explicit in why Sodom and Gomorrah were destroyed and he wrote "Even as Sodom and Gomorrha and the cities about them in like manner, giving themselves over to fornication, and going after strange flesh are set forth for an example, suffering the vengeance of eternal fire".

The reference of Apostle Jude is one of the principles that explains why Christians do not condone the sexuality of homosexuals. Surprisingly, an examination of Jude 1:7 says just as Sodoma (a place in Palestine) likewise Gomorrha

(Amorah, a place near the Dead Sea) likewise the towns surrounding them, men of similar appearance or character, giving themselves over to be utterly unchaste and also after uncertain affinity and human nature with its frailties (physically or morally) and passions of human being are made present to the mind to stand forth as an example or reward, to hold oneself under that is to endure with patience and right judgement of perpetual poverty.

There are seven texts often cited by those in the Christian fraternity in not condoning same-sex relationship: Noah and Ham (Genesis 9:20-27), Sodom and Gomorrha (Genesis 19:1-11), Levitical laws condemning same-sex relationship (Leviticus 18:22; 20:13), two words in the two Second Testament vice lists (1 Corinthians 6:9-10, and 1 Timothy 1:10) and Paul's letter to the Romans (Romans 1:26-27). These quoted references refer not to homosexual relationships between two free, adults, and loving adults. They describe rape or attempted rape (Genesis 9:20-27, 19:1-11), cultic prostitution (Leviticus 18:22, 20:13), male prostitution and pederasty (1 Corinthians 6:9-10; 1 Timothy 1:10) and the Isis cult in Rome (Romans 1:26-27).

Since there is no single word in Hebrew or Greek which can be easily translated into 'homosexual', and it only appeared in the Bible in English for the first time in the 1946 Revised Standard Version. There are only seven textual references to homosexuality (using various nomenclature), with none in the four gospels. No biblical text presents an extensive discussion of same-gender behavior, and none discusses homosexuality in the ministry. Yet cultural attitudes towards gays have affected our interpretation of biblical texts. Some traditions have warmly welcomed gays; one church in the US has ministered to gay people since 1968 and the first openly gay pastor was ordained there in 1972.

Conversely, the Coptic Orthodox Church refers to homosexuals as debased in mind, having rights only to feel shame and to seek repentance, punished appropriately by AIDS, such that a homosexual priesthood is against everything holy. There is surprising unity amongst otherwise divided traditions in their opposition to homosexuality and to non-celibate gay clergy, as Evangelical Protestants, the Roman Catholic Church and the Orthodox tradition line up trenchantly against. Those who evince more charity (notably Anglicans) only highlight the divisiveness of the issue as their tolerance provokes threats of schism from conservative colleagues (particularly from conservative Anglican communities outside the West).

The Church believes that homosexuals can only be accepted and ministered to if homosexuals see themselves as having fallen short of biblical and Christian standards and seek repentance. The belief that current homosexual debate is an attack on the Church, which if not strongly resisted will pollute the Church and weaken its power to preach the Gospel to a permissive society. The Church is particular on sexual expressions due to the perception that the Bible sees sexual intercourse as 'total submission, total nakedness, total unity, total love and total sexual satisfaction within marriage'.

Sexual rights therefore, can only be exercised in godly manner as prescribed by the Church and proscribe the society for exercising that right. Sexual rights broadly defined include the ability to maintain personal preferences regarding whatever ways one exercises his/her sexual feelings in order to attain a high standard of sexuality including the pursuit of a satisfying safe and pleasurable sexual life, and the decision to enter into sexual relations and marriage willingly. Under this premise, each person determines what is best for him/her regarding sexual expressions.

Such laws, as illustrated in the Judeo-Christian tradition in the Ten Commandments (and the expanded version of them in Leviticus 18, 19, and 20 of the Old Testament) are basically directed against incest and parricide, and geared to protecting the boundaries of sexes and generations against massive invasion by regressive polymorphous perverse sexuality under the dominance of primitive aggression. These functions of institutionalized morality in opposition to dangerous regression to primitive group processes would tend to deny the prohibition against incest and parricide.

In addition to the regulation of sexuality, Islam provides all the information required to design a comprehensive sexuality education for all its adherents and converts from the cradle to the grave irrespective of their race or culture since Islam isn't just a religion with laws guiding values, rituals, human transactions and morals but as a way of life. In some sections of Islamic adherents, sexuality education has been misunderstood and interpreted to mean a subject that promotes moral aridity and permissiveness among young people by providing them with information that triggers their curiosity and fuels the desire to experiment with premarital sex.

Amongst Islamic teachings, sexuality is only in conformity when it relates to marriage (nikah)—a union of a man and a woman. Marriage is seen as a religious responsibility to be undertaken by those who are ready to live according to rules guiding the institution. Marriage is traced to the creation of Adam (Alaihi Salaam) and the creation of Hauwa (Eve) as his companion. The Qur'an espouses in Al-Rum Sura 30:21 *'And one of Allah's signs is that He creates for you mates from ourselves, that you may dwell in tranquility with them, and has ordained between you love and mercy'*; and Al-Nahr Sura 16:72 *"And Allah has made for you mates from yourselves and made for you out of them, children and grandchildren"*. Marriage is viewed *"as a means of emotional and sexual gratification, as a mechanism of tension reduction, legitimate procreation and social placement; as an approach to interfamily alliance and group solidarity"*.

According to one Islamic scholar, Imam Ali, what motivates the beasts of prey is their hunger and what motivate women and draw them to men is to extinguish the fire of their shahvat (sexual desire, lust, passion); while Imam Baqir acclaims that Allah has not intended ghairat (sexual honour and jealousy) for women but for men, because for men He has made licit four permanent wives and slave girls but for women only one husband. If a woman shows affection for another man, she is considered zina-kar (fornicator) in the eyes of Allah. Women who show ghairat (when their husbands are polygynous) are those who are faithless, not those who believe in the rules of Allah. In another hadith, he said '*women's ghairat is in reality jealousy and jealousy is the root of heresy; when a woman's ghairat is aroused, she becomes angry, and when she becomes angry, she tends towards heresy. Of course, such women are not Muslim*'.

The difference in men and women' sexuality and the control over women's sexuality finds its legitimacy in the fuqaha's conception of marriage. For Muslims, marriage rights and duties revolve around sexual access and compensation which are embodied in the concepts of tamkin (submission) and nafaqa (maintenance). Tamkin—defined as unhampered sexual access—is a man's right and thus a woman's duty; and nafaqa—defined as shelter, food and clothing—is a woman's right and man's duty. A woman who fails to keep herself covered, to satisfy the sexual needs and other wishes of the husband is believed to be condemned to hell; and if she refuses her husband at night, she will be cursed all night by angels.

To Islam, it's a woman's duty to be sexually responsive at her husband's disposal; she cannot leave the house without her husband's permission, as this would infringe his right of access to her. Nonetheless, other Islamic scholars like Tabataba'i see sexual desires not as fixed and innate but as malleable and social. His perspective is based on the notion that *'man is the slave of his own desire (shahvat) and woman is a prisoner of the man's love (muhabbat)...A man wants to take possession of the person of the woman and to wield power over her, a woman wants to conquer the heart of man and prevail upon him through his heart...A man wants to embrace woman and a woman wants to be embraced...A woman is better able to control her desires than a man. Man's desire is primitive and aggressive, and woman's desire is reactive and responsive'*.

In the spectrum of Islam, sexuality encompasses four main fields—eroticism, reproduction, affectivity and gender. The pleasure couples enjoyed in marital life through foreplay and intercourse were deemed to prefigure one's perfect love of God and the joys that awaited the faithful as their eternal reward in paradise. Tradition has it that the two types of women the Prophet most despised were those who told their husband to wait until later when he wanted to make love, and those who fained impurity by saying that they were menstruating when they were not. Women were enjoined never to deny their husbands erotic pleasure. *'A woman must never refuse him, even if on a camel's back'* and *'A woman must never refuse her husband even on the topmost edge of a burning oven'*, are but two sayings attributed to Muhammad.

Sexual standards in Islam are paradoxical: on the one hand, the exercise of sexuality is allowed and even encouraged but, on the other hand, discrimination is enforced between male and female sexuality, between marital and nonmarital sexuality, and between heterosexuality and homosexuality. To Omar Ben Abdelouaheb, coitus is only validated in marriage and it is evident when he stated that, *'...it is necessary that the husband takes into account the rights of his wife during coitus. Sexual disagreement is the origin of discord between spoused...the meaning of two waters at the same time is the finality of pleasure and the base of affection'*. Sexual position that is only validated in Islam is the 'missionary' or 'normal'—the man on the top of the woman. It is believed that if a woman is on top of a man, it can cause ulcers in the bladder and urethra.

This notion is not medically correct for according to scientists, interstitial cystitis (IC) is a relatively rare condition, although ten times common in women than men, there is no known cause scientifically but one possible cause is the disruption of the lining layer of the bladder (known as epithelium) that causes it to become leaky, allowing toxic substances in urine to irritate the bladder walls as well as an abnormality of the immune response, such as an autoimmune reaction, the presence of an unidentified infection, or increased nervous system activation in the nerves to the bladder; although none of these explanations have been conclusively proven to cause interstitial cystitis (IC).

Anal sex can cause antisperm antibodies (ASA). Antisperm antibodies are immunoglobulins of IgG, IgA, and/or IgM which are directed against sperm antigens (antigens are proteins, peptides, polysaccharides, lipids, nucleic acids or other biomolecules that can bind to a specific antibody or T-cell receptor). ASA can be detected in ejaculate, cervical mucus, follicular fluids, and blood serum of both males and females. ASA can arise whenever sperms encounter the immune system. ASA occur in both women and men, including those who receive anal sex from men or who perform oral sex in men.

ASA have been considered as infertility cause in around 10-30% of infertile couples and in males, about 12-13% of all diagnosed infertility is related to an immunological reason. The incidence can well be higher as the contribution to idiopathic infertility still remain elusive (31% in all cases). Nonetheless, the antibodies are also present in approximately 1-2.5% of fertile men and 4% in fertile women. Only those antibodies directed against antigens involved in the fertilization process impair fertility.

About 40-45% of sex workers test positive for antisperm antibodies and increases for those who do not use contraceptive methods. The causes of ASA include testicular trauma and surgery, orchitis, varicocele, bacterial infections, testicular cancer and unprotected anal intercourse. Nonetheless, the association between aforementioned conditions and ASA production is controversial.

Aside these risks, unprotected receptive anal sex with an HIV positive patient is the sex act most likely to result in HIV transmission. Other infections that can be transmitted by unprotected anal sex are human papillomavirus, typhoid fever, amoebiasis, chlamydia, cryptosporidiosis, giardiasis, gonorrhea, hepatitis A, B and C, herpes simplex, Kaposi's sarcoma-associated herpesvirus (HH-V8), shigella, tuberculosis, pubic lice, salmonellosis and Ureaplasma urealyticum.

Consequently, sodomy in all forms is forbidden especially to the wife as some hadiths attest:

a. Whoever takes a woman from behind is cursed.

b. Sodomy of women is illicit.

c. Whoever takes a woman from behind is not seen by Allah on Judgment Day.

d. Sodomy of the wife, this minor homosexuality.

A justification against sodomy is also reported in 'Madkhal' where Ibn al Hadj gives three 'rational' evidences to prohibit sodomy of the wife: (i) the contact of the penis with faeces is even more harmful than with menstrual blood, hence sodomy is forbidden more severely still than coitus during menstruation; (ii) sodomy does not provide pleasure to the woman, and (iii) the woman suffers physically and psychologically from being sodomised.

Therefore, 'social order' [...] requires male control of women's bodies and sexuality for which female sexuality, if uncontrolled, could lead to social chaos. Homosexuality is a turpitude (fahicha) in the vision of Islam, however, the Qur'an didn't envisage a legal sanction against it, even though Muslims consider it as a major sin (kabira). Even though, homosexuality is punishable by imprisonment, whipping or sentencing to death among Moslems especially according to the doctrines of Sunna and Shi'a, yet the doctrines of Zahirism (a Sunnite doctrine) and Rafida (a Shiite doctrine) affirm that homosexuality should not be punished. In all, sexuality by Islamic texts is partial—it favors men and certain ways of expressing one's sexuality i.e. it constrains sexuality to patterns of masculine and heterosexual domination.

Sexuality which diverts from heterosexuality with its desires outside of marriage is condemned; and marriage defined to be the central institution for erotic pleasure in Islamic culture, and accordingly defines a whole set of practices that defile the marital union's sanctity. Chiefly amongst them is fornication (zin ā), which could manifest in various ways: sodomy (either between men [liw āt] or between women [mus āhaqa], bestiality, transvestitism, necrophilia, masturbation to name a few.

Sodomy in an Islamic setting was first punished in 1735 when a young man, Muhammad ibn Hajj who lived with his mother, Tajia in Aleppo, Syria was accused by twenty-six of his neighbors of having intimate associations with men whom he brought together to fornicate in his mother's house while his mother is suspected to have been pimping him. He was accused due to fact that he was tender, pretty and beardless. Muhammad and his mother were banished from their community and since then sodomy became a capital crime in the Islamic culture; and unmarried men found guilty of sodomy were punished with 100 lashes publicly while married men found guilty of the act were condemned to death by stoning.

Most religious or spiritual people see queer cultures as militantly secular, deluded, mentally unstable or uneducated while queer cultures see religion as intrinsically conservative and repressive. Queer cultures are cultures that emerged from post-structuralist deconstruction while it was also grounded in political agency—in Anglo-American cultures in the HIV/AIDS activism of the 1980s and in contemporary feminism during the early 1990s. Queer cultures seek to place the issue of sexuality as the center of concern, and as a key component through which other socio-political and cultural phenomena are to be understood. A queer critique takes an interest in how organized sexuality is and the continually reproduced, enforcing sociocultural norms of heteronormativity.

There is a sharp and grotesque battle between religious identity and sexual identity. While notions of religious and sexual identities are perceived to belong to different ontological domains, humans in lived experiences should remember that the valued notion of disruption is very wearing. While society needs stable identities in which to live, it is those people (the ill, the poor and the vulnerable) that require certainties of identities. Although queer is an immensely useful critical element, it must be contextual, and not appropriated to defame those who are 'not radical enough' without understanding the particular conditions of existence.

Homonormativity is as essential to the notion of a liberal humanist as are the processes that position the religious as culturally backward, intrinsically homophobic and chauvinistic. Homosexuality historically has been understood pace Freud as a pathologically narcissistic arrested development; thus, queer subculture works to transform this 'diagnosis' of failed adulthood into a conscious and strategic rejection of heteronormative teleology. That is, a queer temporarily is seen as taking full pleasure in and embracing radically the ideas of 'restricted maturity' through a refusal of conventional respectability through reproductive orderliness.

Queerness has a long string of semantic associations; it pricks a discomforting strangeness, provokes uncanny sensations and triggers surprising and unnerving epistemologies. 'Religion is a queer thing'—this is something we 'know' intuitively rather than expressly, hence it is thought as a necessity. The manner of sexual thinking broadly has consequences for repressive hierarchies in the society. The exclusion of other sexuality forms, love and relationships not only make heterosexuality an ideologically compulsive but it further postulates a cultural homogeneity which in practice doesn't exist. As diverse cultures present humanity with different constructions of heterosexuality and other sexual options, economic alternatives and challenges to theology occurs.

Many hurtful words for LGBTQIA+ folks have been religious and in response, LGBTQIA+ cultures have distanced themselves from religion through the trope of anteriority. The main proposition has been that, homophobic views are expressed through religious discourses do not belong in a modern, progressive and secular society. The trope of anteriority attempts to contain injuries. The contentious nature of sexuality-related religious and theological debates often stem from discomforts discussing sexuality in general, confusing and ever-changing language, embedded socialized, heterosexists, cis-gendered, and patriarchal notions of gender dynamics and a pervasive misperception that sexuality may be discussed apart from the embodiment of those participating in the dialogue.

CHAPTER III

PSYCHOLOGY & SEXUALITY

"Man is not a cause of the woman-effect but a specific modality of the relationship between cause and effect."

"Psychical reality is a particular form of existence not to be confused with material reality"—
Sigmund Freud

Sexuality takes on different meanings and significance in different cultures and periods. There are various phases that humanity undergoes to attain mastery of new capacities and abilities. Each stage results in the capacity for the management of more complex functions, the creation of new perceptions of self and the universe, and is mostly accompanied by new anxieties that demand mastery. In the field of psychoanalysis, sexuality is described as a justification against painful effects therefore has nonsexual aspects.

From the perspective of individuals, sexuality can seem the best option available to protect oneself from or perceived harm at any given time or in any given circumstance. Usually, the danger is internal and relates to how a person experiences self and others, and how one perceived danger and vulnerabilities in varied circumstances. These perceptions are to a larger degree influenced by experiences of the past and developmental history. One of the ways to examine sexuality is through attachments. Attachment is that strong affectional bond between the child and the primary caregiver. This bond gives the child a sense of security and lays down a foundation for future attachment behavior.

In its early years, psychoanalysis was at the cutting edge of this progression. Freud bravely noted the damage done by sexual repression, sexual hypocrisy, sexually transmitted diseases and sexual abuse of minors. Freud (1905) was indeed a queer theorist as well as a psychoanalyst. He scandalized Vienna with his proposition that in our unconscious, we are all quite queer ("polymorphously perverse" may be a more scientific term for "queer"). Freud's observations led to vast changes in society, a revolution that is still in progress. But over the years, especially in the mid-twentieth century, psychoanalysis as a whole abandoned its progressive role and became increasingly an enforcer of traditional values, valorizing the supposed normality of middle-class stereotypes. Women who wanted equal rights with men were told they had penis envy. Men who had sexual relations with other men were seen as pathological. Women who had as many sex partners as men were diagnosed as nymphomaniacs. Behaviors that appear similar may have different meanings in different people, and may be prompted by different reasons and etiologies.

Attachment provides the need for proximity, care and security with a separate other. Attachment breeds a positive view of another, reciprocity and trust. People who lack a sense of parental attachment will tend to be anxious and unsecured, making later peer attachment and committed monogamous romantic attachments problematics. Accordingly, attachment proponents view 'sexual promiscuity' as offering a temporary relief for anxiety, insecurity and depression. 'Unrestricted sexual encounters may function as chemical balms for the insecurity wrought by poor attachment experiences'. There is evidence to show also that people who experience weak parental attachment are more involved in unrestricted sexuality as well as more drug usage compared to those who experience stronger parental attachment.

Another perspective is the trauma theory. People who during childhood experienced high frequency of sexual victimization grow up to become sexually compulsive, and in order to cope with their sexual trauma, they dissociate to avoid assimilating the full extent of the trauma experienced. Childhood sexual traumatization mostly involves partial or total amnesia regarding the detail of the abuse and therefore is dissociated from affect and sensations. A trauma survivor could be analgesic as a result of various changes in the central nervous system in conjunction with the trauma; a dissociative person could then view forced sex as a sense of safety in that it creates a sense of control when feeling powerless.

Repeated sexual experiences may serve the role of recapitulating the person's original lesson that the only way to experience intimacy or perceived 'love' is through sex. Sexual exploits therefore give a sense of vengeance and the perceived mastery over what was then beyond control. Accordingly, some scholars have argued that a psychological precondition must exist in order for a person to acquire an addictive pattern of behaviors. Such preconditions include a deep feeling of inadequacy, inferiority, low self-esteem and a positive sense of rejection by parents. The self-induced dissociative state permits the person to detach from the earlier traumatic reality and become so engrossed in subjective fantasy—the ability for one to create and act out roles consistent with the modified or idealized self-image.

Another view to understand the psychology of sexuality is the drive theory. Sex was never seen as an addiction since the beginning of human civilization until the 19th century—around the late 1800s—when it was first suggested by Sigmund Freud. He first used masturbation as the original addiction. Accordingly, Freud argued that intrapsychic conflicts arise unconsciously between the drives (libidos and aggressions) that strive to maintain their expression between the agencies (id, ego and superego) of the mind.

When conflicts are handled through compromises that satisfy these agencies, the resulting behavior is adaptive and expresses aspects of the underlying conflicts but no symptoms arise. However, when the ego capacity is too frail compared to the intensity of either the affective state or drive, there cannot be a reach of compromization therefore symptomatic behaviors occur.

Accordingly, traditional drive theorists argue that all adult disorders could be traced back to previous phases of the psychosexual development (oral, anal, phallic and oedipal) to which the patient either is fixated or regresses. Sexual addiction therefore is seen as repetitive sexual conquests serving as temporary reassurances against inadequacies and impossibilities of ever being able to obtain the love of the longed-for mother.

Another perspective is the ego psychology where perversion is represented as an expression of the ego desire for control and mastery and a means of enhancing ego interests at the expense of instinctual wishes and object interests. Sexual exploits serve to release a frozen anger and feelings of powerlessness since sexual act serves as a drug intended to disperse feelings of violence and of inner death. The sexual partner becomes the container for dangerous parts of the person. Sexual perversion is viewed as 'the erotic form of hatred' in which a person seeks release without genuinely caring about the other.

Also, object relations theory view sexual addiction as the failure to achieve self and other (object) differentiation. Without the capacity for stable memories and images needed for internal regulation of self-esteem and tolerance of being alone, the individual is left vulnerable to unmanageable depression and intense anxiety when solitary. These individuals depend upon others to provide those functions which they lack, but which they need to defend against painful effects. One way the individual with this ego deficit may satisfy their merger need is by sexual behavior. Sex therefore becomes a vehicle for establishing at least transient contact with someone, anyone who can't meet narcissistic needs that help the addict stabilize their internal world and regulate intolerable anxiety or depression.

With the self-psychology perspective, sexual addiction is viewed as repetitive unsuccessful attempts at remedifying central deficits in an uncohesive psychic structure. A sexual addict under this view uses sex to reduce anxiety and increase self-esteem in the absence of adequate intrapsychic resources.

In examining sexual compulsivity, sexual activity gives the addict the feeling that one omnipotently can control the response of another person concordant to one's needs. The sexual addict seeks mirroring self-objects to achieve the feeling of being wanted, desired, alive or powerful. The engagement of habitual sex is perceived as an effort to ameliorate hollowness, sadness and boredom resulting from a shallow and empty existence as well as to ward off impending disintegration of oneself, while sexual excitation is used as a vitalization and strengthening action, as a means to feel alive.

Psychologically, gender is a social construct subject to change, however, the differences inhering in the bodies of men and women are assumed to be pregiven and unchangeable. This was the view held on until the comitant rise in the 17th century of a materialist view of the body, and later addition of Darwinism.

The association between sex and shame is also one of the oldest topics in psychoanalysis and the rationale has been from the understanding of mental functioning being set within a cultural concern with the mores and niceties of fin de siècle 20th century Europe; from the Judaic and Christian culture of its founders and followers and their traditional views of females that supported the coupling of sex and shame; and from the surround of Western cultures that from the 18th century progressively understood individualism and selfhood as valuable psychological acquisitions.

The verbally expression of shame and guilt is based on self-consciousness. The influence of shame is universally signaled psychologically and nonverbally with blushing, downcast eyes, gaze avoidance, and is apparent in all cultures. According to Freud, shame, disgust and morality are massive fortifications of defense against 'sexual excesses' which originates in the shame-free world of early childhood. Freud in 'On Narcissism' captures the baby's beginnings in an untampered omnipotence that must be challenged gradually through parental prohibitions, schooling, and sociocultural moral injunctions to control the urgencies of infantile scopophilic and exhibitionistic sexual drives.

Later in 1933, Freud in *'Femininity'* in New Introductory Lectures, associates shame to female 'genital deficiency' as he called it, their lack of having penises. Freud original observation was that shame is generated very early on as relational and that it is a response to a clash between the individual's internal desire with external personal forces. Furthermore, Lewis in Psychic War in Men and Women (1976) concluded that the feelings of worthlessness and self-attack seen in women are often manifestations of hidden shame in relation to their sexuality, and byproducts of the prevailing phallocentric culture.

One psychoanalyst, Joseph Lichtenberg in "*Sensuality and Sexuality across a Divide of Shame*" defined sexuality as anything (mostly bodily behavior) that is forbidden by the surround, especially by a disapproving parent who activates the child's shame. It also creates the excited tension of the forbidden while defining sensuality to cover all of the bodily touching, holding, caressing, etc. that is exchanged between children and adults and that is permitted by the surround. These amiable constellations become the vehicle of secure attachment and activate systems of inner acceptance of especially expressive bodily interactions as the child grows up into the adult world.

Therefore, the enjoyment of a person's sexual body and gendered psyche depends on this. To him, sensuality is a foundational regulator of the psyche as sexuality seen as distinguishable by shame from 'sensuality'. Although the environment aids regulation that can be absorbed by the child gradually, shame belongs with activity viewed as 'sexual' but not sensual hence great burden in relation to sexuality occurs when a person experiences while growing up multiple interactions encoded from caretakers who are shame-inducing due to their own psychopathology projected or unleashed sexuality towards the child.

Psychoanalysts and their fellow clinicians in dealing with issues of sexuality have allowed their private revulsions at some sexual practices and their own prejudices to interfere in their treatments of patients. Most fail to adopt care and thoughtfulness in dealing with patients. Those who see sexuality as shameful, there are unanswered questions that beg for responses to appreciate the issue of sexuality and shame.

These questions include from whose point of view are people's interactions either sensual or sexual? From whose point of view are they shameful? And how can we distinguish 'sensual' and 'sexual' on the basis of shame that may or may not be present, if not either from the subjects' own conscious vantage points, or in its absence, without some theory that openly acknowledges unconscious conflicts? Shame is also seen as a 'revolutionary feeling' with the aim 'in the public eye' is to generate both speechlessness and attention. Therefore, it is an uphill battle to maintain the wisdom of the centrality of sexuality.

Sexuality is very frightening 'because its biological imperative threatens the symbolic nature of our sociocultural world and personal identity'. Hence, in achieving civilization, it has come at the cost of repressing sexuality; and the repression of sexuality has been necessary for language and symbolic making development. Pollock defined and argued that 'sexuality is not a biological but a psychological effect at the interface of fantasy and the drive. It is a human achievement and not a pre-psychological given'.

Many neurobiologists, psychoanalysts and academics puzzle over the origin of consciousness and attune the brain to be the primary sex organ. While Freud associates shame with women for they lack penises, Pollock notes that the '*suppression that has built an entire phantasmagoria of images, words and modes of actual bodily punishment to terrorize women into a shameful fear of betraying their desire.... Shame is, therefore, a central feminist issue...*' Sex engagement offers three different affects: excitement, enjoyment and contentment.

Like all emotions, sexual feelings tend to be catching—I feel it, you feel it. Feelings arrive at once corporeally and psychically, but corporeality is as much a two-person as a one-body phenomenon. Many have asked 'what makes sexual affect special?' Sexual speech is inherently performative in that it materializes what it aims to describe. Since words are as visceral as psychosocial, speech is always already permeated.

The term '*psychopathology*' was first used in 1913 when the book, General Psychopathology, was introduced by Karl Jaspers, a philosopher and a psychiatrist. Pathological which is the scientific study of the nature of disease including causes, development and outcomes. Here, psychopathologists considered homosexuals based on the use of fear, anxiety, their trouble coping with daily life, thoughts of self-harm or suicide or excessive worry to classify them as people suffering from pathological illnesses needed to be cured.

Psychologists and psychiatrists conceptualize problems based on four key elements: deviance, distress, dysfunction and danger. Deviance is a term used to classify thoughts, emotions or behaviors that deviates from what is common or odds with what is deemed acceptable in society; distress is the negative feelings either felt within a person or that results in discomfort in others around that person. Danger is used to refer to behavior that might put one or another else at some type of detrimental risk. Thus psychopathological behaviors are classified based on how issues are affecting a patients or those around another.

Psychopathological behaviors can be caused by biological factors including genes and brain chemistry, feeling of isolation, lack of social support or traumatic experiences. Hippocrates, the 4th century BC Greek was the first to reject the notion of evil spirits and argued that mental illness was a disease of the brain relating to imbalances of bodily humors or chemicals in the body fluids while Plato argued that mental distress involved issues of virtues, morality, and the soul. This view was carried on till the 19th century.

Such people branded as psychopathological sufferers were either tortured to bring them back to sanity since the notion was to cure the person of demons or evil spirits and once it didn't work, execution was the last option. This continued until the late 1800s when the interest surged in the role of childhood and trauma in the development of mental illness which was championed by Sigmund Freud when he started introducing the talk therapy to deal with those unresolved childhood issues.

In Freud's day, psychoanalysts tried to be knowledgeable about sex, and they were in regular communication with sexologists. These sexologists included: 1. Richard von Krafft-Ebing, who wrote Psychopathia Sexualis in 1886, the single most authoritative treatise on variant forms of sexuality (and who supported Freud's appointment as a university professor, even though they disagreed about many issues); 2. Iwan Bloch, known as the first sexologist, who in 1906 wrote The Sexual Life of Our Time, an encyclopedia of the sexual sciences in their relation to civilization; 3. Albert Moll (1908/1912), whose research on childhood sexuality and whose book, The Sexual Life of the Child had a major impact on psychoanalysis; 4. Magnus Hirschfeld (1914/2000), founder of gay liberation in Germany 60 years before it took off in the United States, and also a scholar of "intermediate sexual conditions" like intersex and crossdressing; 5. Havelock Ellis, who published his series of Studies in the Psychology of Sex, starting in 1897, in which he wrote humanely and with great accuracy about unusual sexual behaviors.

Freud developed his ideas in interaction with these researchers, and they studied the ideas and findings of psychoanalysts. This pattern changed: The turning point was in 1948, when Kinsey published his first scientific study of human sexuality. He was viciously attacked by psychoanalysts for his empirical data showing that approximately 37% of adult American males had engaged in at least one sexual experience with a same-sex partner. From then on, there was a major rift between psychoanalysis and sexology. Edmund Bergler's arrogant 1948 paper: "*The Myth of a New*

National Disease: Homosexuality and the Kinsey Report," which appeared in Psychiatric Quarterly, showed a trend; psychoanalysts felt they could ignore and be contemptuous of scientific studies of sex. Others who attacked Kinsey included Karl Menninger and Arno Karlen.

A rift appeared and expanded between scientific studies of sex and psychoanalysis. For evidence of this disjuncture, consider one of the best-known articles about psychoanalysis and sex: Andre Green's (1995) article, "Has Sexuality Anything to Do with Psychoanalysis?" Green writes: "*If any one of us breathes the air and is alive, it is as a consequence, happily or unhappily, of a primal scene, in other words, to be fully explicit, of a sexual relationship, happy or unhappy, between two sexually different parents, whether we like it or not*" (p. 880). In 1995, when this was written, it was already false; a single woman could receive artificial insemination. Today, it is false in many more ways; modern reproductive technologies, such as in vitro fertilization, make it possible for a child to be conceived and born in many ways without any actual sexual relationship between two sexually different parents.

To be sure, facts can be wrong; Bieber et al., for example, believed the "fact" that homosexuality was caused by a distant father and an overly close mother. They did not consider the alternative—that this pattern of parenting is influenced by the child's homosexuality. But although facts can be wrong or questionable, and need to be considered critically, it is still better to know the data than to dismiss them out of hand. Also, facts of first-hand sexual experience, reported by those with shared sexual patterns, are often more reliable than facts put forth by the clinicians and theoreticians who study them.

Most psychological explanations of sexuality can be attributed to Freud. He studied sexuality during the whole course of his life and did not believe that there were special elements at the basis of homosexuality. In his 1915 edition of the Three Essays, Freud writes:

'Psychoanalytic research is most decidedly opposed to any attempt at separating off homosexuals from the rest of mankind as a group of a special character...On the contrary, psychoanalysis considers that a choice of an object independently of its sex...as it is found in childhood, in primitive states of society and early periods

of history, is the original basis from which, as a result of restrictions in one direction or the other, both the normal and the inverted types develop...A person's final sexual attitude is not decided until after puberty and is the result of a number of factors...But in general the multiplicity of determining factors is reflected in the variety of manifest sexual attitudes in which they find their issue in mankind'.

Freud in explaining homosexuality, came with 4 scenario arguing that during infancy, the child, after a strong fixation phase towards his mother, identifies himself with the female figure, takes himself as the love object and looks for young men like himself whom he can love as his mother loved him. He went on to explain that *'it is true that psychoanalysis has not yet produced a complete explanation of the origin of inversion; nevertheless, it has discovered the physical mechanism of its development, and has made essential contributions to the statement of the problems involved'.*

His second hypothesis of 1910 was based on the stressing that the strong love fixation of the child to his mother, in addition to her unwarranted tenderness and the absence of a strong paternal figure. That is, the male homosexual consciously dislikes and disposes the female figure and looks for love objects able to satisfy his unconscious need for a woman with a penis. In his third hypothesis, Freud (1920) focuses on the role of Oedipus complex. An examination of a normal oedipal constellation, the young girl desires to have a baby with her father, but is disappointed by her mother's pregnancy.

At this juncture, she turns away from her father and her femininity, identifies herself with the male figure and chooses her mother as her love subject. In this form of homosexuality, Freud argues that the final sexual orientation is normally reached after puberty and adds that sexual orientation and sexual characters (i.e. gender identities) are not necessarily connected with the sexual object choice. These factors can defer independently from each other. In his fourth psychodynamic hypothesis, Freud (1922) focuses on strong fraternal jealousy and hostility. Due to repression, these rivals become homosexual love objects. This is completely opposite to the one described for paranoia in which the loved completely becomes the hated persecutor and is associated with a reaction formation that fuels high social instincts.

Furthermore, this type of homosexuality appears late in psychosexual development. In this case, the examined is not identified with parent, is not horrified by either male or female genitalia and can have heterosexual love objects. In conflict with this hypothesis, Freud (1911) argues that in the case of *Senatspräsident Schreber*, paranoia represents a defense against an excruciating situation, which is the anxiety related to the fear of being homosexual.

In appreciating Freud's theories of homosexuality, it is opportune to keep in mind the *Wolf Man* (1918) in which Freud's belief in the omnipresence of homosexual themes is expressed. The role of the Oedipus complex is the central element around which homosexual theme begin and are resolved, and the ideas of activity/passivity and bisexuality (a concept Freud borrowed from Fleiss) are expressed. Freud maintained that the Wolf Man, after a narcissistic phase of identification with the paternal figure, following the episode of seduction by his sister, passes from a phallic masculine active organization to a passive feminine one, with a regression to the anal phase.

Here, the father rather than becoming a figure for male identification becomes the love object of the child. Thereafter, the child connects his mother's intestinal troubles to the primal scene, in which the parents copulate more forearum. The consequent jealousy of his mother and sister induce the child into a new identification with the mother, renouncing his own masculinity. In summary, Freud suggests that a person is homosexual as a consequence of an excessive castration anxiety; strong fixation to the figure of the mother and subsequent identification with her; narcissistic object choice and the negative oedipal complex.

Moreover, Freud repeats that there are several **homosexualities:** *'It is not for psychoanalysis to solve the problem of homosexuality. It must rest content with disclosing the psychical mechanisms that resulted in determining the object-choice, and with tracing back the paths from them to the instinctual dispositions...But psychoanalysis cannot elucidate the intrinsic nature of what in conventional and in biological phraseology is termed 'masculine' and 'feminine'...*Finally, Freud affirmed that homosexuality is not a vice nor an illness in his 'Letter to an American Mother' (1935) and that homosexuality in itself is not sufficient reason to exclude a potential candidate from being a psychoanalyst.

The link and categorization of homosexuality in the realm of the perversion commenced after the death of Freud. This transition towards a pathological view is characterized by the link to the pre-oedipal oral phase with typical character disorders 'observed' in the homosexual patient (such as masochism, aggressiveness, development of a pathological superego), the absence of attribution to constitutional factors and the repudiation of the idea of constitutional bisexuality.

Such proponents include Ferenczi who speaks of subjective homoeroticism—the subject identifies with the feminine figure, and objective homoeroticism—there is the compulsion to avoid sexual relationship with a woman; Rado who argues that there is a primary heterosexuality where heterosexuality is the normal outcome of psychosexual development and that homosexuality must always be considered as a pathological defense in need of cure and conversion into heterosexuality; and Bergler who differentiates perverse homosexuality, a consequence of problems linked to the oral phase, from spurious homosexuality, a consequence of an unresolved oedipal complex.

Klein also considers homosexuality to be an expression of an aggressive object relationship and a consequence of anxiety provoking situations which impedes the psychosexual development of the child. She argues that male homosexual intercourse often satisfies sadistic drives in order to confirm destructive omnipotence and that, there is a paranoid element in every homosexual activity. Behind the positive relationship with the good penis/love object, there is not only hate for the father but also destructive drives against the homosexual partner (and the fear of him).

This means that the love of the father is a defense to appease the persecutor by surrendering to him while simultaneously viewing the fear of the father as the cause of the appearance of the defense of homosexual submission. Interestingly, Thorner links homosexuality with the primitive schizoparanoid position and views homosexuality as neither a disease nor a perversion but a neurotic symptom. Homosexuality is characterized by particular unconscious phantasies and it is always a defense against anxiety that impedes the development of a stable, affective psychic organization.

Rosenfield also links homosexuality with paranoid anxiety and narcissism. He argues that in many cases, homosexuality is a defense against paranoia and it often covers more severe disorders which appear when the homosexual defense cannot contain the psychotic anxiety. The proponents seem to have their focus more on object relationships and the constructive or destructive orientation of the personality and its internal object. They considered homosexuality as an important element of a psychopathological condition characterized by popular object relations. In fact, some Freudian statements induce one to think that the homosexual male perceives himself to be a female because of his unconscious and narcissistic identification with his mother or because of his female submission proclivity (as in the Wolf Man).

Nonetheless, by the 1960s and 1970s, the likes of Foucault and Derrida challenged the binary conceptualization of the human. To challenge the concept that there's a difference between sex and gender, as well as highlight how differences are symbolically conditioned and culturally malleable, discourse was defined as unfixed and recast identity and meaning as fluid. Thus, many new social movement theories seek to avoid exclusionary pitfalls while remaining politically engaged by adopting similar perspectives. For example, queer theory 'does not so much press to abandon identity categories but rethinks them as open to conflicting and multiple meanings and as always interlocking with categories of gender, race, class and so on'.

This theoretical move makes possible newly imagined hybrid or composite and fluid identities which in turn enable coalition building. Sexuality in terms of homosexuality has been one of the most contested issues in the historic annals of socio-psychanalysis. Homosexuality since late 1800s is/was considered as a mental illness. Gays and lesbians have had a complex, often troubled relationship with psychiatry. In the period before 1973, most psychiatrists considered homosexuality to be an 'arrest' in a person's development and likely to cause mental illness.

Nonetheless, Harry Stack Sullivan (1892-1949) considered social prejudice against homosexuals rather than their sexual preference itself, the cause of their mental problems. This is according to the perception of his, that mental illness originates in the socio-cultural 'inhibitions' not in biological 'defects' found in individuals. He argued that, there is no such thing as an individual personality; what we see as individuality is, in fact, an ever-changing product of interpersonal relationships and social interactions. The desire to cure homosexuals emerged in the 1920s when psychiatrists claimed that homosexuals would be better off if 'cured' to become heterosexuals.

Sullivan further argued that social biases against homosexuals and a patient's fear of such biases caused mental illness. Interestingly, in the 1930s, some psychologists began to assume that 'paranoid' schizophrenia and homosexuality were linked casually. Paranoid schizophrenia stems from delusions—firmly held beliefs that persist despite evidence to the contrary—and hallucinations. A person of paranoid schizophrenia is consumed by their delusions or hallucinations where they spend the vast majority of their attention and energy on keeping to and protecting their falsely held beliefs or perceptual distortions.

Homosexuality involves a same-sex object choice, but without gender identity disorders. The Freudian concept of femininity-masculinity does not concern gender identity, but it is a psychic and emotional attitude that centers around the problem of passivity-activity. To Glover the manifestation of homosexual love is indistinguishable from those of heterosexuality; Socarides also is convinced that the normal development outcome is heterosexuality. The homosexual orientation appears first in the three years of a person. While true homosexuality comes from the separation-individuation phase disorder; false homosexuality stems from conflicts of the oedipal phase.

The oedipal phase requires separation and differentiation of the self from the object. As the true homosexual never approaches this phase, he consequently has a borderline character organization and has always damaged personality. Quinodoz views female homosexuality as a resistance acting in duo directions: against going backwards, that would imply psychosis and against going forwards, and working through the Oedipus complex.

Bergeret following Ferenczi's metapsychological concept of homoeroticism sought to replace the term 'homosexual' with 'homophile' in order to describe a narcissistic quality that comes into play in the relational behavior of homoeroticism. He described 4 categories of homoeroticism, but the most commonly encountered in adults are characterized by a fixation with narcissistic homoeroticism in the face of a failure of sexual and oedipal elaboration. Bergeret stresses the narcissistic nature of the erotic satisfaction sought by the homophile that 'does not constitute a truly sexual pleasure in the Freudian sense' but concerns a narcissistic object and not a sexual object. Homosexual people are capable of a mature and healthy love relationship.

Sexuality has a fundamental structuring role in the development of the self and in the acquisition of a personal identity. Sexual orientation, fantasies and wishes constitute a personal identity that should not be changed or coerced by a therapy that ideologically consider heterosexuality to be the only healthy orientation. Homosexuality is constitutional—the homosexual person in his infancy has a specific oedipal constellation (developing love fantasies towards his father and not towards his mother).

Sexuality implies a co-penetration of bodies and thus needs render its infinite variations the ideal instruments for representing desires, conflicts and the way one deals with relationships with others. Sexual orientation and mental health are two distinct subjects hence a homosexual orientation does not necessarily serve as an indicator of pathology. Homosexuality represents a less fully developed psychic condition. Homosexuality develops as a result of an individual's unbroken bond which inhibits the full development of one's personality, such that the individual remains at an 'infantile level'.

Furthermore, the sexual preference of an individual might be the unpredictable result of nearly infinite psychological combinations and positions. Jung considers homosexuality as a state of psychological immaturity, he recognizes how homosexuality often allows certain 'positive' aspects of a person's personality to emerge that would otherwise never be expressed. He says *'Never ask what a man does, but how does it'*. Although, psychoanalysts affirm that a patient's sexual orientation should not be changed, but at the same time they consider homosexuality as a symptom or a developmental arrest.

Roughton also argues that '*Of all the topics that engage psychoanalysts, homosexuality is perhaps the most fraught with ideological, theoretical, historical, cultural, personal, and political differences amongst us*'. To understand the sexuality of a person, psychoanalytically, one can only do so by first considering the biological fundaments. In the early stages of development, the mammalian embryo has the potential to be male or female as its gender as undifferentiated gonads differentiates into either testes or ovaries, depending on the genetic codes represented by the different physiognomies of the 46, XY chromosome pattern for males and the 46, XX pattern for females.

Gonads in the human may be detected from about the 6th week of gestation when under the influence of the genetic code, testicular hormones are secreted in males: The Müllerian duct inhibiting hormone (MIH) which has a defeminizing effect on the gonadal structure, and testosterone, which promotes the growth of internal and external masculine organs, especially the bilateral Wolffian ducts. If a female genetic code is present, ovarian differentiation begins at the 12th gestational week.

Differentiation always occurs in the female direction, regardless of genetic programming, unless an adequate level of testosterone is present—even if the genetic code is masculine, an inadequate amount of testosterone will result in the development of female sexual characteristics. The principle of feminization takes priority over masculinization. During normal female differentiation, the primitive Müllerian duct system develops into the uterus, the fallopian tubes, and the inner third of the vagina while in the males, the duct system regresses, and the Wolffian duct system develops becoming the vasa deferentia, seminal vesicle and ejaculatory ducts.

The internal precursors in both genders' sexual organs are present for potential development, yet the external precursors for the external genitals are unitypic—the same precursors may develop into either masculine or feminine external sexual organs. Without adequate present levels of testosterones and dehydrotestosterones during the crucial differentiation period beginning with the 8-week fetus, a clitoris, vulva and vagina will develop.

However, with adequate levels of androgen stimulation present, the penis including its glands and the scrotal sack will form and the testes will develop as organs within the abdomen. They usually migrate into their scrotal position during the 8th or 9th month of the gestation. During the differentiation phase, there is a dimorphic development of certain areas of the brain taking place under the influences of circulating fetal hormones. Specific hypothalamic and pituitary function that will be differentiated into the cyclic in women and noncyclic in men are determined by this differentiation.

The secondary sexual physiognomies which emerge during puberty are triggered by central nervous system factors and controlled by a significant increase of circulatory androgens or estrogens. Androgens appear to determine the intensity of a clear predominance of psychosocial determinants for sexual arousal. Sexual behaviors in primates are controlled by hormones but somewhat modified by psychosocial stimuli as against low-order mammals' sexual behaviors controlled largely by hormones.

The intensity of sexual arousal, the focused attention on sexual stimuli, the physiological responses of sexual excitements are all under hormonal influences. Oxytocin and vasopressin circuits have a central role in the activation of both female and male sexual arousals and behaviors. Oxytocin and arginine-vasopressin circuits also are key components of maternal nurturance and social bonding disposition, and this system, as well as the attachment-panic systems are involved in the complex development of the capacity for eroticism and sexual love.

The issue of 'reality' is complex hence it is laughable when heterosexuality is bundled around as the reality of human sexuality only especially psychoanalysts who have contributed to the notion of homosexuality as a pathological illness that needs psychoanalysts to help remedify the cause while still holding onto the theories of Freud since Freud in 'The Interpretation of Dreams' (1900:613) writes *'the unconscious is the true psychical reality; in its innermost nature, it is as much unknown to us as the reality of the external world, and it is as incompletely presented by the data of consciousness as is the external world by the communications of our sense organs'*.

To Freud, understanding the emotions of a person entails knowing and respecting the relationship between the real and the imaginary for which he used the phrase 'screen memory'. Screen memories are vivid childhood memories recognized as concealing repressed experiences and fantasies pertaining to a time before or after the scene remembered. They are construction, a compromise formation, combining reality, fantasy and defence.

Freud on 'Screen Memories' ends by saying:

"It may indeed be questioned whether we have any memories at all from our childhood: memories relating to our childhood may be all that we possess. Our childhood memories show us our earliest years not as they were but as they appeared at the later periods when the memories were aroused. In these periods of arousal, the childhood memories did not, as people are accustomed to say, emerge; they were formed at that time".

To understand people who do not subscribe to heteronormativity and its heterosexuality as the only form of relationship and sexuality, we must look at precise reconstruction. To analyze the relations of a homosexual both from conscious and unconscious, we must be able to step by step link the emotions experienced by the homosexual to earliest emotions and relations. The construction of sexual identity is far from straightforward as Freud already pointed out: *"observation shows that in human beings pure masculinity or femininity is not to be found either in a psychological or a biological sense"*.

Every individual on the contrary displays a mixture of the character traits belonging to his own and to the opposite sex; and he shows a combination of activity and passivity whether or not these last character-traits tally with his biological ones'. Therefore, the construction of sexual identity can only be understood within a more general context of the identity construction as espoused by McDougall *"The inherent difficulty facing the infant in his task of becoming an individual is of a more global, more 'psychosomatic' nature than the problems encountered in coming to terms with sexual realities"*.

In the construction of sexual identity, the role of the 'image' (mother) is seen to be centrally involved in this development. The concept of sexuality identity has been described either as the extrinsic designation of the self as opposed to gender identity which is the internal experience of the self as gendered and an integral part of one's self-identity or as something non-conflictual and assigned through a sort of imprinting or attribute its origin basically to labelling or using genital awareness as key bases or seeing it as something that is acquired later and in a more conflictual way.

To Laplanche, 'le sexual' (infantile sexuality) of the parents is the origin of sexuality of a person rather than a biologically given sexuality. Thus, he writes: 'The conceptual distinctions are valid not in themselves but for the conflictual potentialities they conceal'. Although they are binary, they are often the sign of negation and hence of repression. Displacements may hide repressions, thus the displacement of the question of sexual identity onto the question of gender identity.

This displacement onto the question of gender identity may hide the fact that the fundamental Freudian discovery does not lie there, but alongside gender and alongside sex or the sexuated, in the question of le sexual or le sexuel. To Freud, masculinity does not absolutely equate with activity and femininity with passivity. Psychoanalysis is therefore about unconscious desire and not in direct relationship to nature hence the difficulty and complexity surrounding these issues.

The body is itself not a simple notion as there is the real body but also the body as represented, consciously and unconsciously. However, the 'body never stops haunting the presumed autonomy of the unconscious'. The body then comes to represent a reality which cannot be escaped from and which can lead to hatred and attack or extreme procedures to change that reality. The notion of identification is very complicated as it could take the form based on symbolic thinking or as a result of concrete thinking (e.g. the father's penis).

Development isn't a linear progression and that random things happen in life and will affect the course of anyone's development. Recognition is the basic act in cognitive development and the roots of pathology is in misconceptions. Imitation is the earliest form of identification and part of normal development, and imitation and object cathexis go hand-in-hand in development. Hence, 'sexual identity' is the end result of complex phenomena; it may be stable or unstable, it may be congruent or not with the actual body and it is permeated with unconscious phantasy. It is made up of various components related to the body, object, choice, labelling, in an attempt at coherence through repression or splitting.

Many homosexuals are tortured by the fear that they are homosexuals as the fears stem from pervading feelings of inadequacies in relation to their fathers and the feeling that they cannot be 'men'. Since they desperately wish to acquire their fathers' potencies. Their insufficient symbolic functions mean they cannot identify with certain qualities of their fathers and paternal roles and incorporate them in fantasy as they believe it would be through a literal incorporation of a powerful man's penis that he could become a man. His unconscious phantasy is of being penetrated by the powerful penis which would fit him like a glove and enable him to penetrate a woman with the potency they wish for.

They feel drawn to act on the homosexual desires in order to shore up their self-esteem and basically to give themselves the sense of unification in a concrete identification with an 'image', that of the strong penis. However, Olmos de Paz postulates that it is a normative part of development that a fantasy of the boy is to be penetrated by a man in order to acquire potency 'in order to become a man, the boy is confronted with the contradictions of incorporating the object, symbol of potency, bestowed on him by another man, whilst also rejecting the homosexual desire reactivated by the processes introjection and identification'.

Development necessitates introjection as a basic aspect both in relation to the mother and to the father. Freud disputes the naturalness of the heterosexual drive as well as Lacan and asserts that there is no such thing as a pregiven male or female subject, and that the human subject is constructed within the terms of language—from a logic that comes from outside the individual.

According to Carl Jung, to understand human personality, there are 4 major archetypes to grab comprehension of. Archetypes are universal, inborn models of people, behaviors that play a role in influencing human behavior. These archetypes are archaic forms of innate human knowledge passed down from our ancestors. The archetypes represent universal patterns and images that are part of the collective unconscious which is believed to have been inherited same as we inherit instinctive patterns of behavior.

To understand personal unconsciousness of the human, there is the need to better understand the three components of the human psyche—the ego, the personal unconscious and the collective unconscious. The ego represents the conscious mind while the personal unconscious contains memories including those that have been suppressed. The collective unconscious is a component of the human psyche which contains all of the knowledge and experiences that humans share as species. The collective unconscious is where the archetypes exists and the models are innate, universal and hereditary. Archetypes are unlearned and function to organize how we experience certain things.

'All the most powerful ideas in history go back to archetypes' and this is particularly true of religious ideas, but the central concepts of science, philosophy, and ethics are no exception to this rule. In their present form, they are variants of archetypal ideas created by consciously applying and adapting these ideas to reality. For it is the function of consciousness, not only to recognize and assimilate the external

world through the gateway of the senses but to translate into visible reality the world within us'.

It is a misconception to presume that the human mind is a blank slate at birth to be written on solely by experience. The human mind retains fundamental, unconscious, biological aspects of our ancestors and these serve as a basic foundation of how to be human. It is these archetypes which symbolize basic human motivations, values and personalities. The actual way in which an archetype is expressed by man depends upon a number of factors including a person's cultural influences and uniquely personal experiences. These archetypes cannot be observed directly but can be inferred by look at religion, dreams, art and literature.

There are four (4) main archetypes: the persona, the shadow, the anima or animus and the self. The persona is how human beings present themselves to the universe. The word 'persona' is derived from a Latin word translated as 'mask'. It is not a literal mask. The persona represents all of the different social masks that we wear among various groups and situations. It acts to shield the ego from negative image. The persona could appear in dreams and take different forms. Over the course of development, humans learn that they must behave in certain ways in order to fit in with society's expectations and norms. The persona develops as a social mask to contain all of the primitive urges, impulses and emotions that are not considered socially acceptable. The persona allows people to adapt to the world around them and fit in with the society in which they live.

However, becoming too closely identified with this archetype can lead people to lose sight of their true selves. The shadow consists of the sex and life instincts. The shadow exists as a part of the unconscious mind and is composed of repressed ideas, weaknesses, desires, instincts, and shortcomings. The shadow forms out of our attempts to adapt to cultural norms and expectations. The shadow contains all of the things that are unacceptable not only to society, but also to one's own personal morals and values. It might include things such as envy, greed, prejudice, hate and aggression.

The shadow can appear in dreams or visions and may take a variety of forms. This archetype is often described as the darker side of the human psyche representing wildness, chaos, and the unknown. These latent dispositions are present in all of us, although people sometimes deny this element of their own psyche and instead project it on to others. The anima or animus is an archetype. The anima is the feminine image in the male psyche and the animus is a male image in the female psyche. The anima/animus represent the 'true self' rather than the image we present to others and serve as the primary source of communication with the collective unconscious.

The physiological changes as well as social influences contribute to the development of the sex roles and gender identities. Hence the influence of the anima and animus are also involved in this process. These archetypal images are based upon what is found in the collective and personal unconscious. The collective unconscious may contain notions about how women should behave while personal experience with wives, girlfriends, sisters and mothers contribute to more personal images of women.

Even though in many cultures, men and women are encouraged to adopt traditional and often rigid gender roles, there should be the discouragement of it as the discouragement of men exploring their feminine aspects and women exploring their masculine aspects served to undermine psychological development. The combination of anima and animus is syzygy or the divine couple—represents completion, unification, and wholeness. The self represents the unified unconsciousness and consciousness of the individual.

The creation of the sole occurs through a process, individuation, in which the various aspects of personality are integrated. The disharmony between the unconscious and the conscious mind can lead to problems. Therefore, bringing these conflicts into awareness and accommodating them in conscious awareness is a crucial phase of the individuation process. The ego makes up the center of the consciousness, but it is the self that lies at the center of the personality of humanity.

The word "perversion" has its roots in religion. The definition of "perversion" in the Oxford English Dictionary is *"turning the wrong way; corruption, distortion; specifically, change to error in religious belief."* There is therefore a basic problem with the concept of perversion: in orthodox religion, there is a right way to do things, and if one does things differently, even if it makes one happy and one does not harm anyone, one is still wrong, perverted, and sinful. Many clinicians have bought into such a translation from sin to psychopathology, even if the connection between pathology and sin is not fully conscious. That has caused a lot of clinical mischief and a good deal of suffering for patients

Indeed, Freud defined perversion as any sexual act that did not lead to genital intercourse: *"Perversions are sexual activities which either (a) extend, in an anatomical sense, beyond the regions of the body that are designed for sexual union, or (b) linger over the intermediate relations to the sexual object which should normally be traversed rapidly on the path towards the final sexual aim."* Thus, oral sex was considered a perversion if it led to orgasm, but not if it was preparatory to penis-in-vagina intercourse. It may be that if one thinks perversion, one is also implicitly thinking, "I know the right way to behave." Not just the right way for me to behave, but the right way to behave. Or, as one scholar puts it, "I may not know the right way to behave, but I do know the wrong way to behave."

Saketopoulou has attempted to salvage the term "perversion" as a sexual experience that is overwhelming, without retaining its pathologizing connotations. She writes: "Anal sexuality, for example; penis-in-vagina sex; acrobatic sex while suspended from the ceiling are all equally viable candidates for perversion as long as they are subjectively experienced as overwhelming". Her definition of perversion comes close to (some might say is synonymous with) "great sex," which is overwhelming, destabilizing to the ego, and often mixes pleasure with disgust, danger, and taboo. Harry Stack Sullivan gives an important alternative to the pathologizing inherent in the psychoanalytic view of perversion. Sullivan tried to formulate a view of sexuality that would evade old religious formulas and would instead define sexual health in practical terms.

He argued that there are many sexual practices and preferences, and what is most important for psychoanalysis about these practices is how much they allow for pleasure and intimacy. One example was mutual oral sex, which Sullivan called "synstomixis." Freud considered mutual oral sex leading to orgasm a perversion, but Sullivan saw it as a good path toward intimate and mutual satisfaction. Sullivan tried to establish a way of looking at sexual practices without being limited by religious and cultural taboos. In Sullivan's own words, in the Interpersonal Theory of Psychiatry: *"In this culture the ultimate test of whether you can get on or not is whether you can do something satisfactory with your genitals or somebody else's genitals without undue anxiety and loss of self-esteem."*

If one really takes this postulate seriously, one may have to reconsider many judgments of sexual health and pathology. Sullivan does away with the religious idea that healthy sexuality must culminate in at least the potential for pregnancy, as well as the psychoanalytic derivative of this, so-called "mature genitality." Sullivan does not judge whether any sexual desire is in itself healthy or pathological; instead, he focuses on how feasible it is to realize any particular sexual desire, without excessive anxiety or danger. Odd forms of sexuality are not a problem if one can find a way to satisfy one's desire without danger to oneself or someone else.

We should uphold the right of every person to experience pleasure, as long as it is consensual and no one is damaged. If a psychoanalyst insists on pathologizing and trying to change another person's nonharmful sexuality, especially when that person has no desire to change that sexuality, the psychoanalyst is committing a crime against that person. Sexuality is too important an aspect of life to yield to another person's arbitrary sense of right and wrong. Sullivan's postulate needs some revision, because it implies that anxiety is the enemy of sexual excitement. Yet for some people most of the time, and for most people some of the time, a certain amount of anxiety or other "unpleasant" affect can heighten sexual excitement.

It is one of the great paradoxes of sexuality that any emotion that inhibits arousal— including anxiety, guilt, shame, fear, disgust, humiliation— can, under different circumstances, intensify arousal. Can we develop an affective neuroscience of sexuality? Can we specify which affects, with what intensity, and under which circumstances, enhance or diminish excitement? These are the affective dimensions of the "sexprint" or "lovemap", the personal pattern of sexual excitement and satisfaction.

Is the relationship of negative affect and sexual desire unique for each person, or can we spell out any general laws or principles about the relationship of multiple affects and sexual excitement? And to what degree, if at all, can the sexprint be modified by psychotherapy or by experience? Within Sullivan's postulate, are any forms of sexuality inherently problematic? Anything that is nonconsensual or coercive or seriously damaging another person remains problematic, such as coercive voyeurism.

"Without undue anxiety and loss of self-esteem—these are large caveats. Psychoanalysts must attend to the level of the patient's anxiety and loss of self-esteem when it comes to sexual experience. Is the sexual experience followed by affects such as shame, regret, abjection, and hatred? When that is the case, an analysis of unconscious aspects of the sexual experience may reveal the sexual pattern as an attempt to master anxieties and other unpleasant affects.

CHAPTER IV

SCIENCE & SEXUALITY

"Males do not represent two discrete populations; heterosexual and homosexual. The world is not to be divided into sheep and goats, and not all things are black nor all things white. It is a fundamental of taxonomy that nature rarely deals with discrete categories. Only the human mind invents categories and tries to force facts into separated pigeon-holes. The living world is a continuum in each and every one of its aspects. The sooner we learn this concerning human sexual behavior, the sooner we shall reach a sound understanding of the realities of sex"—Alfred C. Kinsey.

Living organisms evolved from one or a few simple forms of life through the process of natural selection. The essence of this process is that, the individuals that comprise a population differ in the number of viable offspring they produce during their lifetimes, the more fecund individuals owing their relative reproductive success to features of structure, behavior, or psyche not possessed, or possessed in differing degree, by the less fecund members.

Since progeny tend to resemble their parents, there is constant selection for characteristics that result in successful reproduction. An organism is reproductively successful or unsuccessful only compared with other members of the population, and in this sense reproductive "competition" is inevitable. This does not imply that organisms themselves will necessarily engage in overt reproductive conflict, but it does imply that sexual intercourse will not normally be random. In Darwin's words (1871:362): "promiscuous intercourse in a state of nature is extremely improbable."

Human sexuality is not unique, nor is human sexual behavior totally different from that of other animals. For, despite our large brains, lofty intellectual capacities, and cultural complexity, we are animals too, and our species share the tree of life with millions of other organisms, all of which are the products of evolution by natural (and sexual) selection. Among the Old World anthropoid primates, it is not unusual to see members of the same sex mounting one another or making hindquarter presentation postures in a variety of social contexts.

Such interactions are much less frequent in New World monkeys and have been recorded only rarely for any of the prosimians. In many species of Old World monkeys and apes, sexual patterns have become incorporated into the broader realm of social communication; this is the essence of "socio-sexual behavior." Mounts may occur between males, or between females, as affiliative (distance reducing) displays, for "reconciliation" (e.g., following aggressive interactions), and to reduce "social tension" between group members.

Although mounts and presentations occur in rank-related contexts, it is not the case that higher ranking individuals always mount lower ranking ones, or that presentations are always submissive in nature. Socio-sexual communication is subtler than this, and more complex. Same-sex mounts and presentations occur in at least 17 genera of Old World monkeys and apes. For 13 of these (76 percent) at least one species in each genus is known to engage in male–male mounting, and in 12 (70 percent) the females mount one another.

Baboons, macaques, mandrills, talapoins, langurs, bonobos, and many others show these kinds of socio-sexual patterns, both in the wild and in captive groups. Because monkeys or apes of the same sex may mount or present to one another, this does not mean that they are "homosexuals" in the sense that a small percentage of the human population is "gay" or homosexual. Homosexuals exhibit exclusive, or almost exclusive, erotosexual preferences for members of the same sex. Old World monkeys and apes, by contrast, engage in same-sex interactions, but also solicit copulations and mate with members of the opposite sex.

Moreover, mounts and presentations are frequently seen in infants and juveniles; males mount one another more often than females do, and females exhibit presentations at higher frequencies. These sexually dimorphic traits thus begin to be expressed from infancy onwards. The sex difference in mounting is affected by androgenization of the male brain during fetal life, and the resulting infant patterns of socio-sexual mounting play a crucial role in ensuring normal development of social and sexual behavior (e.g., in the rhesus monkey).

There is no a priori reason to reject the possibility that nonhuman primates might engage in same-sex activities, at least in part, because such behavior is positively reinforced by pleasurable (hedonic) feedback during mounting and genital stimulation. Female stump-tail macaques sometimes exhibit orgasmic responses during same- sex mounts. Female Japanese macaques mount one another "jockey style" in order to maximize stimulation of the mounter's vulval, perineal, and anal area. The genital rubbing (G–G rubbing) which occurs during isosexual mounting between female bonobos also involves clitoral and vulval stimulation, but in this case tactile stimulation is possible for both partners as mounts occur in a ventro-ventral position.

These examples serve to emphasize that there is not a rigid dichotomy between the "sexual" and "socio-sexual" functions of isosexual behavior. The propensity for monkeys and apes to exhibit bisexual capacities is considerable, especially where the Old World monkeys (Cercopithecoidea) and apes (Hominoidea) are concerned. As Homo sapiens is also a member of the Hominoidea, and derives from ape-like (australopithecine) ancestors, it is likely that we might share some capacity for the expression of a bisexual orientation with the other Old World anthropoids due to common descent. Examples of same-sex (e.g., male–male) sexual relationships between individuals who are primarily heterosexual in orientation is not uncommon, in indigenous societies, and in accounts of Euro-American cultures.

The dominance of sexual reproduction is still an unresolved enigma in evolutionary biology. The enigma of the evolution of sex comprises two processes, the origin and the maintenance of sex. Theories on the advantages of sex mainly refer to the improvement of the progeny's fitness in sexual populations despite reducing the overall number of offspring. Nevertheless, one of the enduring mysteries of biology is the prevalence of sexual reproduction in eukaryotes. Because parthenogenetic species do not waste resources in producing males (the now-classic "two-fold" advantage) and do not break up favorable gene combinations, they should rapidly out-compete sexual species in most environments.

These differences in male and female behavior are considered to stem from a simple thing: anisogamy. Anisogamy refers to the difference in size of the sex cells, or gametes. Males of many taxa produce multiple, motile, tiny sperm cells while females produce only a few, large, immobile, nutrient-loaded egg cells. 'Males' are members of a species that produce microgamete seekers (sperm), and females as those that produce macrogamete providers (eggs). Humans are sexually dimorphic (size and body shape differences between men and women), more than some great apes (i.e. other members of the Family Hominidae: the gorilla, the common chimpanzee, the bonobo or pygmy chimpanzee, and the orangutan), and less than in others.

Men are generally taller and heavier than women; they have more upper body strength, higher metabolic rates, more facial and body hair, deeper voices, larger brains, higher infant mortality, later sexual maturity and die younger. Human beings are anisogamous: the human egg is 85,000 times larger than the human sperm cell. Men produce large ejaculates (an average of 2.75 ml, containing 280 million sperm: about two trillion in a reproductive life of 60 years) and females produce one egg *per* lunar month (13 per year: about 500 in a reproductive life of 40 years). Record lifetime reproductive success is enormously different between men and women.

Humans become sexually mature when they enter puberty and become fertile. For both males and females, this is due to hormonal events that are triggered by physiological condition. For girls, it is generally considered that they need to exceed about 50 kg in weight before they can enter menarche. Importantly, young women need to exceed a certain percentage of body fat before menstruation can be maintained. A sixteen-year-old woman must have over about 20% body fat to be fertile.

Interestingly, there is some evidence that many pre-technical societies are fully aware of this, and girls about to enter puberty are encouraged to eat more to hasten the event and to ensure high fertility. At puberty, the hypothalamus starts to produce gonadotrophin releasing hormone (GnRH) that stimulates the pituitary to secrete hormones that, in turn, initiate the production of estrogen and testosterone in the gonads. At the same time, the gonads begin the conveyor belt of sperm and egg production. Much is often made of the fact that, from birth, a baby girl has a stock of ovarian follicles already present in her tiny gonads and the description of this is often associated with negative terminology such as how this 'stockpile' 'degenerates' up to menopause at about 50 years old.

In fact, although spermatogenesis continues throughout a male's reproductive life, the sperm-producing tissue has also been present from before birth, waiting for the hormonal kiss of life.

Hormone production not only influences fertility, it also affects the outward appearance of boys and girls. Both sexes have androgens and estrogens, but in different ratios. At about thirteen or fourteen when boys experience a testosterone peak from their testes making them look more like adult men, they are actually experiencing their second dose of testosterone. The first occurs in the womb, at about two months into development as the testes differentiate from the fetal proto-gonads. This testosterone-burst ensures that at birth the parents are able to identify their child as a son.

The second burst of testosterone produced by their gonads at about fourteen results in all the classic symptoms of puberty: growth spurts, body hair, body odor, and the development of an 'adult' face. Testosterone encourages the growth of the lower face and brow ridges, both indicators of 'masculinity'. A higher ratio of estrogen in girls suppresses this growth but apparently induces growth of the lips, a 'feminine' indicator. Girls born with a male twin are the only ones that are exposed to testosterone in the womb, and according to some studies, are more 'masculine' in appearance and behavior, but what exactly constitutes 'male behavior' can be strongly culturally influenced. It certainly influences female twins in other species: in cattle, such females are known as 'freemartins' – masculinized females.

The onset of puberty, ovulation and sperm production does not mean that young humans are truly 'adult', and most of our cultural mores reflect this. Unlike most animals, pubertal humans have yet to reach their full fertility. A thirteen-year-old boy may be a raging mess of hormones and sperm production, and a twelve-year-old girl may be gaining an 'adult' female shape and menstruating, but peak fertility is not reached until about nineteen years old (slightly later for men than for women).

In women, studies have shown that a small lower jaw and the lower part of the face are regarded as attractive by men. In men, studies have shown that a large lower jaw regarded as dominant by women. As these are indicators of 'femininity' and 'masculinity', this is highly suggestive of a role in sexual selection. Even more interesting is that these high dominance indicators in highly masculine men are not perceived by women to be as attractive as lower dominance men.

What other features might influence mate choice? Humans like symmetry. Faces that are more symmetrical are more attractive to us. Babies like faces and particular components that signal human faces: curves, strong contrasts of light and dark, moving lips. Babies will stare longer at more symmetrical, more 'attractive' faces than at 'unattractive' faces. Maybe, as most people's faces are relatively symmetrical then symmetrical faces look more human, and hence we like them. However, it has been suggested in multiple studies that symmetry also reflects 'developmental stability'.

In other words, the more symmetrical the features (and this can apply to any bilaterally symmetrical structure: hands, feet, legs, arms, fingers etc.) the 'fitter', the 'healthier', the individual would be. In a world where sexual selection acts upon individuals, symmetry could have a role in mate choice. In humans, symmetry appears to predict male sexual behavior. Men who are more symmetrical report attracting more sexual partners, have sexual intercourse earlier in life, have more partners outside of their primary relationship, tend to have more offspring, tend to have fewer serious diseases, are heavier for their height and are more muscular.

Joan Roughgarden, an evolutionary biologist, has produced a compelling thesis in which she claims that the argument for 'unnaturalness' of same sex sexuality can be dispelled by dropping Sexual Selection (Darwin 1871) for her own 'Social Selection'. As simply as possible, what Social Selection says is that sex is not just about exchanging gametes, but about forming bonds within societies and negotiating for access to resources necessary to reproduce. The argument then follows that this negotiation will take place as much within sexes as between sexes.

For instance, a couple with two children, who have enjoyed a fifty-year monogamous relationship with an average of twice-weekly intercourse, have had 2,700 copulations per child. That is why non-reproductive sexual behavior such as homosexuality occurs, because, according to social selection, homosexuality ultimately functions in the same way as heterosexuality: negotiating social bonds and access to resources.

Regardless of the above, what evidence is there of a genetic component to homosexuality? One study found that if one dizygotic male twin is homosexual; his brother has a one in four likelihoods of also being homosexual. If one monozygotic male twin is homosexual, his identical brother has a 50% likelihood of also being homosexual. If true, this alone suggests that there is a sizeable genetic component to homosexuality. There is also some evidence that homosexuality is inherited from the maternal (X chromosome), not paternal line (i.e. homosexual uncles are more likely to be from the maternal side of the family).

The pursuit of a 'gay gene' is sociologically problematic. Traditionally, those on the right of the political spectrum have embraced genetic determinism while those on the left have repudiated it. With homosexuality, the positions have generally been reversed. Those on the left have accepted the 'gay gene' as support that homosexuals should not be persecuted for their lifestyle, while those on the right have rejected it, claiming that homosexuals 'choose' to follow their lifestyle, or that it is environmentally (socially) induced.

Other aspects of 'abnormal' sexuality come from one's personal observation that most people are clearly either male or female. Some people may be more 'feminine', some more 'masculine'. This is intuitive, and most of us are aware that men are genetically different from women (XY chromosomes versus XX). In fact, the two sexes are closer than many of us might care to think. As fetuses developing in the womb, both males and females develop along very similar lines until a certain point. This is reflected in our physiology: both sexes have nipples; in males, they are not, generally, functional. Both sexes have the same basic genital plumbing: clitoris and glans, ovaries and testes. The genital structure of women, with a vaginal opening bordered by labia majora and minora is mirrored in the male penis.

Until puberty, and for many men, beyond, there is a visible dark line along the base of the penis, known as the median raphe. This is the 'sealed' homologue of the female genital slit. This differentiation begins in the womb when male fetuses begin to produce testosterone and, for a while, develop faster than female fetuses. At puberty the testes again produce a burst of testosterone. For some children, genetically male, the testes do not produce a burst of testosterone in the womb and the fetus continues to develop along the 'female' plan. Born with undescended testes, unfused scrotal tissue like labia and reduced penises, these boys appear indistinguishable from girls and are often raised as such.

With puberty, the testes produce testosterone, facial hair grows, the penis often enlarges, and the testes attempt to descend. Semen is also produced, ejaculating from beneath the penis. Once again, such an 'abnormal' sexuality is abnormal in the sense that it is statistically extremely uncommon, but where gender identification is a sliding scale (multiple types of intersexual) rather than a bi-categorical state (male: female), it is not to be unexpected.

Analogously, the literature is full of observations on other species where sexual role switching takes place, even gender identity. Many group-living fish compete to become males; if the 'male' dies, the dominant 'female' changes color, switches from egg to sperm production and fertilizes the other females. However, is that comparable to what we see in human societies? Roughgarden gathers an impressive review of apparent abnormal intersexual behavior across cultures. She emphasizes the difference between traditional cultures that view 'gender—and—sexuality-variant' people positively or neutrally and the modern Western view that, although often accepting in its outlook, has a history of defining physical and behavioral sexual ambiguity as pathological.

She gives examples such as 'Two-spirited' people in North American Indian groups (both men and women who flout traditional roles, e.g. warrior women who take female lovers), 'Mahu' in Polynesia (boys who are raised amongst and as women) and 'Hijra' in the Indian sub-continent (a religious caste/sect made up of men-to-women transgenders). It is worth emphasizing again, what has been evident throughout that it is difficult to have any certainties about human sexuality, whether as biologists or sociologists. Science, of course, revels in uncertainty: it is one of its greatest attributes. Judgement, condemnation and conservatism have no place here. The cause of psychoanalytic ignorance about sex may be dated to the mid-20th century, when psychoanalysis effectively broke relations with scientific sexology.

Sexual orientation has biological underpinnings and considers the involvement of epigenetic mechanisms. Sexual orientation is more concordant in monozygotic twins than in dizygotic ones and male sexual orientation is linked to several regions of the genome. Sexual orientation is perceived to be caused by a complex interplay of genetic, hormonal and influences from the environment.

Homosexual men are believed to have been exposed to little testosterone in key regions of the brain, or had different levels of receptivity to its masculinizing effects, or experienced fluctuations at critical times. In women, it is perceived that high levels of exposure to testosterone in key regions may increase likelihood of same-sex attraction. This is supported by studies of the finger digit ratio of the right hand. Digit ratio (2D:4D) is the ratio of the lengths of different fingers. Usually, the ratio of the index finger is to the ring finger of the same hand. When the index finger is shorter than the ring finger, its results points to a higher exposure to testosterone in the uterus. The ratio is affected by fetal exposure to hormones in particular to testosterone and other androgen.

Women whose ratio of 2D: 4D are lower have greater assertiveness. "Sexual differences in 2D:4D are mainly caused by the shift along the common allometric line with non-zero intercept, which means 2D:4D necessarily decreases with increasing finger lengths, and the fact that men have longer fingers than women" which may be the basis for the sex differences in digit ratios and/or any putative hormonal influences on the ratio. The formation of the digits in humans, in utero, is thought to occur by 13 weeks, and the bone-to-bone ratio is the 'consistent' from this point into an individual's adulthood.

During this period, if the fetus is exposed to androgens, the exact level of which is thought to be sexually dimorphic, the growth rate of the digit is increased, as can be seen by analyzing the 2D:4D ratio of opposite sex dizygotic twins, where the female twin is exposed to excess androgens from her brother in utero, and thus has a significantly lower 2D:4D. Women with congenital adrenal hyperplasia (CAH) which results in elevated androgen levels before birth have lower, more masculinized 2D:4D on average. Other possible physiological effects include an enlarged clitoris and shallow vagina. Maternal immune responses—the immune tolerance shown towards the fetus and placenta during pregnancy— during fetal development are strongly demonstrated as causing male homosexuality and bisexuality.

Research since 1990s has demonstrated that the more male sons a female has, there is a higher chance of later born sons being homosexual. During pregnancy, male cells enter a mother's blood stream which are foreign to her immune system. In response, her body develops antibodies to neutralize them. These antibodies are then released on future male fetuses and may neutralize Y-linked antigens which play a role in brain masculinization, leaving areas of the brain responsible for sexual attraction in the female-typical position, or attracted to men. This effect is estimated to account for between 15% and 29% of gay men, while other gay and bisexual men are thought to owe sexual orientation to genetic and hormonal interactions.

Around 1900s, socialization theories favored ideas that children were born 'undifferentiated' and were socialized into gender roles and sexual orientations. The effect led to medical experiments in which newborn and infant boys were surgically reassigned into girls after accidents such as botched circumcisions. Incidents of injury resulting from the circumcision procedure can range from excessive bleeding to significant tissue loss and even partial amputation. These males were then reared and raised as females without telling the boys, which contrary to expectations, did not make them feminine nor attracted to men.

These demonstrate that socialization effects don't induce feminine type behavior in males, nor make them attracted to men, and that organizational effects of hormones on the fetal brain prior to birth have permanent effects. The INAH3 region is thought to be a crucial region in sexual behavior. INAH3—interstitial nucleus of the anterior hypothalamus—is the sexually dimorphic nucleus of human. The INAH3 is significantly larger in males than in females regardless of age and larger in heterosexual males than in homosexual males and heterosexual females.

INAH3 is smaller in volume in homosexual men than in heterosexual men because homosexual men have a higher neuronal packing density in the INAH3; there is no difference in the number of cross-sectional area of neurons in the INAH3 of homosexuals as against heterosexual men. This difference in INAH3 between homosexual and heterosexual men is because it is present prenatally or in early life and aided in establishment of the men's sexuality.

A study on brain imaging technology found that heterosexual men had right hemisphere 2% larger than the left; heterosexual women has the 2 hemispheres the same; in homosexual men, the two hemispheres were also the same, or sex atypical, which in lesbians, the right hemisphere were slightly larger than the left, indicating a small shift in the male direction. Moreover, autosomal genetic contribution to development of sexual development has been proven to help in understanding the sexuality of the human race.

There is an 'unusually high' proportions of homosexuals both female and male of the Rh negative in comparison to heterosexuals; also there was found a statistically significant difference in the frequency of blood type A between homosexuals and heterosexuals. Female fertility is explained as also a reason for sexual orientation. A research of 4600 people who were the relatives of 98 homosexuals and 100 heterosexual men showed that female relatives of the homosexual men tended to have more offspring than those of the heterosexual men.

Female relatives of the homosexual men on their mothers' side tended to have more offspring than those of the father's side. This evidence was used to conclude that there was genetic material being passed down on the X-chromosome which both promotes fertility in the mother and homosexuality in her male offspring. These connections discovered would explain about 20% of the cases studied. Across cultures, 2% to 10% of people report having same-sex relations. In 2019, geneticist Andrea Ganna at the Broad Institute of MIT and Harvard and colleagues analyzed the DNA of close to half a million of people and concluded that 8% to 25% of same-sex behavior is influenced by genes.

However, there isn't one particular gene responsible for causing homosexuality. Numerous researches have established that sex is not just male or female; rather it is a continuum that emerges from a person's genetic makeup. Sexuality is linked to the presence or absence of a section of the X-Chromosome and it is perceived to be caused by a gene called SLITRK6, which is active in the brain region called the diencephalon, which differs in size between heterosexuals and homosexuals. Genetic studies in mice have uncovered additional gene causing candidate that could influence sexual preferences. A 2010 study linked sexual preference to a gene called fucose mutarotase. When the gene was deleted in female mice, they were attracted to female orders, and preferred to mount females rather than males.

Other studies have shown that disruption of a gene called TRPC2 can cause female mice to act like males. Male mice lacking TRPC2 no longer displayed male-male aggression, and they initiated sexual behavior towards both males and females. Expressed in the brain, TRPC2 functions in the recognition of pheromones— chemicals that are released by one member of a species to elicit a response in another. Males with a genetic condition, androgen insensitivity syndrome can develop female genitalia and are usually brought up as girls, despite being genetically male—with an X and Y chromosome—and they are attracted to men.

This suggests that testosterone is needed to 'masculinize' a prenatal brain; if that doesn't happen, the child will grow up to desire men. In the same vein, girls who have a genetic condition called congenital adrenal hyperplasia are exposed to unusually high levels of male hormones like testosterone while in the womb, which may masculinize their brain and increase the odds of lesbianism. It is also possible that hormonal shifts during gestation stage could affect how a fetus' brain is configured.

Sexual behavior is widely diverse and governed by sophisticated mechanisms throughout the animal kingdom. As with other complex behaviors, it is not possible to predict sexuality by gazing into a DNA sequence as if it were a crystal ball. Such behaviors emerge from constellations of hundreds, perhaps thousands of genes, and how they are regulated by the environment—i.e. not physio-social environment. Homosexuality is largely biologically determined, not environmentally influenced. This is because decades of psychiatric research into social and cultural causes show 'small effect size and are causally ambiguous'.

In a research carried by Pillard and Bailey where they examined identical and fraternal twins- as well as nonrelated brothers who had been adopted – in an effort to see if there was a genetic explanation for sexuality (homosexuality). They found that if one identical twin was gay, 52% of the time, the other was also; the figure was 22% for fraternal twins and only 5% for nonrelated adopted brothers. However, the researchers were quick to point that how sexuality is determined remains a mystery. Also, 5 chromosomes have been identified to be causing homosexuality. Sexuality is a sexually differentiated trait; it is a behavioral trait which displays one of the largest degrees of sexual differentiation given that 90-97% of individuals of one sex display an attraction that is different from that of the other sex.

Human data demonstrate that the prenatal endocrine environment has profound and irreversible effects on a variety of morphological, physiological and behavioral features of a person. Since males and females' embryos are exposed to a different hormonal milieu during specific phases of their intrauterine life, male and female newborns are substantially different on the day of birth. Estrogens are often unable to activate female-typical behaviors in males and vice versa testosterone does not reliably activate male-typical copulation behaviors in females even after its conversion to estradiol. It is not the type of adult hormones that determine the behavior that will be expressed (male or female typical); it is the nature of the neural substrate on which the hormone acts.

The phenotype represents a reasonable model of human sexuality yet it is imperfect. Sexuality isn't affected by activational effects of steroids in adulthood. Gonadectomy does not also influence sexual orientation nor does adult treatment with androgens and estrogens. Numerous studies have clearly established that plasma concentration of sex steroids are perfectly 'normal' (typical of the gonadal sex) in both homosexual genders. Exposure to a high concentration of testosterone during a critical phase of development would lead to a male-typical orientation (attraction to women), where as a lower embryonic exposure to steroids would lead to a female-typical orientation (attraction to men).

Childhood gender conformity, or behaving like the other sex is a strong predictor of adult sexual orientation that has been consistently replicated in research, and is thought to be strong evidence of a biological difference between heterosexuals and non-heterosexuals. A review authored by J. Michael Bailey states:

'childhood gender nonconformity comprises the following phenomena among boys: cross-dressing, desiring to have long hair, playing with dolls, girls as playmates, exhibiting elevated separation anxiety, and desiring to be-or believing that one is-a girl. In girls, gender nonconformity comprises dressing like and playing with boys, showing interests in competitive sports and rough play, lacking interests in conventionally female toys such as dolls and makeup, and desiring to be a boy'.

This gender nonconformist behavior typically emerges at preschool age, although is often evident as early as age 2. Children are only considered gender nonconforming if they persistently engage in a variety of these behaviors, as opposed to engaging in a behavior of a few times or on occasions. It is also not a one-dimensional trait, but rather has varying degrees. Children who grow up to be non-heterosexual were, on average, substantially more gender nonconforming in childhood. This is confirmed in both retrospective studies where homosexuals, bisexuals and heterosexuals are asked about their gender typical behavior in childhood, and in prospective studies, where highly gender nonconforming children are followed from childhood into adulthood to find out their sexuality.

A review of retrospective studies which measured gender nonconforming traits estimated that 89% of homosexual men exceeded heterosexual males level of gender nonconformity, whereas only 2% of heterosexual males exceeded the homosexual median. For females' sexuality, the figures were 81% and 12% respectively. A variety of other assessments such as childhood home photos, videos and reports of parents also confirmed the finding.

Nonetheless, the critiques of this study argue that the research serves as a way of confirming stereotypes. Many non-heterosexuals often deny they were gender nonconforming in childhood because they may have been bullied or maltreated by peers and parents for it, and because they often do not find femininity attractive in other gay males and thus would not want to acknowledge it in themselves. The research carried does not mean all non-heterosexuals were gender nonconforming, but rather indicates that long before sexual attraction is known, non-heterosexuals, on average are noticeably different from other children.

There is little evidence to support the notion that gender nonconforming children have been encouraged or taught to behave that way; rather, childhood gender nonconformity typically emerges despites conventional socialization. Medical experiments in which infant boys were sex reassigned and reared as girls did not make them feminine nor attracted to males. Although we are all members of one species, human beings display remarkable differences. Adults can be less than 3 feet tall or more than 7, and they can weigh under 100 pounds or well over 400.

Facial features vary greatly from race to race and from individual to individual. Most families have at least a few obvious genetic characteristics they can trace back through many generations, and a few families seem to be 'cursed' with more serious disorders such as albinism, color blindness, hemophilia or Huntington's diseases and all of which are based on genetic mutations. Such pronounced variations amongst members of our own species and the underlying patterns of inheritance that explain them are the concerns of human genetics. Most human traits seem to be determined through more complex gene interactions.

In a test cross, the phenotype is known for both parents, yet the genotype is certain for only one of them, and is revealed by the appearance of the offspring. When both parents have dominant alleles, the genotype usually expresses itself and doesn't skip generations; that is offspring will not express a trait determined by the dominant allele unless one or both parents have that allele. A recessive allele can skip generations. Normally, a trait determined by a recessive allele usually expresses itself only in homozygotes; occasionally, however, a dominant allele is masked by some other allele or process, so that its recessive partner is expressed in the phenotype. In analyzing any generation for a particular trait, there is always the possibility of finding a propositus—the person with the trait who first came to the attention of the person constructing the pedigree analysis—after two generations.

CHAPTER V

SEXUALITY AND LAWS

"Civility is the recognition that all people have dignity, that's inherent to their person, no matter the religion, race, gender, sexuality, or ability"—Opal Tometi

The term 'homosexuality' was coined in the 19th century by the psychologist, Karoly Maria Benkert. The term is of recent yet the discourse of sexuality in general and same-sex attraction have occasioned philosophical discourses ranging from Plato's Symposium to modern queer theory. The understanding of same-sex attractions in societies can only be understood from histocultural understandings. To appreciate why most legislations are made against same-sex attraction, one must appreciate the references to natural law as it still plays an important function in why there are so much hostilities against non-heterosexuals. The existence of laws concerning sexualities emanate from the conflict that exists between and amongst societies and cultures of whether sexuality is constructed socially or purely driven by biological forces.

The history of today's understanding of sexuality especially the case of homosexuality can be traced to ancient Greeks. The ancient Greeks did not have terms or concepts that correspond to the present dichotomy of human sexuality. There are vast resources on sexuality from ancient Greece ranging from dialogues of Plato, such as the Symposium, to plays by Aristophanes and Greek artwork and vases. Although, the concept of sexuality amongst the ancient Greeks were vague, there were regional variations. For instance, in parts of Ionia, there were general strictures against same-sex eros, while in Elis and Boiotia, it was approved of and even celebrated.

To the ancient Greeks, sexual orientation of a person was approvable when responded erotically to beauty no matter the sex of the person whose beauty was being appreciated. For example, Diogenes Laeurtius wrote of Alcibiades, the Athenian General and Politician of the 5th Century BC, '*in his adolescence he drew the husbands from their wives, and as a young man, the wives from their husbands*".

Others were also noted for their exclusive interests in persons of one gender. Alexander the

Great and founder of Stoicism, Zeno of Citium for examples were known for their exclusive interests in boys and other men. Moreover, the issue of what biological sex one is attracted is seen as an issue of taste or preference, rather than as a moral issue. A character in Plutarch's Erotikos (Dialogue on Love) argues that *'the noble lover of beauty engages in love wherever he sees excellence and splendid natural endowment without regard for any difference in physiological detail'*.

In ancient Greece, gender was irrelevant and instead the excellence in character and beauty was the most important. Although the gender that was erotically attracted to was not important, other issues were salient, such as whether one exercised moderation. Status concerns were also of the highest importance. Only men (free men) had full status could have sex with women and male slaves because women and male slaves were not problematic sexual partners. Nonetheless, sexual intercourse between two free men was problematic for status.

The central distinction in ancient Greek sexual relations was between taking an active or insertive role versus a passive or penetrated role. The passive role was acceptable only for inferiors, such as women, slaves, or male youths who were not yet citizens. Therefore, the cultural ideal for a same-sex relationship was between an older man, probably in his 20s or 30s, known as the 'erastes', and a boy whose beard had not yet begun to grow, the 'eromenos or paidika'. In such relationship, there was courtship rituals, involving gifts such as roosters and other norms.

The erastes had to show that he had nobler interests in the boy, rather than a purely sexual concern. The boy was not to submit too easily, and if pursued by more than one man, was to show discretion and pick the more noble one. Penetration was often avoided as the erastes could only face his beloved and place his penis between the thighs of the paidika, known as intercrural sex. The relationship was to be temporary and should end upon the boy reaching adulthood.

To continue in a submissive role even while one should be an equal citizen was considered problematic, although there were many adult male same-sex relationships that were known and noted, and not strongly stigmatized. While the penetration of a man was seen problematic, to be attracted to men was seen as a sign of masculinity; and Plato in the Symposium argues for an army to be comprised of same-sex lovers. Thebes in Boiotia did form such a regiment, 'The Sacred Band' of Thebes formed 500 soldiers, and they were renowned in the ancient world for their valor in battle.

However, Ancient Rome had many parallels to ancient Greece in its understanding of same-sex attraction and sexual issues more generally. This understanding is what has shaped the modern world's understanding of sexuality. For example, under the Republic yet under the Empire, Roman society slowly became more negative in its views towards sexuality due to socioeconomic turmoil even before Christianity became influential. Although, the early fathers of Christianity were much more outspoken about their condemnation of same-sex attraction evident in their writings, in a few generations these views eased in part due to doubt to practical concerns of recruiting converts.

By the 4th and 5th centuries, the mainstream Christian view allowed only for procreative sex. The viewpoint, that procreative sex within marriage is allowed, while every other expression of sexuality is sinful is expressive in the writings of St. Augustine. This understanding of permissible sexual relationships leads to concern with the gender of one's partner that is not found in previous Greek or Roman views, and it clearly forbids homosexual acts. Soon this attitude, especially towards homosexual sex, came to be reflected in Roman law.

In Justinian's code, promulgated in 529 AD, persons who engaged in homosexual sex were to be executed, although those who were repentant could be spared. This is the genesis of the criminalization of the world's stance of homosexuality. With the decline and demise of the Roman Empire, and its replacements by various barbarian kingdoms, a general tolerance (with the sole exception of Visiogothic Spain) for homosexual acts prevailed. This tolerance of homosexual acts prevailed until the middle of the 13th century. While some Christian theologians continued to denounce nonprocreative sexuality, among the clergy developed a genre of hemophilic literature in the 11th and 12th centuries.

The latter part of the 12th through the 14th centuries however saw a sharp rise in intolerance towards homosexuality, alongside persecution of Jews, Muslims, heretics and others. This intolerance can be traced to two causes: the class conflict alongside the Gregorian reform movement in the Catholic Church. The church itself began to appeal to a conception of 'nature' as the standard for morality, and drew it in such a way so as to forbid homosexuality as well as extramarital sex, nonprocreative sex within marriage and often masturbation.

For example, the first ecumenical council to condemn homosexual sex, Lateran III of 1179 stated *'Whoever shall be found to have committed that incontinence which is against nature' shall be punished, the severity of which depended upon whether the transgressor was a cleric or layperson"*. This appeal to natural law became very influential in the Western tradition and then passed unto other nations through colonialism. It is important to know that a sodomite differs from the contemporary idea of homosexual.

A sodomite was understood as an act-defined not as a type of person. Someone who had desires to engage in sodomy, yet didn't act upon them, was not a sodomite. Also, persons who engaged in the heterosexual sodomy were also sodomites and there are reports for persons being burned to death or beheaded for sodomy with a spouse. Finally, a person who had engaged in sodomy, yet who had repented of his sin and vowed to never do it again, was no longer a sodomite. The gender of one's partner was not decisively important when looking at the worst type of sexual crime during the medieval period. Enforcements were episodic and in some regions, decades would pass without any persecutions.

However, the Dutch in the 1730s mounted a harsh anti-sodomy campaign even using torture to obtain confessions. As many as 100 men and boys were executed and denied burial. Also, the degree to which sodomy and same-sex attraction were accepted varied by class, with the middle class taking the most restrictive view, while the aristocracy and nobility often accepted public expressions of alternative sexualities. However, in the 19th century, there was a significant reduction in the legal penalties for sodomy. The Napoleonic code decriminalized sodomy, and with Napoleon's conquests that Code spread.

Furthermore, in many countries where homosexual sex remained a crime, the general movement at this time away from the death penalty usually meant that sodomy was removed from the list of capital offenses. Between the 18th and 19th centuries, the discourse of same-sex attraction moved from theological frameworks to secular arguments and interpretations. The most secular domain for discussion of homosexuality was medicine including psychology. This was linked up with considerations about the state and its need for growing population, good soldiers, and intact families marked by clearly defined gender roles.

Doctors were called in by the courts to examine sex crime defendants; and at the same time the dramatic increase in school attendance rates and the average length of time spent in school, reduced transgenerational contact and the frequency of transgenerational sex influenced same-sex relations between persons of roughly the same age become the norm. Instead of specific acts defining a person, as in the medieval view, an entire physical and mental makeup usually portrayed as somehow defective or pathological is ascribed to the modern category of homosexual.

Although there are historical precursors to these ideas such as Aristotle's description of the physiological explanation of passive homosexuality, medicine gave them greater exposure and credibility. This has led to the view that since homosexuality is not chosen, it makes less sense to criminalize it. People are not choosing evil acts. However, persons may be expressing a diseased or pathological mental state, and hence medical intervention for a cure is essential.

This influenced doctors especially psychiatrists to campaign for the repeal or reduction of criminal penalties for consensual homosexual sodomy yet intervened to 'rehabilitate' homosexuals. They sought also to develop techniques to prevent children from becoming homosexual, for example by arguing that childhood masturbation caused homosexuality, hence it must be closely guarded against.

In the 20th century, sexual roles were redefined again. For a number of reasons, premarital intercourse slowly became common and accepted. With the decline of prohibitions against sex for the sake of pleasure even outside marriage, it became more difficult to argue against gay sex. These trends were very strong especially in the 1960s, and it was in this context that the gay liberation movement took off.

Although gay and lesbian rights groups had been around for years, the subtle approach of the Mattachine Society and the Daughters of Bilitis had not gained much grounds and this changed on June 28, 1969 when the patrons of the Stonewall Inn, a gay bar in Greenwich Village rioted after a police raid. The post-Stonewall era has also seen marked changes in Western Europe, where the repeal of anti-sodomy laws and legal equality for homosexuals has become common.

T.H. Marshall's classic definition of citizenship provides a useful starting point. Marshall suggested that *"[c]itizenship is a status bestowed on those who are full members of a community. All who possess the status are equal with respect to the rights and duties with which the status is endowed. There is no universal principle that determines what those rights and duties shall be...."* Citizenship was thus associated with the possession of full adult status and equality in relation to that status, but this outline notion does not in itself tell much about the content of the connected rights and duties.

In reality, this can clearly vary: as Marshall observed, citizenship *"can be based on a set of ideals, beliefs and values."* Marshall's own three part scheme of rights—defined as civil rights (associated with individual freedom: liberty of the person, freedom of speech, the right to own property, and the right to justice), political rights (relating to participation in the political process), and social rights (the right to economic welfare and security through to the right to share in the social heritage and to live in civilized circumstances according to the standards prevailing in one's society)—was tied to political, economic, and social history.

Marshall suggested that different types of right had been more powerful at particular times and were tied to particular theories of society, rights and constitutional law and politics. The specific notion of "sexual citizenship" has attracted wide attention in the past twenty years. Brenda Cossman has argued that citizenship has been "increasingly sexed up" to incorporate

> "once abject sexualities [i.e., the female] and once deviant sexual practices [i.e., lesbian and gay]. Sexual discourses now saturate the public sphere, as the subject of political contestation and cultural representation." On

this view, while citizenship *"has traditionally been focused on the relationship between the individual and the state,"* it has more recently *"been deployed to capture a broader range of social practices of belonging"* through which *"sexual practices are a central dimension of contemporary citizenship."*

There has been a normalization of sexual citizenship in popular culture, with "the sexual subject" being *"reconstituted and reframed within the privatizing, domesticating, and self-disciplining discourses of contemporary citizenship."* Not only "the subjects," but also *"citizenship itself,"* are *"changed through the process of inclusion . . . as explicitly sexualized subjects are incorporated into its folds."* Perhaps in parallel with the growing acknowledgement of the sexual in popular and political culture, citizenship has been expressly associated with arguments made by sexual minorities in U.S. Supreme Court case law.

Thus, in Romer v. Evans, in which a state-level constitutional amendment which sought to preclude public authorities from acting to protect lesbians and gays against discrimination was held to fail Fourteenth Amendment equal protection standards, Kennedy J. made clear for the majority that equal protection *"explains why laws singling out a certain class of citizens for disfavoured legal status or general hardships are rare. A law declaring that in general it shall be more difficult for one group of citizens than for all others to seek aid from the government is itself a denial of equal protection of the laws in the most literal sense."*

In similar vein, in her concurring judgment in Lawrence v. Texas based on equal protection analysis, O'Connor J. noted that *"the State cannot single out one identifiable class of citizens for punishment that does not apply to everyone else, with moral disapproval as the only asserted state interest for the law."*

Kennedy J.'s majority judgment in Lawrence obviously rested on due process analysis, but Cossman suggests that it may still be understood in terms of sexual citizenship. Viewed against a changing cultural backdrop in which lesbians and gay men, and same-sex couples, have become publicly much more visible, Lawrence might be seen as highlighting "the transformation of sodomite as outcast to gay subject engaged in sodomy as sexual citizen." Since the litigants had been having sex at the time of their arrest, their "newly acquired sexual citizenship is not one that disavows sex but, rather, is forced to embrace sex within its folds." Even though Kennedy J. was able to characterize the entry into a same-sex relationship as a private, domestic matter, being sexual has in many contexts simply become a part of being a citizen.

For example, Senator Orin Hatch, a vocal supporter of the proposal, argued in a 2004 Senate debate that:

"[o]ur attempt to protect traditional marriage laws has nothing to do with the private choices of gay and lesbian citizens." Cossman thus suggests that *"[a]s gay and lesbian subjects cross borders for some purposes, as they unbecome sexual outlaws, the language of border control itself changes. Social conservative opponents of same-sex marriage must appropriate the discourse of those who have sought to advance the citizenship rights of gay and lesbian subjects."*

A more mixed picture is nonetheless apparent from the dissenting judgments in Lawrence, which unsuccessfully sought to uphold the Supreme Court's earlier decision in Bowers v. Hardwick that the criminalization of consensual same-sex sexual activity survived due process analysis.

On the one hand, Thomas J. was keen to emphasize his disagreement on the merits with *"[p]unishing someone for expressing his sexual preference through non-commercial consensual conduct with another adult,"* but believed that the legislature should repeal the statute concerned rather than the Court finding it unconstitutional. However, Scalia J. (with whom Thomas J. joined) strove to defend the conclusion in Bowers that *"homosexual sodomy is not a fundamental right deeply rooted in this Nation's history and tradition."* Cossman suggests that Bowers was characterized by many of the hallmarks of border patrol of sexual citizenship.... Good citizens were familial, marital, heterosexual. Sodomites were not. The Court expressly stated its border anxieties: that recognizing a right to engage in consensual gay sex would make it difficult if not impossible to continue to police other forms of consensual sex like adultery and incest.

On this view, Scalia J. could be seen as seeking in Lawrence to maintain the existence of that border: "inclusion" of gay men and lesbians within the realm of permitted sexual activity would, in Cossman's words, undermine the "security of sexual citizenship." Such a conclusion might suggest that, there may not have been an across-the-board attribution of sexual citizen status to lesbians and gay men by moral conservatives. More generally, Nancy Cott has argued that assumptions about the appropriate forms of marriage have long established "terms for the inclusion and exclusion of new citizens". Furthermore, Cott suggests that "[a]t the same time that any marriage represents personal love and commitment, it participates in the public order" and that [p]ublic preservation of marriage on this [traditional life-long monogamous heterosexual] model has had tremendous consequences for men's and women's citizenship as well as for their private lives.

Men and women take up the public roles of husbands and wives along with the private joys and duties. These roles have been powerful, historically, in shaping both male and female citizens' entitlements and obligations. For Cott, by *"incriminating some marriages and encouraging others, marital regulations have drawn lines among the citizenry and defined what kinds of sexual relations and which families will be legitimate."* While campaigners for the recognition of same-sex marriage continue to make the exclusion of same-sex partnerships politically visible where it exists, a jurisdiction's failure to grant legal recognition might be thought to highlight the persistence of a boundary between groups of citizens given the public role of marriage as a social and legal status. Brenda Cossman builds on Cott's argument, noting that marriage grants access to a range of public and private rights and responsibilities. From actual legal citizenship through immigration and naturalization laws, to private support to Social Security, marriage is the basis for the recognition of relational rights and, with them, access to many dimensions of civil and social citizenship.

Sex, then, or more specifically—natural heterosexual intercourse—continues to formally mediate access to a full panoply of rights and responsibilities and, in turn, to full social citizenship. The entitlement to marry might thus be thought to help define who counts as a full citizen, full citizenship being a far from universal status. Nonetheless, sexual citizenship *"has begun to transform: heterosexuality no longer operates as a preemptive bar to all forms of citizenship. Gay and lesbian subjects have begun to cross the borders of citizenship, unevenly acquiring some of its rights and responsibilities and performing some of its practices."*

In the 21st century, the legal recognition of same-sex marriages has become widespread. Those who argued for the decriminalization of same-sex attraction and relationships have argued based on history by putting forward lists of famous historical figures. Such lists imply a common historical entity underlying sexual attraction whether one called it 'inversion' or 'homosexuality'. This approach is closely related to the approaches of essentialism. Essentialists claim that categories of sexual attractions are observed rather than created. For example, the ancient Greece did not have terms that correspond to heterosexual/homosexual division, persons did note men who were only attracted to persons of a specific sex, hence the lack of terminology need not to be taken as evidence of a lack of continuity in categories.

Through history and across cultures, there are consistent features, albeit with meanings variety over time and space, in sexual attraction to the point that it makes sense to speak of specific sexual orientations. According to this perspective, homosexuality is a specific, natural kind rather than a cultural or historical product. There are cultural dissimilarities in how homosexuality is expressed and interpreted, but they emphasize that it does not prevent it from being universal category of human sexual expression.

The essentialists argue that sex is organized in a given cultural and historical setting and is irreducibly particular. The emphasis on the social creation of sexual experience and expression led to the labeling of the viewpoint as social constructionism. There is no given mode of sexuality that is independent of culture, argues the social constructionists. Even the concept and experience of sexual orientation itself are products of history. Advocates of this view hold the perspective that the range of historical sexual diversity and the fluidity of human possibility is simply too varied to be adequately captured by any specific conceptual scheme. Social constructionists view heterosexuality/homosexuality as conservative, perhaps even reactionary, and forecloses the exploration of new possibilities.

Today, natural law theory offers the most common intellectual defense for differential treatments of homosexuals, and as such it merits attention. The natural law is a very long and complicated story and it is traced to the dialogues of Plato, for this is where some of the central ideas are first articulated, and significantly enough, are immediately applied to the sexual domain. For the Sophists, the human world is a realm of convention and change, rather than of unchanging moral truth.

The theory of natural law offers the most common intellectual defense used by both heterosexuals and their opponents; but it is normally used by heterosexuality advocates who find non-heterosexuality conducts disdainful. Central to this perspective is an account of human goods that are seen as good in themselves, and as rational bases for choice and human action. In relation to sexuality, the 2 most important goods from this perspective are those of marriage and personal integration.

Under the natural law perspective, there is the belief that there are genuine human goods that are least partially universally in scope and partially in commensurable, and a conviction that these goods help establish reasons for action and criteria by which to judge actions. In the 13th century, Thomas Aquinas made the most influential formation of natural law theory based on the teachings of Aristotle. Integrating an Aristotelian approach with Christian theology, Aquinas emphasized the centrality of certain human goods, including marriage. At the center of his view of marriage is the idea of fides, which in part means monogamy (it is the Latin root for fidelity) but which encompasses mutual regard and love.

Aquinas writes about marriage as the 'greatest friendship' which while realized in marital sex is oriented towards running a household, procreation and the nurturing of children. For Aquinas, sexuality that was within the bounds of marriage and which helped to further the distinctive goods of marriage: love, companionship and legitimate offsprings as permissible ad even good. All sex outside the bounds of marriage, whether premarital or extramarital are immoral. In contrast, loving, non-contracepted vaginal intercourse within a marriage is not merely permissible, it is good in itself, even apart from the pleasure and intimacy it brings.

Aquinas did not argue that procreation was a necessary part of moral or just sex; married couples could enjoy sex without the motive of having children, and sex in marriages where one or both parties is sterile, is also potentially just (given a motive of expressing love). This view actually need not rule out homosexual sex. However, for a sex is to be moral, it must be of a generative kind—only the emission of semen in a vagina can result in natural reproduction, only sex acts of that type are generative, even if a given sex act does not lead to reproduction, and even if it is impossible due to infertility.

Personal integration is the idea that humans, as agents need to have integration between their intentions as agents and their embodied selves. Hence, to use one's or another body as a mere means to one's own pleasure, as happens with masturbation, causes 'dis-integration' of the self—one's intention is just to use a body as a mere means to the end of pleasure, and this detracts from personal integration. The argument is not against pleasure but what is harmful and therefore immoral—instead of having as the end a real human good or goods, such as the goods of marriage and openness to procreation, pleasure in and of itself has become the end.

This is what is dis-integrating. Marriage should center on procreation as its 'natural fulfillment' for the committed relationship and sex to be 'just'.

Natural law advocates believe that immoral acts can be prohibited by laws, even if they only involve self-harm. The goal is therefore the cultivation of virtues in citizens, and failing that, at least the prevention of greater vice. Natural law advocates believe that laws must be responsive to the conditions of the populace-whether it is generally virtuous or vicious.

Laws will help to mold and habituate citizens and citizens-to-be into greater virtue, allowing even more moral legislations to be enacted. From this perspective, moral legislation holds out the hope of a virtuous circle of citizen improvement, where stricter laws help to properly shape citizens, which would then alter the prudential considerations, allowing even stricter moral laws.

Plato argued that unchanging truths underpin the flux of the material world. Reality, including eternal moral truths, is a matter of phusis. Although there is clearly a great degree of variety in conventions from one state to another, there is still an unwritten standard or law that humans should live under. In the Laws, Plato applies the idea of fixed, natural laws to sex and takes a much harsher line in the Symposium or the Phraedrus. In

Book One, he writes about how opposite-sex acts cause pleasure by nature, while same-sex sexuality is 'unnatural'. In Book Eight, Plato considers how to have legislation banning homosexual acts, masturbation, and illegitimate sex widely accepted. He then states that this law is according to nature. To understand the stance of Plato, it should be in the context of his overall concerns with the appetitive part of the soul and how best to control it.

Aristotle also played an important role in the development of the natural law theory. Aristotle, with his emphasis upon reason as the distinctive human function, and the Stoics, with their emphasis upon human beings as a part of the natural order of the cosmos, both helped to shape the natural law perspective which says that "True law is right reason in agreement with nature". To Aristotle, change is allowable to occur according to nature, and therefore the way that natural law is embodied could itself change with time.

They argue that Socrates, Plato and Aristotle all reject homosexuality and its associated conducts as the commitment of a man and woman to each other in the sexual union of marriage is intrinsically good and reasonable, and is incompatible with sexual relations outside marriage; homosexual conducts are radically and specifically non-marital and for that, intrinsically unreasonable and unnatural; homosexual acts have a unique similarity to solitary masturbation, and both types of radically non-marital acts are manifestly unworthy of the human being and immoral. The contention is on the phrase 'para phusin' as used by Plato in the Laws.

While those who agree and disagree on the Laws agree that the phrase translates to be 'unnatural', Plato was referring to the morality of sexual conduct, evidenced by the Republic, and the Phaedrus as well as by the Laws were substantially the same as the positions maintained in the catholic tradition's understanding of natural law as against 'para phusin' rejects that translation as tendentious as the phrase talks about 'any normative moral sense'. A look at the position of Plato, Aristotle and Musonius Rufus' conceptions of the inseparable double goods of marriage all find marriage as a union not of mere instinct but of reasonable love, and not merely for procreation but for mutual help, goodwill and cooperation for their own sake.

The core of this perspective can be clarified by juxtaposing it with St. Augustine's treatment of marriage in his 'The Bono Coniugali' where the good of marital communion is an instrumental good, in the service of the procreation and education of children so that the intrinsic, non-instrumental good of friendship will be promoted and realized by the propagation of the human race, and the intrinsic good of inner integration be promoted and realized by the 'remedying' of the disordered desires of concupiscence.

In the consideration of sterile marriages, Augustine had identified an additional good of marriage, the natural societas (companionship) of the two sexes. Had he truly integrated this into his synthesis, he would have recognized that in sterile and fertile marriages alike, the communion, companionship, societies and amicitia of the spouses—their being married—is the very good of marriage and is an intrinsic, basic human good, not merely instrumental to any other good. This communion of married verve, the integral amalgamation of the lives of the two persons, has as its intrinsic elements as essential parts of one and the same good, the goods and ends to which the theological tradition, following Augustine, for a long time subordinated that communion.

It took a long and gradual process of development of doctrine, through the catechism of the Council of Trent, the teachings of Pius XI and Pius XII, and eventually those of Vatican II—a process brilliantly illuminated by Germain Grisez—to bring the tradition to the position that procreation and children are neither the end (whether primary or secondary) to which marriages are instrumental, nor instrumental to the good of the spouses, but rather parenthood and children and family are the intrinsic fulfillment of a communion which because it is not merely instrumental, can exist and fulfill the spouses even if procreation happens to be impossible for them.

Sexual acts cannot in reality be self-giving unless they are acts by which a man and a woman actualize and experience sexually the real giving of themselves to each other—in biological, affective and volitional union in mutual commitment, both open-ended and exclusive—which like Plato and Aristotle and most people call marriage. Every society draws distinctions between behaviors found merely offensive and behaviors to be repudiated as destructive of human character and relationships.

Homosexual relationships are repudiated because they are not simply sterile, and dispose the participants to an abduction of responsibilities for the future of mankind; nor are they simply that they can nor really actualize the mutual devotion which some homosexual individuals hope to manifest and experience by it, and that it harms the personalities of its participants by its disintegrative manipulation of different parts of their one personal reality. It is also that it treats human sexual capacities in a manner which is deeply hostile to the self-understanding of those members of the community who are willing to commit themselves to real marriage in the understanding that its sexual joys are not mere instruments or accomplishments of marriage's responsibilities but rather enable the spouses to actualize and experience their intelligent commitment to share in those responsibilities, in that genuine self-giving.

All societies are made up of the communication and cooperation between their members. There are 3 types of common goods: (i) the affectionate mutual help and shared enjoyment of the friendship and communio of 'real friends'; (ii) the sharing of husband and wife in married life, united as complementary, bodily persons whose activities make them apt for parenthood—the communion of spouses, and if their marriage is fruitful, their children; (iii) the communio of religious believers cooperating in the devotion and service called for by what they believe to be the accessible truths about the ultimate source of meaning, value and other realities, and about the ways in which human beings can be in harmony with the ultimate source.

The fundamentally instrumental character of the political common good is indicated by both parts of the Second Vatican Council's teaching about religious liberty, a teaching considered by the Council to be a matter of natural law. The first part of the teaching is that everyone has the right not to be coerced in matters of religious beliefs and practice. To know the truth about the ultimate matters and adhere to and put into practice the truth, one has come to know, is so important a good and consequently a responsibility, and the attainment of that 'good of the human spirit' is so inherently and non-substitutably a matter of personal assent and conscientious decision that if a government intervenes coercively in people's search for true religion, beliefs in people's expression of the beliefs they suppose true, it will harm those people and violate their dignity even when its intervention is based on the correct premise that their search has been negligently conducted and/or had led them into false beliefs.

Religious acts, according to the Council,

> 'transcends' the sphere which is proper to government; government is to care for the temporal common good, and this includes acknowledging and fostering the religious life of its citizens; but governments have no responsibility or right to direct religious acts and 'exceed their proper limits' if they presume to do so. The second part of the Council's teaching concerns the proper restrictions on religious freedom, namely those restrictions which are 'required for [i] the effective protection of the rights of all citizens and of their peaceful coexistence, [ii] a sufficient care for the authentic public peace of an ordered common life in true justice, and [iii] a proper upholding of public morality. All these factors constitute the fundamental part of the common good and come under the notion of order public'.

St. Aquinas also played a critical role in promoting the natural law theory with his writings and teachings. To Aquinas, although sexuality that was bound within marriage and which helped to further what he saw as the distinctive goods of marriage, mainly love, companionship and legitimate offspring, was permissible and good; procreation was not a necessary part of moral or just sex; married couples could enjoy sex without the motive of having children, and sex in marriages where one or both partners is sterile is also potentially just given a motive of expressing love. For Aquinas adds, any given sex act to be moral, it must be of a generative kind.

Thomas Aquinas' treatise, On Princely Government, advocates that government should command whatever leads people towards their ultimate end, forbid whatever deflects them from it, and coercively deter people from evil-doing and induce them to morally decent conduct. Aristotle also sees the state as a mere mutual insurance arrangement for which the common good of the state is insufficient—self-sufficiency (autarcheia) is a life lacking in nothing of complete fulfillment. Hence, integral human fulfillment is nothing less than the fulfillment of all human persons in all communities and cannot be achieved in any community short of the heavenly kingdom—a community envisaged not by unaided reason but only by virtue of divine revelation and attainable only by a divine gift which transcends the capacities of nature. Therefore, to Aristotle, '*[T]he polis was formed not for the sake of life only but rather for the good life...and...its purpose is not [merely] for the sake of trade and business relations...any polis which is truly so called, and is not one merely in name, must have virtue/excellence as an object of its care [peri aretes epimeles einai; be solicitous about virtue]. Otherwise a polis sinks into a mere alliance, differing only in space from other forms of alliance where the members live at a distance from each other. Otherwise, too, the law becomes a mere social contract [syntheke covenant]—or (in the phrase of the sophist Lycophan) 'a guarantor of justice as between one man and another—instead of being, as it should be, such as will make [poiein] the citizens good and just...The polis is not merely a sharing of a common locality for the purpose of preventing mutual injury and exchanging goods. These are necessary preconditions of the existence of a polis...but a polis is a communio [koinonia] of clans [and neighborhoods] in living well, with the object of a full and self-sufficient [autarkous] life...it must therefore be for the sake of truly good (kalon) actions, not of merely living together'. The state is therefore seen as a cooperation which undertakes the unique tasks of giving coercive protection to all individuals and lawful associations within the domain, and of securing an economic and cultural environment in which all persons and groups pursue their own proper goods. This common good of the political community make it far more than a mere arrangement for 'preventing mutual injury and exchanging goods'.*

Sexual health is fundamental to the physical and emotional development of the individual and ultimately to the social development of communities. Nonetheless, the achievement of sexual health and its associated development is influenced by the access to comprehensive information about sexuality—knowledge about the risks faced and vulnerabilities to the adverse consequences of sexual activities; and an atmosphere that affirms and promote sexual health.

Legislations and public policies that are applied to sexuality-related matters play a critical function in fostering or worsening sexual health, and in promoting and safeguarding the individuals" human rights to sexual health. According to the World Health Organization (WHO) Technical

Report series in 1975, sexual health is defined as '*the integration of the somatic, emotional, intellectual and social aspects of sexual being, in ways that are positively enriching and that enhance personality, communication and love*'.

However, there has been drastic changes in understanding human sexuality and sexual behavior since that period due to elements such as the HIV pandemic and the toll taken on health of societies by other sexually transmitted infections (STIs). In the last three decades at least, there has been a rapid increase in the documentation and understanding of the nature of discrimination and inequality related to sexuality and sexual behavior in relation to health.

This includes information about the marginalization, stigmatization and abuse of those perceived as having socially unacceptable sexual characteristics or practices. Moreover, there has been a rapid expansion of the application of human rights to sexuality and sexual health matters, especially relating to protection from discrimination and violence, and protection of freedom of expression and association, privacy and other rights for the marginalized. This has resulted in the production of an important body of human rights standards promoting sexual health and human rights.

Also, according to the World Health Organization, '*sexuality is a central aspect of being human throughout life; it encompasses sex, gender identities and roles, sexual orientations, eroticism, pleasure, intimacy and reproduction. Sexuality is experienced and expressed in thoughts, fantasies, desires, beliefs, attitudes, values, behaviors, practices, roles and relationships. While sexuality can include all of these dimensions, not all of them are always experienced or expressed. Sexuality is influenced by the interaction of biological, psychological, social, economic, political, cultural, legal, historical, religious and spiritual factors*'.

Furthermore, sexual health is '*a state of physical, emotional, mental, and social wellbeing in relation to sexuality; it is not merely the absence of disease, dysfunction or infirmity. Sexual health requires a positive and respectful approach to sexuality and sexual relationships, as well as the possibility of having pleasurable and safe sexual experiences, free from coercion, discrimination and violence. For sexual health to be attained and maintained, the sexual rights of all persons must be respected, protected and fulfilled*'.

Ill-health related to sexuality represents a significant disease burden globally. This includes morbidity and mortality related to HIV and other sexually transmitted infections; morbidity and mortality linked to lack of access to contraception and safe abortion services; erectile dysfunction; the sequelae of sexual violence and female genital mutilation; and sexual and reproductive cancers. Sexually transmitted infections are significant causes of acute illnesses, infertility, long-term disability, and death, with serious medical and psychological effects for millions of people.

For instance, people between 15 and 49 years, an estimated 448 million new cases of four curable sexually transmitted infections—chlamydia, gonorrhea, syphilis and trichomoniasis—occurred in 2005 and the numbers are not diminishing; an estimated 38 million people are currently living with HIV or AIDS with 1.5 million people becoming newly infecting with HIV in 2020. Since 1981, 79.3 million people have become infected with HIV/AIDS with 36.3 million people having died from AIDS-related illnesses; and 1.7 million children between 0-14 years living with HIV as at 2020. Out of those about 38 million living with HIV/AIDS as at 2020, 53% were women and girls.

Law is seen as patriarchal, hierarchical, and rigidly formal in ways that does violence to women's claim as well as the claims of homosexuals. However, rights and laws are essential-incredibly so-and often used in given contexts. Laws and rights provide aspirational norms that can be mobilized to hold institutions accountable and to provide material benefits to those excluded from systems of power. Legal discrimination based on sexuality is not anything new to societies of today.

England for example after Parliament's decriminalization of private adult homosexual conduct by the Sexual Offences Act, 1967, the highest court (the House of Lords) reaffirmed that a jury may lawfully convict on a charge of conspiring to corrupt public morals by publishing advertisements by private individuals of their availability for (non-commercial) private homosexual act. The Court of Appeal has constantly reaffirmed notably in 1977, 1981 and 1990 that public soliciting of adult males by adult males fall within the statutory prohibition of 'importun[ing] in a public place for an immoral purpose'.

England's Parliament has peacefully accepted both judicial interpretations of the constitutional, statutory and common law position. It has also voted more than once to maintain the legal position whereby the age of consent for lawful sexual intercourse was 21 as at 1967 following the recommendations of the Wolfenden Report for homosexuals but 16 years for heterosexual intercourse; in February 1994, its House of Commons voted to make the homosexual age of consent 18 in the Criminal Justice and Public Order Act, 1994 which would reduce but retain the differentiation between heterosexual/homosexual conducts; and finally lowered to 16 in the Sexual Offences (Amendment) Act 2000.

These laws have been enacted to protect children's rights as well as prohibits a person in a position of trust from performing sexual acts with someone who cannot consent, including minors and very vulnerable people. Today, modern standard position of European sexuality laws is consistent with the view that (apart perhaps from special cases and contexts, it is unjust for A to impose any kind of disadvantages on B simply because A believes (perhaps correctly) that B has sexual inclinations (which s/he may or may not act upon) towards persons of the same-sex. The position does not give B the widest conceivable legal protection against such unjust discrimination (just as it generally does not give wide protections against needless acts of adverse private discrimination).

However, the position does not itself encourage, sponsor or impose any such unjust burdens; and it is accompanied by many legal protections for homosexual persons with respect to assault, threats, unreasonable discrimination by public bodies and officials, among others. Laws are enacted in relation to sexuality due to concerns for public morality and the education of young ones towards truly worthwhile and against allowing but bad forms of conduct and life. Nor have such states renounced the judgment that a life involving homosexual conduct is bad even for anyone unfortunate enough to have innate or quasi-innate homosexual inclinations.

States regulate sexuality because they deem it necessary to supervise the public realm and the reasons deduced include: this is the environment in which young people (of whatever sexual inclination) are educated; it is the context in which and by which everyone with responsibility for the wellbeing of young people is helped or hindered in assisting them to avoid bad forms of life; it is the milieu in which and by which all citizens are encouraged and helped, or discouraged and undermined in their own resistance to being lured by the temptation into falling away from their own aspirations to be people of integrated good characters and to be autonomous, self-controlled persons rather than slaves to impulse and sensual gratification.

Whenever there is an advocacy of a repeal of laws on sexuality, the focus as always been on homosexuality. However, the critical question to be answered is can these be defended by reflective, critical, publicly intelligible and rational arguments? Even the advocates of 'gay rights' do not seriously assert that the state can never have any compelling interest in public morality or the moral formation of its young people or the moral environment in which parents, other educators and young people must undertake this formation.

The first and earliest known law condemning the act of male-to-male intercourse is the Middle Assyrian Law Codes of 1075 BC which states: if a man has intercourse with his brother-in-arms, they shall turn him into a eunuch. In the Roman republic, the Lex Scantinia, imposed penalties on those who committed a sex crime against a freeborn male minor. For adult male citizens to experience and act on homoerotic desires was considered permissible, as long as their partner was a male of lower social standing.

Pederasty in ancient Rome was acceptable only when the younger partner was a prostitute or slave. Starting in 1200s, the Roman Catholic Church launched a massive campaign against sodomites, especially homosexuals which became radically criminalized in most of Europe even punishable by death. Interesting, there are few countries in the world that sodomy has never been illegal and these include Ivory Coast, Laos, Madagascar, Mali, Niger, North Korea, Rwanda, South Korea, Philippines, Poland, Taiwan, Benin, Burkina Faso, Cambodia, Central African Republic, Congo, DR Congo, China, Djibouti, Equatorial Guinea, Indonesia and Vietnam.

In 1786, Pietro Leopoldo of Tuscany abolished the death penalty for all crimes thus becoming the first ruler to abolish death penalty for sodomy and was replaced by prison and hard labor; then followed by France during the French Revolutionary penal code issued in 1791 which struck for the first time down sodomy as a crime and decriminalizing it together with all 'victimless crimes' (sodomy, heresy, witchcraft, blasphemy) and during the first Czechoslovak republic (1918-1938), the heterosexuals became a movement and asked to repeal sodomy laws.

Many countries that have decriminalize homosexuality have based their rulings on the fact that they are two consenting adults and are above the consenting age irrespective of gender orientation as found in the case of Naz Foundation v National Capital Territory of Delhi which was overturned by the Supreme Court of India on 11th December, 2013; the fact that, 'there is no place for the state in the bedrooms of the nation'; the equality rights, for example in the 1995 Court of Appeal for Ontario case R. v. M. (C) the judges ruled that the law was unconstitutional on the basis that the specific exemptions based on marital status and age infringed on the equality rights guaranteed by section 15 of the Charter of Rights and Freedoms, and constituted discrimination based on sexual orientation'; that the enact of the act is voluntary as in the Chinese Supreme Court ruling in 1957; that such laws are discriminatory towards a section of the public i.e. homosexuals and infringes on their fundamental rights.

A large part of the international community continues to deny many of the protections of human rights law to homosexuals, bisexuals, and other sexual minorities. Few states do so in the conviction that sexual minorities lack the same basic human needs as everyone else. Nor, if they are forthright, do states deny them human rights because they believe sexual minorities undermine national security, economic prosperity, or other legitimate state interests. Nor yet do they do so because sexual minorities infringe on the human rights of others by their intimate personal choices and conduct. They do so primarily because political elites or their constituents, or both, are offended by unconventional sexuality for cultural and religious reasons.

Far from offering clear guidance on the content of human rights law relating to sexuality, these documents merely state general norms of personal and familial privacy and free association intended to protect individuals from arbitrary government intrusion into intimate relations. Most of these instruments include express guarantees of freedom of association, rights against arbitrary or unlawful interference with privacy, and protection of family life and the right to marry.

In this context, the right to privacy is usually construed not merely as the freedom to maintain secrecy, but as freedom of intimate conduct, association, and expression without fear of arbitrary state interference. These rights have implications also for those of sexual minorities. Another accepted norm of international human rights law is nondiscrimination in the protection of human rights or grant of state benefits based on specific intellectual, cultural, or physical attributes of a class of persons, such as race or sex.

The major human rights instruments do not necessarily guarantee uniformly the same kinds of rights or interests from the same kinds of discrimination, but they contain catch-all protected categories requiring state parties to guarantee all of the human rights set forth in the respective instruments without distinction based on sex, birth, or "other status".

The source of contention may be traced to a qualification to many human rights expressed in the relevant treaties that include explicit exceptions for measures taken by the state to maintain public morals and welfare. The ICCPR allows states to restrict the exercise of association by any laws that *"are necessary in a democratic society in the interests of national security or public safety, public order (ordre public), the protection of public health or morals or the protection of the rights and freedoms of others."*

The UDHR does, however, provide generally that the rights set forth therein may be limited by state action necessary for "meeting the just requirements of morality, public order and the general welfare in a democratic society. *"Even where textually absent, however, these same exceptions are typically and understandably considered implicit in both privacy rights and the right against discrimination. In interpreting the ICCPR, for example, the U.N. Human Rights Committee has concluded that discrimination may be justified"* if the criteria for such differentiation are reasonable and objective and if the aim is to achieve a purpose which is legitimate under the Covenant.

On the other hand, there is always a risk that states will rely on these broadly drawn exceptions to intrude into interpersonal relations unnecessarily. The flexibility inherent in the ordre public and morality exceptions has long been used by states to justify the systemic oppression of and discrimination against classes of persons defined as sexual "deviants" and repression of masturbation, fornication, oral or anal intercourse, and other sexual practices.

For example, the state may claim that outlawing the use of contraceptives in private sexual relations advances an important public policy of maintaining population growth or preventing condemned fornication, and thereby constitutes permissible state regulation of sexuality and other intimate relations. Although the ICCPR contains no specific limitation on the privacy right based on "morality" or ordre public, in 1985, the SubCommission on Prevention of Discrimination and Protection of Minorities of the U.N. Economic and Social Council (ECOSOC) adopted the Siracusa Principles on the Limitation and Derogation of Provisions in the ICCPR (Siracusa Principles), which interpret the term "public order" as limited to the rules that "ensure the functioning of society or the set of fundamental principles on which society is founded."

The Sub-Commission interpreted "public morals" somewhat more expansively as "*essential to the maintenance of respect for fundamental values of the community*." This interpretation, besides suggesting that universal human rights are not universal at all (unless by "community" the Sub-Commission intended the world community), leaves undefined what kind of communal "fundamental values" are worthy of respect and justify derogation of human rights, what kind of regulation is essential to ensure the maintenance of those values, and so forth.

For example, it says nothing about whether a society in which undeviating adherence to a state-sponsored religion is a "fundamental value" that could justify the expulsion or execution of apostates, much less the systematic denial of public sector jobs to them, in derogation of principles of freedom of religion, conscience, and speech. The answer to these questions suggested by the Siracusa Principles reminds us that even the core principles supporting international human rights law remain contested by many states. The denial of these rights not only prevents sexual minorities from engaging in peaceful advocacy to persuade the public and political elites of the legitimacy of their claims to human rights. It also shuts down their ability to organize in order to support and assist one another in dealing with legal disadvantages and detrimental social prejudices by criminalizing their organization.

Specifically, states discriminating against sexual minorities or unconventional sexuality in one way or another have had to justify this discrimination to their domestic populations and to the international community as consistent with the exceptions in human rights instruments for public morality and ordre public. The most difficult forms of regulation to justify are criminal prohibitions on unconventional sexual behavior, as these entail the most intrusive form of state regulation into the most private and personal of behaviors. Criminal prohibitions consequently represent the fastest receding area of state discrimination against sexual minorities.

Other forms of discrimination have, however, proven more tenacious. Among these are discrimination in the age of legal consent to sex, bans on military enlistment, and state tolerance of private persecution of sexual minorities. When sexual minorities seek state license on equal terms for benefits provided freely to heterosexuals, such as marriage and parental rights, states have shown the most recalcitrance.

Same-sex intercourse remains subject to criminal penalties in 41 of the 192 United Nations member states for women and in 71 states and 3 sub-state provinces for men, including almost all of Africa and the Middle East, and much of Asia. This number includes some states that have no laws forbidding homosexual intercourse eo nomine but that nonetheless prosecute it under nebulous prohibitions on "immorality," "debauchery," "obscenity," or "hooliganism." In these countries, homosexuality is as illegal de facto as it is in countries that formally forbid homosexual conduct.

As at 2008, laws and policies indirectly regulate the behavior of some 2.5 billion of the world's 6.7 billion people, more than a third of the world's population. Penalties for homosexual conduct in most of these countries are disproportional to whatever harm the crime is imagined to cause, and range from long terms of imprisonment (up to life) to physical punishment to execution. At least seven countries are known to prescribe the death penalty for homosexual conducts—Afghanistan, Iran, Mauritania, Pakistan, Saudi Arabia, Sudan, and Yemen.

Other forms of unconventional sexuality may receive lesser but still harsh punishments. For example, in addition to capital punishment for sodomy, the Iranian penal code prescribes a punishment of one hundred lashes for the offense of Tafhiz ("the rubbing of the thighs or buttocks" between two men), sixty lashes for male kissing, and one hundred lashes for the first three convictions for the offense of Mosaheqeh (lesbianism) and death for the fourth. While reliable calculations of actual executions do not exist, Iran has reportedly imposed the death penalty on homosexuals numerous times.

Beginning in 1982, the trend toward decriminalization of unconventional sexuality was buttressed and accelerated by two European developments. The first was the Parliamentary Assembly of the Council of Europe's Resolution 924, which urged member states to decriminalize homosexual intercourse and to ensure equality of treatment between heterosexuals and homosexuals.

This was followed in 1984 by the European Parliament's adoption of recommendations to eliminate workplace discrimination based on sexual orientation.

These resolutions established the first Europe-wide public policy of treating some kinds of discrimination based on sexual orientation as inconsistent with state policies respecting personal freedoms and the limits of governmental regulation. The second development was the ECtHR's 1981 decision in Dudgeon V. United Kingdom. In Dudgeon, the court heard a challenge to Northern Ireland's criminal prohibition on oral and anal intercourse, described in the statutes at issue as "buggery" and "gross indecency.

"In considering whether this invasion of the private life of the applicant could be justified for the protection of morality, the court found that none of the various social and political factors it considered could qualify the legislation as "necessary or appropriate" in a democratic society. Instead, the court held: Although members of the public who regard homosexuality as immoral may be shocked, offended or disturbed by the commission by others of private homosexual acts,

> this cannot on its own warrant the application of penal sanctions when it is consenting adults alone who are involved".

The basis of the decision-a violation of the Article 8 right of privacy without reference to Article 14 (discrimination)--evidences an approach concerned with protecting sexual liberty in general from unjustified state interference. The ECtHR (European Court on Human Rights) has reiterated the Dudgeon holding on this point several times since, striking down statutes in Ireland and Cyprus criminalizing adult, consensual homosexual intercourse. The court's decision on the matter binds all forty-seven member states of the Council of Europe. A steady stream of liberalizations followed Dudgeon over the next two decades. Domestic courts and legislatures around the world began striking down prohibitions on adult, consensual homosexual conduct with great rapidity.

Northern Ireland was the first following Dudgeon in 1982 to decriminalize homosexual intercourse, while France repealed its law making homosexuality an aggravating circumstance in the offense of public indecency. In 1984, Cuba decriminalized same-sex intercourse, and in 1986, New Zealand did as well. In 1991, Hong Kong decriminalized oral and anal intercourse. After liberation from communist dictatorship in the early 1990s, almost all of the former Soviet republics of Eastern Europe, the Baltics, and several in Central Asia decriminalized homosexual intercourse as well.

In 1994, the U.N. Human Rights Committee put an international spin on these mostly isolated events. In Toonen v. Australia, the U.N. Human Rights Committee found that prohibitions on homosexual intercourse constituted a violation of Articles 17(1) (privacy), 26 (equal protection of the laws) and 2(1) (nondiscrimination) of the ICCPR. After acknowledging that adult, consensual sexual activity conducted in private falls within the scope of Article 17 privacy, the Committee stated that interference in such a right could only be justified if "reasonable in the circumstances"-a phrase the Committee interpreted in harmony with the ECtHR's interpretation of Article 7 of the ECHRv8 to mean *"proportional to the end sought and ... necessary in the circumstances of any given case"*.

The Committee rejected Tasmania's proffered justification for the legislation as necessary to secure public morality on the ground that such a rationale could justify virtually any invasion of privacy. " The Committee found that, because the criminal law prohibiting homosexual intercourse went mostly or entirely unenforced, it could not be deemed "necessary" or "essential" to protect morality. In concluding, the Committee opined that discrimination based on sexual orientation was forbidden by Articles 26 and 2(1) under the rubric of discrimination based on "sex".

The Human Rights Committee now often includes prohibitions on homosexual intercourse among the state measures condemned in its reports. More recently, it has broken a new barrier, calling for the United States to outlaw employment discrimination based on sexual orientation altogether.' Neither the Toonen guidance nor the HRC's subsequent practice, however, further accelerated the trend toward decriminalization. Decriminalization proceeded on an individual state basis largely as before.

In 1994, Australia reacted to the Toonen guidance by enacting a blanket prohibition on provincial laws prohibiting "[sexual conduct involving only consenting adults acting in private." Also in 1994, the European Parliament called expressly for the decriminalization of homosexual intercourse in all EU member states. In 1995, Albania, Cyprus, Macedonia, and Moldova repealed their bans on homosexual intercourse. In 1996, the Colombian Constitutional Court struck down that country's laws criminalizing adult, consensual homosexual sex, and Iceland repealed a similar law.

In the following year, the People's Republic of China repealed its laws forbidding *"hooliganism,"* which had often been used to persecute homosexuals, while the Constitutional Court of Ecuador struck down that state's antisodomy law. In 1998, the South African Constitutional Court, referring to the U.N. Human Rights Committee's decision in Toonen, struck down a similar law on constitutional grounds. Beginning in 2000, the Council of Europe's Parliamentary Assembly formalized the trend by announcing a policy of accepting for membership only those states that had abolished criminal prohibitions on homosexual intercourse.

This pushed the last of the Eastern European holdouts into liberalization. Romania soon thereafter decriminalized homosexual intercourse after threats of sanctions from the Council of Europe overcame strident church opposition. The United States is a relatively late bloomer. Until 1961, every U.S. state outlawed homosexual conduct between consenting adults; that number was halved by 1986 when the Supreme Court decided in Bowers v. Hardwick *that adult homosexuals had no constitutional right to engage in "sodomy"*.

In the 2003 decision in Lawrence v. Texas, the Supreme Court overruled Bowers, finding state statutes criminalizing homosexual conduct to be an unconstitutional intrusion on freedom and privacy. India in 2018 through its Supreme Court ruled that gay sex is no longer a criminal offence 'which at one stroke cut in half the world's male population being subjected to laws criminalizing same-sex intercourse (homosexual intercourse between females is not illegal in India)". Very few of these states have bucked the trend and recriminalized homosexual intercourse after decriminalizing it. In the historic judgement of the Indian Supreme Court, the apex court in its ruling said: "Criminalizing carnal intercourse is irrational, arbitrary and manifestly unconstitutional"; and that "history owes an apology" to LGBT people for ostracizing them.

Countries have decriminalized non-heterosexual sexuality and its accompanied acts because of the protection of the rights of such people is set out to be enjoyed without discrimination on any grounds such as 'sex, race, color, language, religion, political or other opinion, national or social origin, association with a national minority, property, birth or other status'. Opponents of the decriminalization have argued that such a 'remedy' would work significant discrimination and injustice against and would indeed damage families, associations and institutions which have organized themselves to live out and transmit ideals of family life that include a high conception of the worth of truly conjugal, sexual intercourse.

Law does have a role to play in sex and sexuality, but it should aim to steer a path between (i) untethered individualism in how these concepts and categories manifest in the public sphere and (ii) dogmatic conservatism, masquerading as realism, that artificially and oppressively constrain such manifestations. Laws can exert both proximal social consequences and distal social consequences. Laws regarding sexuality is necessary to determine and punish violence as well as distribute rights equitably across all citizens as in the Fricke v. Lynch, 1980 where the federal district court of Rhode Island decided 2 young men were entitled to attend prom together and that the school must provide enough security at the dance to ensure that the young men were safe while attending the dance.

Laws and policies regarding sexuality can determine what children learn about sex in schools as a way of governing and ensuring the circulation of sexual knowledge; legislating types of couples are allowed to marry, govern family formation and for some reproduction. Laws on sexualities are made to protect young people because young people are often perceived to be the neediest of and the most vulnerable to sexual information. The focus on sexual knowledge is influenced by the interest in regulating and standardizing knowledge about sexuality. Such a policy has interest in regulating how a person imagines sexual scenarios.

These focal policies are organized around age and consider the child or minor as needing education or protection from the sexual knowledge of adults. Laws and policies regulating sexual behavior are mostly concerned with what a person does with their or another's body, with or without a partner, which may or may not include one's genitals. Such legislations violate privacy, further complicating expectations around sexual privacy and when sexual bodies are public or private matters of concern. Criminalizing non-heterosexual sexuality inflict psychosocial harms on the individuals to which such laws apply. Specifically, by criminalizing same-sex relationships, homosexuals and bisexuals are denied access to sexual intimacy which is a key component to psychological health development of close relationships.

Hence, such laws exclude homosexuals from attaining fundamental aspects of the human experiences as well as further promoting discrimination of and violence against sexual minorities. Sexuality is regulated because the state is concerned on how a person reproduces or forms a family. 'Sexuality is most certainly a hugely symbolic, social affair...But it is also a lusty, bodily, fleshy affairs'. Sexuality related based on the concept of the sexual body sees the sexual body as the material body—the flesh, blood, and genitals of a person who has sexual experiences.

The sexual body is usually imagined as a vulnerable space that needs protection from harm, and therefore, is the location of several primary types of policies, including sexual health, safety and wellbeing. The sexual body is a matter of public concern in the sense that it moves around and has the potential to affect other sexual bodies through infection, reproduction and relationality. Bodies have often been the marker of devaluation resulting into seeing specific bodies as pathological or deviant or marginalized and needing the guidance and protection of policy, resulting in the surveillance of certain bodies and not others.

For example, in 1982, Crystal Chambers, an unmarried Black woman in her early twenties, worked for the Girls Club of Omaha as an arts and crafts instructor. After becoming pregnant, she was fired from her job for offering a 'negative role model' to the young girls in the club when she became a single, pregnant, working woman. Chambers sued and lost—the court ruled that it was a violation of the club's Negative Role Model Policy, which stated that *'single persons who become pregnant or cause a pregnancy would no longer be permitted to continue employment at the Girls Club'*.

Here, the policy is aimed at regulating the visibility and spectatorship of specific sexual bodies—pregnant while unmarried was seen to carry with it the danger that other young girls would follow suit. Furthermore, other policies aim to criminalize specific bodies and deem certain bodies inherently dangerous regardless of whether they are ill or contagious. Example, majority of U.S. states have criminalized HIV exposure through sex, shared needles, and even exposure to 'bodily fluids' including saliva—regardless of intent or actual transmission. As of 2010, more than 600 people had been convicted of criminal HIV exposure or transmission.

Spitting and biting have been used as proof to apprehend people even though HIV was not transmitted. Again, men who have sex with men are excluded automatically from donating blood, semen or organs by the CDC regardless of their HIV status or relationship history. Sexuality as a sexual infrastructure is one area that policies and laws are made to govern. To understand sexual infrastructure, there is the urgency to understand the concept of 'thick desire' as proposed by McClelland and Fine. They argued that thick desire encourages people to thread the sexual experiences and wants of young people to the ideologies, policies, power relations, institutions, families and schools in which they live and develop.

Thick desire highlights the need for a set of enabling conditions that links a person's capacity to desire and engage sexually with a set of necessary sexual infrastructures including to [a] develop intellectually, emotionally, economically and culturally;[b] imagine themselves as sexual beings capable of pleasure and cautious about danger without carrying the undue burden of social, medical, and reproductive consequences;[c] have access to information and health-care resources;[d] be protected from structural and intimate violence and abuse; and [e] rely on a public safety net of resources to support youth, families, and community. Infrastructures in this sense are structures that hold up a system, a community or a state.

Laws and policies focused on sexual infrastructures aim at a larger structural level, influencing how social institutions organize themselves and determine agreed-upon social norms. Example, the Gay, Lesbian and Straight Education Network examined school environments for LGBT and gender nonconforming youth in its National School Climate Survey of 2011 which included responses from 8,584 students aged 13-20 years from all 50 states and the District of Columbia and represented more than 3000 school districts, the findings showed that a majority of LGBT youth faced verbal harassment (e.g. called name or threatened) because of their sexual orientation (81.9%) or gender expression (63.9%); a third of respondents reported missing at least a day of school in the past month because they felt unsafe or uncomfortable; 56.9% of LGBT students reported hearing homophobic statements and negative remarks about gender expression from their teachers or other school staff.

As a result of this, 2 anti-bullying bills were proposed in Congress in 2011/12, both of which specifically mentioned gender identity and sexual orientation as characteristics for which bully victims have been singled out: The Student Non-

Discrimination Act (SNDA, 2011) and the Safe Schools Improvement Act (SSIA, 2011) and as of July, 2011, all but 3 states (Michigan, Montana and South Dakota) had enacted anti-bullying laws that required school districts to adopt an anti-bullying policy.

Some states have lists of specific behaviors—such as Florida's list, which include teasing, social exclusion, threat, and stalking—and other states such as Delaware and Mississippi, have a bullying policy that refer more generally to 'any intentional written, electronic, verbal or physical act or actions against another student, school volunteer, or school employee; and Tennessee has a policy that refers simply to bullying in terms of its consequences [i.e. interfering with students' educational benefits] without elucidating specific behaviors.

These laws and policies are essential because victimization at school has been linked to numerous negative psychological outcomes, including depression, loneliness, suicides, and low self-esteem as well as alcohol and tobacco use, poor academic achievement, and poorer relationships with classmates.

Certain policies are based on rationales surrounding perceived need for control of women's sexuality and reproductive decision-making abilities such as laws on contraceptives and abortion; other rationales are based on a desire to 'protect' the larger society from what policy makers consider 'morally corrupt' sexual behaviors, bodies and actors such policies directed as same-sex sexualities and HIV and abortion [which implicitly represents a desire to protect the unborn—when envisioned as yet to be a member of the society]. This protection discourse provides the avenue and resources for policy makers to determine what and who is seen as dangerous as well as who is seen as vulnerable.

At the center of such policies aimed at regulating sexuality are the notions of being a good, healthy, sexual citizen; defining specific bodies and groups, and individuals as worthy of protection and others as needing surveillance control and punishment to diminish their influence; the collective preservation of national healthy as a civil obligation. Hence, policies on sexualities as a public health matter sits at the intersection of fears over contamination, morality, hygiene, reproduction and religion.

However, regulations on sexuality has become an avenue to enforce policies aimed at punishing those who become ill for failing in their duties as good citizens, rather than helping people remain healthy. Societies have decriminalized sexuality [non-heterosexuality conducts] because it is important as law reforms is a useful tool in combatting social prejudice; that institutions ought to serve as liberators in the face of existing social and legal discriminations.

For instance, in the European Community, homosexuality was decriminalized by historical antecedents. Homophobia, the most extreme manifestation of which was the mass slaughter of non-heterosexuals in Nazi Germany is an example of the type of prejudice and injustice committed against non-heterosexuals in modern history. Therefore, a state which professes noble aims, cannot hope to achieve them if it turns a blind eye to prejudice, discrimination and sometimes even to the oppression of some 2-10% of its citizens.

In contrast, this is simply a slippery slope of increasingly draconian laws that infringe upon important freedoms as seen in Nigeria and proposed bill in Ghana. According to the

International Covenant on Civil and Political Rights (ICCPR), there is non-discrimination norm modeled on the Universal Declaration on Human Rights (UDHR) Article 2. ICCPR Article 2(1) states: '*Each State Party to the present Covenant undertakes to respect and to ensure to all individuals within its territory and subject to its jurisdiction the rights recognized in the present Covenant without distinction of any kind, such as race, color, sex, language, religion, political or other opinion, national or social origin, property, birth or other status*'.

Article 26 provides a further non-discrimination norm '*All persons are equal before the law and are entitled without any discrimination to the equal protection of the law. In this respect, the law shall prohibit any discrimination and guarantee to all persons equal and effective protection against discrimination on any grounds such as race, color, sex, language, religion, political or other opinion, national or social origin, property, birth or other status*'. Unlike article 2(1) which provides for non-discrimination only with regards to the 'rights recognized in the present Convention', article 26 reaches considerably further, providing for 'equal protection of the law'—that is arguably, of 'all' law—within the jurisdictions of the State Parties.

The ICCPR provided for the creation of the Human Rights Committee, whose functions include issuing comments on reports submitted by State Parties, and examining individual complaints. The first global sexual revolution occurred from the 16th through the 19th centuries through European colonialism. Germane to the depiction of colonized people as savages was the depiction of their sexuality, including, in many cases, same-sex or transgender practices, as sinful, primitive or bestial. Native inhabitants of Asia, Africa and the Americas were burned, tortured or punished for 'deviant' and 'sinful' sexual practices during the 16th and 17th centuries.

Subsequent attempts to 'mainstream' colonized peoples, enduring into the 20th century included the thoroughgoing eradication of 'un-Christian' social and sexual norms. Yet, today, in defense of discrimination against sexual minorities, a characterization of, for instance, homosexual conduct is 'un-African' is promoted by political elites in non-Western States routinely relying upon European colonial statutes.

Most African countries maintain the 19th century penal codes prohibiting 'carnal knowledge against the order of nature'. Such a vocabulary has more to do with Victorian readings of the Old Testament Sodom and Gomorrha story than with anything that can clearly be called 'traditional African values'. As a result of maintaining the language of 'carnal knowledge' or as replaced with homosexuality, African states have enacted draconian laws, for example as in the case of Mozambique, where homosexuality is punishable with up to 3 years' imprisonment and hard labor for purposes of 're-education; and Nigeria punishing homosexuality with up to 14 years' imprisonment with hard Labour.

Underestimate nor overestimate the significance of such laws, for such laws were enacted to substitute some forms of sexual oppression with others. Yet when post-colonial political elites speak of their pre-colonial ancestors as having categorically condemned homosexuality or transgenderism, they perpetuate the self-same colonial worldview they accuse Europeans of having imposed.

The notion of minority sexual orientation as 'un-African' or 'un-Asian' is the embodiment of European-style racism, for it does exactly what

Europeans were accused of doing: it ignores the histories of thousands of different African and Asian people, throughout thousands of years of history, each with their own changing patterns of social and sexual norms. It perpetuates the distinctly colonial idea that Africans or Asians are all alike, that their pre-colonial existence was frozen in time.

CHAPTER VI

SOCIOLOGY & SEXUALITY

"According to the prevailing view human sexual life consists essentially in an endeavor to bring one's own genitals into contact with those of someone of the opposite sex"—Sigmund Freud

Sexuality as a social construction is defined as "*the genitally-based distinctions between men and women accompanied by culturally defined appropriate sexual tastes, partners and activities*". Sexuality is the result of a dialectical process between individuals. A person's sexuality is a negotiated social fact—what you think is your sexuality versus what others think is your sexuality. Sexuality can be seen as a set of similar boundaries dividing populations; sexual identities are negotiated, situational and shifting as well as socially constructed.

Sexuality has always played a major role in the power and class struggles of any society. A classic example is found in the roots of contemporary racism and racial conflicts in early American history and slavery. Both thrived in the environment of lust, greed and demeaning sexual stereotypes. Sexuality demonstrates the plasticity of human behavior and attitudes for which man constructs his own nature. Sexuality is seen as a representation of humanity at its stratums of social classifications.

Sociologists such as Gagnon and Simon consider sexuality as a desire of social constitution which is located in mundane actualities of everyday life which is continually constructed and reconstructed throughout adolescence and adulthood. Therefore, variability of human sexuality cannot be explained and understood through the repression or modification of pre-social drives but rather must be understood as socially situated meaningful conduct.

Sexuality is therefore seen as a sexual conduct and not sexual behavior since behaviors imply a response to inner drives or external stimuli but rather conduct as it conveys the meaningfulness of human sexuality as well as the reflexive processes of negotiations through which meanings emerge. Acts, feelings and body parts are not sexual in themselves but only become so through the application of sociocultural scripts that imbue them with sexual significance.

"Scripts are involved in learning the meanings of internal states, organizing the sequences of specifically

sexual acts, decoding novel situations, setting the limits on sexual responses, and linking meanings from nonsexual aspects of life to specifically sexual experience". Sexuality is culturally inherent, interpersonal and intrapsychical. It is fluid and contigent as well as emergent from the actualities of everyday practices which ensures avoidance of dangers of ungrounded abstractions common in other forms. "*It is easy to see how social the sexual is when one notes that the patterns of idiosyncratic desires flow from all that which is social—racism, sexism, ageism, romanticism, etc. all social values and beliefs are complexly present and visible*".

The sociology of sexualities has experienced growth. In its infancy and early childhood, the sociology of sexualities was mainly the terrain of scholars interested in 'deviance' of one sort or another, and especially of the homosexual sort; the coping mechanisms of discredited and discreditable sexual beings. As sexuality liberation movements soared, the sociology of sexualities became more interested in sexuality as a basis of community and political life. The sociology of sexuality relayed heavily on the social constructionism donated by symbolic interactionists, phenomenologists, and labeling theorists.

The sociology of sexuality became tightly linked to denaturalizing project, demonstrating as "*sexual meanings, identities, and categories were intersubjectively negotiated social and historical products—that sexuality was, in a word constructed*". Sociologists demonstrated the variability of sexual meanings, identities, and categories, many shifted their focal point from "the homosexual" as a fixed, natural, universal sort of being to "homosexual" as a social category that "should itself be analyzed and its relative historical, economic and political base be scrutinized".

By the mid-1990s, "queer theory" began to make its mark on academic studies of sexuality. Its poststructuralists roots were revealed in its claims that sexual and other identities are "arbitrary, unstable, and exclusionary" and in its interests in "those knowledges and social practices that organize 'society' as a whole by sexualizing". Since the late 1990s, there has been something of a reconciliation between sociology of sexuality and poststructuralist queer theory as sociologists began more assertively to make their own contributions to a "queer sociology".

Rather than conceiving of heterosexual and homosexual identity and community as "monolithic empirical units of analysis, sociologists have been challenged to sharpen their analytical lenses to grow sensitized to the discursive production of sexual identities, and to be mindful of the insidious force of heteronormativity as a fundamental organizing principle throughout the social order".

The advances of queer theory are based on 4 hallmarks:

"a notion that sexual power runs throughout social life, and is enforced through "boundaries and binary divides"; a "problematization" of sexual and gender categories as "always on uncertain ground"; a rejection of civil rights strategies in favor of "deconstruction", decentering, revisionists readings, and antiassimilationist politics; and a "willingness to interrogate areas which normally would not be seen as the terrain of sexuality".

The notion that sexuality would not simply be understood through the presumptive binary categories of "homosexual" and "heterosexual" resonated with much earlier sociological constructionism. Nonetheless, queer theory pushed further arguing that sexual identities, desires and categories are fluid and dynamic, and that sexuality is inevitably intertwined with even sometimes constitutive of power relations.

Identities are neither stable nor unified across time and space; they vary in "duration, durability, and dominance". Amongst homosexual gays, there are several "ideal types" of identity such as **"peacocks"**—those who live and work in exclusively gay circles, and for whom being gay is a full-time master identity; **"chameleons"**—those who live and work in the suburbs, and commute to hardcore, urban gay lives for sex and socializing; and **"centaurs"**—those who live and work in the conurbations and mix that with gay social and sexual activities here and there.

Peacocks treat "gayness as a noun", chameleons treat their identity as a verb, and centaurs treat it as an adjective. The analysis of sexual identities is not static hence *"collective actors do not exist de facto by virtue of individuals sharing a common structural location"*, but are *"created in the course of social movement activity"*. Fixed identities are seen as the basis for oppression and the basis for political powers.

Others have argued that to understand homosexuality, there should be a "third way" between the closet of invisibility, the cloistered ghetto, and "the dubious status of public spectacles". In this manner, homosexuality as an identity is understood as "never singular...but as also never separate from the vicissitudes of commercialization and heterosexual, mainstream culture" and homosexuals are citizens just as anyone in a state that is basically altered by their inclusion and forced to *"rethink and reimagine marriage, family, partnerships, sexual and gender identity, friendships, love relationships"*.

To sociologists of sexualities, gender and sexuality are linked systems to the more difficult task of specifying how sexuality intersects and interacts with other systems of oppressions. Sexuality has in recent years been linked to race and class for which there has been active investigations of the sexualization of race, the racialization of sexuality, the classing of sexuality and the sexualization of class. For example, black sexuality has become *"constructed as an abnormal or pathologised heterosexuality"* through the female jezebel and the male rapist images and subjected to *"sexualized racism" that justifies segregation and racial containment*.

Leaders in power use languages of sexuality to naturalize oppression based on race, class, and gender, such as in racist understandings of black women as sexually voracious, Asian women as sexually erotic, black men as sexually predatory, and white women as sexually innocent. These have influenced policies as broad as colonization, marriages, and welfare law, healthcare and education. A definition of sexual preference based only on the gender of the desired neglects the many factors that contribute to a person's experience of sexual attraction. The desires of a person by another is not based on only gender but also by constructions of race, ethnicity, age and class.

Therefore, identities cannot be understood as simply an accumulation of the effects of different categories. Nationalism and colonization "*suggests that building nations and national identities involves inspecting and controlling the sexualities of citizens and condemning the sexualities of noncitizens and those considered outside the sexual boundaries of the nation.*" While others see sexuality as enduring and acultural, others have argued that it cannot be separated from the world outside and that sexuality is often shaped by political and economic conditions.

To such scholars, sexuality as affected by and reflect global political-economic and political policies has led to the commercialization of sex—"the rapidity of change is increasing the sex trade" and the various ways in which sexual mores and values have changed as "societies have come into contact with outside influences and new technologies." Others have argued that the political economy of tourism and development shape sexual possibilities and identities, therefore creating new sexual types such as **'internacional'**- someone whose sexual identity reflects North American sexual category and cosmopolitanism.

With the transformation of the gay and lesbian movements into a niche market, there has been market for greater visibility for "homosexual with money "sort of "unintended disenfranchisement on the basis of race, class and gender that is an effect of conceiving of political rights as market-based rights". This assertion ignores "differences among homosexuals, such as those of gender and race", a parallel tendency toward a "nationalist" pseudoethnic paradigm, since the group must be a definable and identifiable market segment.

Homosexuality and other minority groups are seen as lazy, slothful and morally suspects who are getting special rights, circumventing the channels that reward those who work hard. In the 21st century, sex is seen as a recreational culture especially in the political economy due to the rise of the service sector. In a postindustrial service sector, a culture has emerged that sees commercial sex indoors as legitimate while seeing lower-price, outdoor prostitution as bad—exploitative, addictive and criminal.

This street level policing and cultural normalization has facilitated the rise of a postindustrial service sector and the information economy, helping to create the clean and shiny urban spaces in which middle-class men can safely indulge in recreational sexual consumption. Colonialism has also been blamed for the misunderstanding on gender and sexuality as it is deemed to have led to the creation of a new gender system whereby colonialists created for—and imposed upon—the colonized very different arrangements compared to their while bourgeois colonizers. A typical example is found in the colonial and independent history of the US where differential gender arrangements led to the criminalization of the rape of white women as a violation of their womanhood, while black women could be raped with impunity.

Under the dual gender framework, only Europeans were gendered, and so civilized and fully human. Against this, the enslaved and the colonized were judged as excessively sexual and improperly gendered. This is seen as the genesis of the "*long process of subjectification of the colonized toward adoption/internationalization of the men/women dichotomy as a normative construction of the social*".

In the 18th century, there were epistemological shifts provoked by the emerging sciences as well as the political challenges of women excluded from formal power led to a growing emphasis on the two-sex model with an increasing biologization of male and female as two distinct sexes that belonged in two separate spheres, in which men only were suited for the public sphere, while women belonged in the private sphere. This biologised sex distinctions became the basis for emerging definitions of the two distinct sexualities—heterosexuality and homosexuality.

In pre-enlightenment Europe and Africa, understanding of sex was in the context of power and class. Contemporary western notions of sexuality and particular types of people were absent. Nonetheless, from 1500s, male travel writers constructed the monstrosity of humanity via a focus on the bodily and sexual deviances of their women from normative European standards. Before the coming of European Portuguese Catholics in Africa, Africans accentuated balance, centeredness and order with sexuality seen as necessary for a happy life as well as women considered as autonomous beings with a presence in public life and some level of access to power and authority.

However, the Catholics saw these as impediments to conversion and thus translated Christian notions of gender and sexual hierarchy via African moral tropes. These worked often hand-in-hand with the roles of globalizing capitalism and earlier colonial states, which used emerging racializations to organize the various forms of free and unfree labor they constituted and managed. Colonial narratives about gender and sexuality were central to how Africans were incorporated into slavery.

By the 1700s, a number of problematic assertions about African women's bodies and behaviors including tolerance for pain, their propensity for easy and painless childbirth and breastfeeding justified their dehumanization and enslavement. If African women had easy and painless childbirth for instance, they did not require rest after delivery and could be put directly back to work. This denial of the "privileges of gender" was extended to African men. While men enjoyed power and authority within their own households, black men did not; likewise, while white families were considered the cornerstone of society, black families possessed none of these rights.

Colonization buoyed the need to shore up and perform civilizational narratives of sexed difference, binary gender and (hetero)sexuality both "abroad" and "at home". Colonialism was not only consequential for the development of sexual regimes in the trucial states and metropoles, it served to deny the power and authority traditionally held by women as well as had the effect of displacing local conceptions of balance, centeredness, and independence with hierarchical categories of good and evil, god and devil, and male and female. For instance, while West African Yoruba social order had been organized traditionally by principles of seniority, British colonization introduced gendered ideologies and asymmetries.

The system of indirect rule by the British recognized only the male chief's authority at the local level, thereby excluding women from colonial state structures. *"The very process by which females were categorized and reduced to "women", then, made them ineligible for leadership roles"*. The historical sociology of sexuality adopted the dichotomies of civilized/primitive, rational/irrational that characterized the broader colonial conditions—masculinity became associated with rationality and femininity became the irrational. Both became integral components of the heteropatriarchal family as the necessary locus of "civilized" sexuality.

The marital and sexual customs of different people were a marker of their progress from savage and barbarous stages to civilization, hence the beginning of the heteropatriarchal family fulfilled the law of Evolution. However, to the father of sociology, Auguste Comte, the character of modern society and the demands it made on men made the patriarchal family critical since modern society required the containment of irrational desires or sexual passions, and the solution was the heteropartriarchal family.

Family was indeed central to Comte's social statics. Social statics is the synchronic study of all the elements out of which societies are made. Accordingly, one of the goals of social statics is to identify the elements constitutive of social phenomena—individuals, families, and societies themselves. Individuals are described as endowed with a natural instinct for sociability, characterized by the preeminence of affective faculties over intellectual ones, and led in their actions by the consideration of their well-being.

As for the family, it constitutes the first form of society, for only such an association enables the social dispositions inherent in individuals to thrive. They develop by way of the rudimentary division of labor existing between husband and wife, which foretells the hierarchical cooperative system to be found in societies proper. As Comte put it, *"the family spontaneously presents us with the genuine necessary germ of the diverse essential dispositions characterizing the social organism"*, *"domestic life [being] the constant basis of social life"*.

Accordingly, since the family, as conceived by Comte, is a strictly patriarchal association (in which the husband — or the father - provides for the needs of his dependents and supervises all activities, while the wife takes care of the household), and given that society is just a development of the organizational features of the domestic realm, subordination — of wife to husband, of children to parents — is to be mirrored at the level of society itself:

> *"Whatever empty notions are to be formed today about social equality, any society, even the most limited, necessarily and obviously presupposes not only diversities but also some inequalities: for there could not exist a genuine society without a permanent cooperation to a general operation, carried on by way of distinct and suitably subordinated means. Now, the most complete realization possible of such elementary conditions inevitably belongs to the family only, in which nature has borne all the essential costs of the institution".*

Obviously, the practicability of Comte's organizational proposal depends on the availability of knowledge of human capacities and abilities that would enable him to cash out empirically his factual premise ("males are fit for supervision and women for obedience"). Accordingly, if one wants to refute his argument, perhaps it would be worth leaving aside the first premise (which is not entirely counter-intuitive and benefits from some empirical support) and taking the second as the primary target.

What Comte needs in order for his argument to be sound is a premise establishing that men are endowed with specific character traits enabling them to carry out supervision duties in ways unavailable to women. The hierarchical organization should be based on natural differences in capacities, if such differences exist. These features, Comte finds in the biological make-up of individuals.

"The sound biological philosophy, especially with regard to the important theory of Gall, begins to be able to treat as it scientifically deserves these chimerical revolutionary pronouncements concerning the alleged equality of the two sexes, by demonstrating directly, either by way of anatomical examination, or by way of physiological observation, the radical differences, both physical and moral, which, in all animal species, and particularly within the human race, separate one from

the other, notwithstanding the common preponderance of the specific type".

Nonetheless, Mill disagrees with the assertions made by Auguste Comte especially on women. Mill regards women's education as one of the main causes of their subjection, which usually takes the form of them being confined to the household and its domestic chores, with no hope for an independent existence. He details this reproductive mechanism when he comes to inquire into the "means by which the condition of a married woman is rendered artificially desirable". After having set aside unlikely explanations (it cannot be because of an improvement of women's legal or civil condition subsequent to marriage, for there is none), he points out what he thinks is the main cause of the enduring attraction of marriage: "*It is not law, but education and custom which make the difference. Women are so brought up, as not to be able to subsist in the mere physical sense, without a man to keep them*".

Since girls are brought up in the idea that they are destined to be men's dependents in all decisive regards (security, subsistence, affection), they do not feel—and they are prevented by their parents and acquaintances from realizing it—the urge to develop character traits such as self-reliance, fortitude, or initiative. To the contrary they are prompted to cultivate alleged feminine character traits such as patience, temperance, or benevolence for relatives, which suit their social position. Therefore, they end up being convinced that they do not partake of these qualities so highly praised in men, and imagine that their mere existence is impossible without them.

Such is the trick of men-governed societies: to convince women that they are not fit for autonomy because of their intellectual capacities and that they benefit from the system of dependence to which they are subjected. If women are to further their social position, they must be educated so as to be able to earn by themselves their livelihood, that is by getting trained in a certain profession. By the same token, they might be able to develop the character traits associated with such a training (perseverance, ingenuity, etc.), which are certainly elements partly constitutive of autonomy and independence, and might be able to express, on a par with men, the full range of their intellectual capacities.

Now, in a society where marriage has become a matter of choice and not of necessity, what about divorce? Mill lists three main arguments in favor of indissolubility. First, he acknowledges the fact that repeated failures in finding the light match may contribute to the moral debasement and disillusionment of those who fail to encounter the appropriate partner. Secondly, in case the couple has children, he invokes the necessity of guaranteeing for them a familial environment in which they will thrive. Thirdly, he underlines the fact that if one is not bound and can substitute one partner for another, that could tend to prevent one's moral improvement, for one could always put the blame on the other.

Mill maintains one should not fear that people will part with each other on the burst instance of disagreement. For, in a "tolerably moral state of society", promiscuity will still be an object of moral reprobation. As for children, Mill ventures that the new modalities of marriage (in which the partners are free to enter or not into the relation), by elevating the morality of individuals, will lead couples to have children if and only if they are sure that their affection for each other is true and durable. And if they decide to divorce, they will eschew total separation for the children's good. But Mill sees no serious reasons for refusing the possibility of divorce. Hence his conclusion:

> *"The arguments, therefore, in favor of the indissolubility of marriage, are as nothing in comparison with the far more potent arguments for leaving this like the other relations voluntarily contracted by human beings, to depend for its continuance upon the wishes of the contracting parties".*

Mill viewed the issue of women's emancipation as a central social question deserving a full-length analysis. Just as Comte, Mill thought that the practical issue of divorce, and by extension that of the appropriate structure of family, could only be settled by an inquiry into the nature of women's intellectual capacities, which would rely primarily on an ethological basis. Once this knowledge would be made available to the public, it would bring drastic reforms with regard to women's social position. As far as Mill was concerned, he surely hoped the "scientificisation of politics" would lead to such an outcome.

Nonetheless, Weber and Durkheim argue that modernity requires a routinization of sexuality via monogamous heterosexual marriage and that in "civilized" modernity, women who in the past were little different from men in terms of morphological characteristics of height, weight and even brain size must be entrenched. Therefore, civilized sex was marital, heterosexual coitus; even though Weber viewed sexual love as the greatest irrational force in life positing an evolutionary divide between raw, unembarrassed, pre-modern, primitive sexuality and rationalized sexuality.

Earliest sociologists contend that societies with the greatest gender distinctiveness were the most civilized. Early historical sociology elaborated the character of the modern in relation to two, interrelated oppositions: a temporal opposition to a primitive or traditional past, wherein certain gender and sexual bodies and practices were cast as anachronistic; and spatial opposition to primitive or traditional spaces, wherein certain gender and sexual bodies and practices were rendered outside the space of modernity.

Everything matters and nothing alone ever simply matters. The sexual activities of both males and females and genders are very important to individuals irrespective of age. A survey conducted by Wiley and Bortz revealed that men below 70 years are mostly troubled about their feelings about decreased sexual frequency when compared to women—85% of men compared to 63% of women. Also, those above 70 years were synonymous in their sexual conducts, i.e. 21% of men are very troubled compared to a 0% of women above 70 years. Although both below 70 and above 70 wish to have regular sexual encounters and satisfactions at least once a week.

In nation-states, citizenship is associated with heterosexuality as it is implicitly the heterosexual citizen who symbolizes an imagined national community and underlies the construction of a notion of a shared collective national identity. This is so because, for instance, the term "homosexual" has long been associated with the charge of treachery and treason, usually "justified" with the claim that homosexuals are liable to blackmails. This image of the "homosexual" as a potential traitor has been used to signal fear of a threat to national security.

Thus, this specific historical construction of homosexuality, based upon a presumed risk of betrayal, undermines the position of 'homosexuals' as legitimate members of a nation-state. While the notion of nation-state is constructed as heterosexual, this does not mean that all forms of heterosexuality are necessarily regarded equally. It is heterosexuality as marriage and the traditional, middle class nuclear family which is commonly held up as a model of good citizenship necessary for ensuring national security and a stable social order. Moreover, women have often been identified as closer to 'nature', they have also been at risk of exclusion from 'civilized' society.

The process of such dehumanization operates through the exclusion of those deemed to be closest to nature, and more 'animal-like', in the case of sexuality; it also operates to exclude those who are not a part of nature so defined (as heterosexual) who are constructed as unnatural (homosexual). The naturalization of heterosexuality not only serves to dehumanize lesbians and gay men; it also provides the context in which the right to existence of lesbians and gays may be questioned.

The primacy of gender has often been reduced to a one-sided understanding of gender difference. This is the bane of homophobia. Nonheterosexuality oppressions have been on the rise in societies, and such oppressions are difficult to fully understand.

In some situations, they are described as disadvantageously positioned by sexual prejudice, but always advantageously positioned on the grounds of gender; yet this situation is blurred by recent accounts of the many ways in which gay men are denied the privileges that attach to dominant forms of masculinity as well as large numbers of lesbians having developed an effective social distance from the domestic exploitation and physical dangers of intimacy with heterosexual men.

Evidence about the exceptional vulnerability of gay men to acts of serious physical assaults and murder appear to defy a common-sense structural understanding of various levels of group oppression. Evidence further shows that lesbians are subject to disturbing levels of homophobic harassment and violence in public places, as well as the levels of physical violence against gay men are even higher. To society, the violence committed against lesbians and gays is justifiable because same-sex desire not only disregard the conventions that accord supremacy to heterosexuality, it also challenges gender axioms that define masculinity and femininity as encompassing a sexual attraction to each other.

Lesbian violence is gendered and can be categorized into three broad sphere: feminization of the lesbian subjects through enforced acts of heterosexuality, the characterization of lesbians bodies as unhygienic and the association of lesbianism with masculinity. Survey researches indicate that in terms of age and socioeconomic status, homosexual men have much higher rates of victimization compared to heterosexual men, and are more frequently the victims of random public attacks. A classic example is a Brazilian study of the killings of gay males, lesbians and 'transvestites' which found a high level of complicity with police and military officials pointing to the links that can exist between this violence and the masculinist culture of the larger society.

For example, in 1993, a transsexual dressed in a wig, dress and high heels and wearing makeup, went walking along a public cycleway near Wollongong. He was approached by young male strangers and then tortured and killed in a lengthy attack. According to one youth convicted, he approached what he thought was a young woman in the darkness only to be subjected to a sexual advance provoking violence.

In his statement to the court, it emerged that his rage against the deceased concerned the issue of public feminine appearance as evident in his words:

> "I was coming around the corner and someone jumped out behind me and I've turned around and he said 'ah, I'm gonna get you' or 'hello young gentleman' or something like that ... he was going on about something, just looked really weird to me ... he's just started saying his stuff and just going on. I was just throwing me hands and they, they were, just hitting him. He had something on his face. I think, I think he had make-up on. I'm not sure because he just looked – ah it just made me feel sick ... and then he's grabbed me and it just went on from there".

Most people who engage in violence against homosexual men are men in a marginal location of social class with the masculine claim on power undermined by economic and social weaknesses. Such perpetrators are young men with little education, minor criminal histories and bare survival through laboring jobs. Gay bashing serves a dual purpose of constructing a masculine and heterosexual identity through a simultaneous involvement with violence and by establishing homosexuals as an oppressed group of social outsiders.

CHAPTER VII

THE INTERSEX: ARE WE NORMAL?

"In adopting a patently false but stubbornly clung to mythology of human sexuality that makes demons out of natural drives, we've entered a stage of moral sickness, not of moral health"—Jesse Bering

"Sexual desire was a play of signifiers, an infinite determent and displacement of anticipated pleasure which the brute coupling of the signified temporarily interrupted"—David Lodge

Michel Foucault's notion of conceptual genealogy is quite useful in understanding contemporary medical views of intersex as pathological. During the early years of the Enlightenment, in the late 18th century, the medical establishment began to gain authority over the body. This was, in large part, related to the developing science of taxonomy. This scientific focus on classification had a major impact on how clinicians viewed and treated human bodies, especially when bodies or body parts seemed to defy typical categorization.

Cary Nederman and Jacqui True reviewed 12th century theological and medical writings that characterized sex as continuous rather than binary. Unlike later, 12th century contentions that an intermediate intersexed state is not truly possible, it appears that, during the 12th century in Western Europe, hermaphrodites were regarded as a discrete third sex. This idea was based on Galen's second-century theory claiming that there were gendered differences in body temperature, especially in the reproductive and sexual organs.

According to this theory, sex distinctions were based on a continuum of heat, with males being internally hotter than females, thus creating the impetus for male external reproductive organs and female, "colder," internal organs. In Thomas Laqueur's analysis, this differential temperature theory actually provided the basis for a one sex conceptual model, with females being seen as the inverse of males. (That is, the vagina was viewed as an inverted penis, the uterus as a scrotum, the fallopian tubes as seminal vesicles, the ovaries as internal testicles, and so on).

In the early 17th century, scientific thought about apparent females masculinizing at puberty was associated with Galen's temperature model. The esteemed seventeenth-century surgeon Ambroise Pare viewed an excessive amount of internal heat as the cause of this female pubescent masculinization. According to Pare's writings of 1634, this heat was typically brought on by the activities of children, such as jumping and playing roughly, which then led to the "pushing out" and transition of internal female organs into external male organs. Laqueur disagrees with both Pare and Galen. He claims that Pare's theory is based on "reading" male anatomy onto female bodies and that Galen viewed men not only as "hotter" than women but also as superior to them.

The widely read and highly acclaimed pseudo-Galenic De Spermate further defined sex differentiation in reproduction. According to De Spermate, both the male "seed" and the female uterus played active roles in determining the sex of the offspring. The uterus and testicles were seen as divided into hot (right) and cold (left) sections, with both having a mysterious indeterminate middle section. When male "seed" was planted in the warmer, right section of the uterus, the baby was a boy. A girl was produced by implantation in the colder, left side of the uterus. If the "seed" planted itself in the midsection, a hermaphroditic baby was produced.

In this sense, with the uterus having a separate, "neutral" chamber for nurturing hermaphroditic fetuses, hermaphroditism was conceptualized as a natural, if not expected, state. Further evidence of the definition of three distinct sexual categories comes from the late-twelfth-century Italian civil jurist Portius Azo, who wrote in his Summa Institutionum (1610): *"There is another division between human beings, namely that some are male, others are female, others are hermaphrodites"*. Although attitudes toward hermaphroditism varied widely in twelfth-century Europe, from viewing hermaphrodites as monsters to seeing hermaphroditism as natural, hermaphroditism was seen as a separate, third sex category.

Since this period precedes the separation of church and state, the writings of theologians had great influence. On the moral regulations applied to the hermaphrodites of the twelfth century, the Parisian, Peter the Chanter, wrote:

> *'The church allows a hermaphrodite--that is, someone with the organs of both sexes, capable of either active or passive functions -to use the organ by which*

(s)he is most aroused or the one to which (s)he is most susceptible. If (s)he is more active, (s)he may wed as a man, but if (s)he is more passive, (s)he may marry as a woman. If, however, (s)he should fail with one organ, the use of the other can never be permitted, but (s)he must be perpetually celibate to avoid any similarity to the role inversion of sodomy, which is detested by God'.

This widely accepted tolerance of hermaphrodite choice in her/his sex/gender/sexuality stands in striking contrast to the rigidity of contemporary sex assignment. It appears that although physiological ambiguity was allowed to persist in premedicalized times, the forms in which sexual identity could be displayed or expressed were culturally mandated. In contemporary and historic times, legal concerns related to sex ambiguity are located within a system of gendered rights and obligations. In Epstein's normative breaching, "*Hermaphrodites highlight the privilege differential between male and female precisely because they cannot participate neatly in it*".

Throughout history, family, church, and state have exercised control over overt expressions of gender such as choice of occupation, gender of marital/sexual partner, and type of clothing as a means to distinguish between women and men and to decrease the sex/gender/sexual ambiguity presented by hermaphrodites. For example, in the mid-twelfth century, a person's ability to serve as a legal witness depended on her/his predominant gender. As women were excluded from providing court testimony, voting privileges, and property rights, hermaphrodites who presented as more female than male were also precluded from exercising the legal rights accorded to males at the time.

Early surgical attempts to solder sex, such as lowering abdominal testicles, appeared in the beginning of the 19th century. A primary motive for the social insistence upon outward displays of gender clarity was fear of homosexuality, or hermaphroditism of the soul, a threat that was present in the sexually ambiguous (or, quite literally, bisexual) body of the hermaphrodite. By appearing, outwardly, to be of the "other" sex, it was feared hermaphrodites would tempt heterosexual partners into homosexual relations.

The legal motivation for making precise sex distinctions was, and is, grounded in a morally based attempt to preserve the heterosexual institution of marriage, which is predicated on sex difference. By the end of the 18th century, "*The sex of husband and wife was beset by rules and recommendations. The marriage relation was the most intense focus of constraints; it was spoken of more than anything else*". Regardless of the time period, demarcations for lawful marital unions are precise even when legal definitions of sex are lacking.

According to Roger Ormrod, "To constitute a valid marriage the parties must be of different sexes, for the simple reason that is what the word [marriage] means". Although overt legal discourse surrounding the validity of marital unions concentrates on sex (as in genitals, gonads, and chromosomes), the underlying motive for the insistence upon "opposite" sex wedlock appears to be social insurance against sodomy. This is evidenced by legal clauses relating to the traditional penile-vaginal heterosexual consummation of marriage vows. Ormrod and Donna Hawley note that an inability to consummate a marriage in this manner provides legal grounds for annulment.

Additional reasons for requiring legal registration and classification of sex at birth include the prevention of fraud; restriction for the carrying out of sex-specific rights, duties, and obligations; and the preservation of morality and family life (otherwise known as the prevention of homosexual relations). In Alexander Capron and Richard D'Avino's words, *"To enforce the prohibition (and, incidentally, public sexual displays) between members of the same sex, society needs a legal means of classifying all individuals by sex"*.

In the same article, the authors reiterate the importance of maintaining a stable sex once it is proclaimed: *"The state's insistence on a dual classification [of sex] is usually accompanied by a requirement of permanency in the designation"*. In fact, transgressions of sex/gender stability have been met historically by punishments as severe as death. In early seventeenth-century France, hermaphrodites were allowed to marry a person "opposite" of their predominant sex. Once a hermaphrodite made this type of visible gender choice, they were morally and legally expected to adhere to that decision—to uphold the ascribed social status in gender.

Echoing Peter, the Chanter's statement above, if a hermaphrodite turned against their sex/gender decision in a sexual relationship, they were charged with sodomy, publicly whipped, hanged, and/or burned. In contrast with twelfth-century allowance of social gender choice, in eighteenth and nineteenth-century western Europe, female pseudohermaphrodites who gained access to male privilege through outwardly male displays such as marriage to women and performing "male" occupations were often charged with fraud or usurping male privilege and subjected to public punishment such as whipping, hanging, and burning.

A "natural" and "invariant" properties of reality. Members of any society will regard some of their own rules, practices, or customs as more or less arbitrary than others. Some will be seen as alternative, variable, or optional: others will be the "only," the "natural," and the "imperative" ways in which the world is constituted. This "taken-for-granted," "couldn't-be-otherwise" quality of some aspects of culture is reflected in the level of awareness people have of them. That people everywhere maintain relatively unconscious assumptions regarding time and space, customs, attitudes and values, meanings of all kinds, and language itself, is common anthropological knowledge.

One such assumption, which is probably universal, is that the world consists of two biological sexes—men and women. That the world should be so constituted is taken for granted as the natural, normal and necessary way of things. Of course, it is commonly recognized that biological men and biological women may fail to behave in ways appropriate to their sex—may be too masculine, too feminine or even become transvestites—but such persons are nevertheless always known to be biological men or women, even though they may have "gone wrong." It is always understood that a person is born with a male or a female body, and despite a lifetime of acts that compromise or even reverse normal sex role expectations, this person will continue to live in the body of a man or woman.

Occasionally, however, children are born that do not have a clearly male or female body. These are the cases of hermaphroditism or, as it is now known, intersexuality—that is, persons possessing some degree of anatomical or physiological sexual ambiguity. It is now recognized that in terms of chromosomal sex, gonadal sex, hormonal sex, the predominant internal accessory reproductive structures, and the external genital morphology, gender occurs along a continuum rather than in a pair of discrete binary opposites.

While medical knowledge of these sexual conditions permits the ranking of individuals along such a continuum, knowledge in the vast majority of non-Western societies is confined to the common sense understanding of the phenotypic expression of sex-facial hair, voice, breast development, general body configuration, and preeminently, the external genitalia. In these societies, when infants are born, the external genitals provide the only evidence for intersex. The incidence of marked intersexuality in man is estimated to be 2-3%, but, of course, in societies where the only criterion is the external genital morphology, this rate would drop considerably.

Still, the condition (and the problem) is probably known to all societies. If it is true, as it seems to be, that societies are organized on the fundamental and unspoken assumption that there are only biological males and biological females, and that such a reality is natural and necessary, then the birth of intersexed infants must pose a fundamental problem. The occurrence of intersexuality is thus an unnatural incongruity for which societies must provide a practical and moral resolution.

Intersex also known as hermaphroditism is a group of conditions where there is a discrepancy between the external genitals and the internal genitals (the testes and ovaries). This group of condition is today known as disorders of sex development (DSDs). Intersex is divided into four different categories: 46, XX intersex, 46 XY intersex, true gonadal intersex and complex or undetermined intersex.

The 46, XX intersex: The person has the chromosomes of a woman, the ovaries of a woman but external genitals appear as male. This most often is the result of a female fetus having been exposed to excess male hormones before birth. The labia fuse, and the clitoris enlarges to appear like a penis. This condition used to be called female pseudohermaphroditism. Such conditions are influenced by several possible causes: congenital adrenal hyperplasia (the commonest cause); male hormones (such as testosterone) taken or encountered by the mother during pregnancy; male hormone-producing tumors in the mother—these are often ovarian tumors; and aromatase deficiency (that may not be noticeable until puberty).

Aromatase is an enzyme that normally converts male hormones to female hormones. Too much aromatase activity can lead to excess estrogen; too little to 46 XX intersex. At puberty, these XX children who had been raised as girls, may begin to take on male characteristics.

46, XY intersex: The person has the chromosomes of a man, but the external genitals are incompletely formed, ambiguous, or clearly female. Internally, testes may be normal, malformed or absent. This condition is also called 46, XY with undervirilization or male pseudohermaphroditism. Formation of normal male external genitals depends on the appropriate balance between male and female hormones. Thus, it requires the adequate production and function of male hormones.

46 XY intersex causes include:

- Problems with the testes. The testes normally produce male hormones. If the testes do not form properly, it will lead to undervirilization and one of

such possible cause include XY pure gonadal dysgenesis.
- Problems with testosterones formation. Testosterone is formed through a series of steps. Each of these steps requires a different enzyme. Deficiencies in any of these enzymes can result in inadequate testosterones and produce a different syndrome of the 46 XY intersex.
- Problems with using testosterone. Some people have normal testes and make adequate amounts of testosterones, but still have 46 XY intersex due to conditions such as 5-alpha-reductase deficiency or androgen insensitivity syndrome (AIS).
- People with 5-alpha-reductase deficiency lack the enzyme needed to convert testosterone to dehydrotestosterones (DHT). There are at least 5 different types of 5-alpha-reductase deficiency. Some of the babies have normal male genitalia, some have normal female genitalia, and many have something in between. Most change to external male genitalia around the time of puberty.
- Androgen Insensitivity Syndrome (AIS) is the most common cause of 46, XY intersex. It has also been called testicular feminization. Here, the hormones are all normal, but the receptors to male hormones don't function properly.

True Gonadal Intersex: The person must have both ovarian and testicular tissue. This may be in the same gonad (an ovotestis) or the person might have 1 ovary and 1 testis. The person may have XX chromosomes, XY chromosomes, or both. The external genitals may be ambiguous or may appear to be female or male. This condition used to be called true hermaphroditism. In most people with true gonadal intersex, the underlying cause is unknown, although in some animal studies, it has been linked to exposure to common agricultural pesticides.

Complex or undetermined intersex disorders of sexual development. Many chromosomes configurations other than simple 46, XX or 46, XY can result in disorders of sex-development. These include 45, XO (only one X chromosome), and 47, XXY, 47, XXX. These disorders do not result in a condition where there is discrepancy between internal and external genitalia. However, there may be problems with sex hormone levels, overall sexual development, and altered numbers of sex chromosomes.

Symptoms associated with intersex include ambiguous genitalia at birth, micropenis, clitoromegaly, partial labia fusion, apparently undescended testes in boys, labial or inguinal (groin) masses in girls, hypospadias, electrolyte abnormalities, delayed or absent puberty, unexpected changes at puberty. In approximately one out of every 100 births, seemingly tiny errors occur during the various stages of fetal sex differentiations, causing a baby's body to develop abnormally. Problems in the formation of chromosomes, gonads or external genitals can lead to a range of intersex conditions and the most common of these conditions include:

Congenital Adrenal Hyperplasia (CAH) which occurs in one in 13,000 births. Here, two hormones are critical in normal sex differentiations. The testes of normal 46, XY males secretes both Müllerian Inhibiting Substance (also known as MIS or antiMüllerian hormones) and masculinizing androgenic hormones, while the ovaries of a normal 46, XX females secretes neither. In CAH, the absence of a critical enzyme allows a 46, XX fetus to produce androgens, resulting in ambiguous external genitals. A CAH individual may have an oversized clitoris or fused labia.

Testosterone Biosynthetic Defect which occurs in one out of 13,000 births. In a condition related to CAH, some 46, XY individual do not have the properly functioning enzymes needed to convert cholesterol to testosterone. When such enzymes prove completely incapable of creating testosterone, the genitals appear female; when the enzymes function at a low level, ambiguous genitals form.

Androgen insensitivity syndrome (AIS) which occurs 1 out of 13,000 births. AIS affects the section of the 46, XY population that is physically unable to react to androgens. In Complete AIS, testes exist in the abdomen while the external genitals are female. The Wolffian, or male, duct structures do not form because of the lack of response to androgens. The Müllerian, or female, duct structures do not evolve because the testes still release MIS. At puberty, Complete AIS individual grow breasts but do not menstruate. The testes are sometimes removed from the abdomen because they may develop cancer. Partial AIS (PAIS) is marked by a limited response to androgens. The external genitals are ambiguous and duct development is incomplete.

Depending on the selection of hormone treatment, PAIS individuals may exhibit partial male or partial female development at puberty. During development, the testes also make a hormone (MIS) that prevents formation of the uterus, fallopian tubes, and a small part of the upper vagina. Due to the fact that testes do not make estrogen, and the body can turn androgens into estrogen, people may have traits like breast development from their own hormones at puberty, and often supplement with synthetic hormones to fully develop. The risk of cancer development before puberty in CAIS (Complete Androgen Insensitivity Syndrome) is very low, and it is accepted medical practice to leave CAIS testes in place for a more natural puberty, and because androgen also influences sperm formation, some adult men do not discover that they have minimal PAIS until they see a doctor for infertility.

Gonadal Dysgenesis which occurs in one in every 150,000 births. In gonadal dysgenesis, the androgen receptors are intact while the androgen-secreting testes are not. Complete Gonadal Dysgenesis (or Swyer syndrome), in which neither androgens nor MIS are produced, yields female genitals and Müllerian duct formation, despite a genetic profile suggesting maleness. During prenatal development, these babies develop a vulva and a small uterus. The underdeveloped, would-be testes become fibrous tissues called "streaks" which are neither testis or ovary.

With estrogen treatment, female puberty can be achieved. Nonetheless, because there is an increased risk of cancer developing in streak glands, removal is commonly recommended. Partial Gonadal Dysgenesis results in ambiguous genitals and duct development, as some androgens and MIS are produced. Like PAIS, the choices of hormone treatments determine the physical gender of the adult with Partial Gonadal Dysgenesis. Babies' genitals can vary in appearance depending on how much the testes function. Tumors occur about 20-30% of the time.

Undescended and streak gonads present a 30% probability of gonadoblastoma and dysgerminoma. The incident increases with age, at 10% by age 20 and 19% by age 30. In dysgenetic male, pseudohermaphroditism, the incidence of tumor formation is 3% in patients younger than 20 years and 46% by age 40 years. Reported tumor formation rates in intra-abdominal dysgenetic testes and streak gonads are 27% and 31% respectively. Tumor formation in an intra-scrotal gland is rare, only three cases have been reported, with one each of seminoma, intratubular germ cell neoplasm and teratoma.

5-Alpha Reductase Deficiency. 5-Alpha Reductase is the enzyme that facilitates the conversion of testosterone to another hormone, dehydrotestosterones (DHT). When a genetic male is deficient in 5-Alpha Reductase, the powerful DHT hormone is not produced. While testes and Wolffian ducts do exist, the male external genitals are similar in size to those of a normal female. If left intact, an adult 5-Alpha Reductase Deficiency individual will appear generally male but with small genitals and no facial hair.

Micropenis. In order to create the proper penis in 46, XY individual, androgens must be secreted twice during fetal life. First, the androgens help to shape the basic structures into a penis and scrotum; later the androgens enlarge the penis. A micropenis is the result of normal androgen secretion in the first stage and little or no androgen secretion in the second. The penis is normal in shape and function, but extremely small in size. Individuals with intact micropenises are often given testosterone to stimulate masculinizing puberty.

Klinefelter syndrome (or XXY syndrome) which occurs in 1 out of 1,000 births. Sometimes chromosomes join but do not form standard 46, XX or 46, XY combinations. Individuals with Klinefelter Syndrome are genetically 47, XXY and live as men. Small penis and testes, low androgen secretion, and possible female breast development are characteristics of this syndrome. Klinefelter syndrome is a genetic condition in which a person has an extra copy of the X chromosome. Klinefelter syndrome isn't inherited, but rather occurs only as a result of a random genetic error after conception. People with Klinefelter syndrome may have low testosterone and reduced muscle mass, facial hair, and body hair. Most people with this condition produce little or no sperm.

Turner syndrome. Like Klinefelter syndrome, Turner Syndrome (TS) is marked by an abnormal karyotype, 45, XO. Turner Syndrome happens when a person has one complete X chromosome, and their second X chromosome is absent or smaller than usual. This happens in about 1 in 2000 live births. Turner syndrome is sometimes found prenatally with amniocentesis. While Turner women have female external genitals, the individuals lack properly formed ovaries. Without estrogen treatment, no breast growth occurs. Other possible features of Turner syndrome include short stature, webbing of the neck, and misshapen internal organs.

In TS, the level of hormones needed to start puberty is unusually low because of a difference in development of the ovaries, which are called "streak gonads". TS can also be discovered in adolescence when puberty does not happen as expected. Many people with TS are petite, often under 5 feet tall. Other organs in the body, such as the heart, may also develop atypically. Some people only have one X chromosome in some of their cells. This is called "mosaic Turner Syndrome". The other cells can have XX or XY chromosomes. Physical difference in mosaic TS will depend on what proportion of the cells and tissues have typical XX or XY chromosomes.

Timing Defects. If all of the proper stages of normal male sex differentiation occur, but the timing is incorrect by just days, errors may arise.

This occasional outcome is a 46, XY individual with this timing defect is ambiguous external genitals.

Hypospadias and Epispadias. Hypospadias happens when the urinary opening (urethra) is located below the usual position on the tip of the penis. It is one of the most common and visible genital variations. Hypospadias is the most common birth difference in children with XY chromosomes, seen in 1 out of every 125 to 300 live births. The cause of hypospadias is unknown. The location of the opening of the urethra can vary from just below the tip of the penis down to just in front of the rectum. Bending of the penis, or chordee, is often seen with hypospadias, although they can occur separately.

Epispadias is similar to hypospadias because the urinary opening is not in the usual position. In epispadias, the urinary opening is located on the upper surface of the penis or the middle of the clitoris. It is much less common than hypospadias. Epispadias usually happens in conditions called exstrophy, where the bladder, abdominal wall, and pelvis are not closed in the front as usual, but epispadias can occur by itself. Characteristics of epispadias include a very short and wide penis, often classified as complete epispadias when the entire urethra is exposed from the abdominal wall to the tip of the penis.

Epispadias although usually happen in males, but it can also occur in females, where it is manifested as a split clitoris and displacement of the urinary opening. Epispadias is caused by malformation of the embryonic genital tubercle and cloacal membrane sometime in the 5th or 6th week of pregnancy. It is not related to hypospadias, which is thought to be a hormonally moderated defect of penile formation and closure of the urethral plate, which takes place about 8 weeks after conception. Estimates are that epispadias with exstrophy occurs about once every 30,000 births, isolated epispadias, without exstrophy in males about once in 120,000 and isolated epispadias in females about once in 500, 000.

Mayer-Rokitansky-Küster-Hauser (MRKH). Children with 46, XX chromosomes and ovaries may have atypical development of internal structures such as the vagina, the uterus, and the Fallopian tubes. MRKH sometimes also involves differences in development of the skeleton, internal ears, and in rare cases, the heart, fingers and toes.

The number of births with ambiguous genitals is in the range of 0.02% to 0.05%. Intersex people were previously referred to as 'hermaphrodites' or 'congenital eunuchs'. The concept of taxonomic classification system of intersex conditions began in the 19th century and continued into the 20th century. However, in the latter part of the 20th century, the terms associated with hermaphrodites were discarded as they were considered to be misleading, stigmatizing and scientifically specious in reference to humans.

In biology, the term 'hermaphrodite' is used to describe an organism that can produce both males and female gametes. In clinical settings, the term 'disorder of sex development' (DSD) emerged and has been used since 2006, a shift in language considered controversial since its introduction. Intersex people face stigmatization and discrimination from birth, or following the discovery of intersex traits at stages of development such as puberty. Intersex people may also face infanticides, abandonment, and the stigmatization of their families.

The term 'intersexuality' as used to describe the sexuality of intersex people was first used by Richard Goldschmidt in 1917 in reference to a variety of physical sex ambiguities. However, the popularity of the term is attributed to Anne Fausto Sterling when she published her article, *"The Five Sexes: Why Male and Female Sex Are Not Enough"* in 1993. The term 'hermaphrodite' in modern-day society was first used in law to refer to people whose sex were in doubt. The 12th century Decretum Gratiani states that "Whether an hermaphrodite may witness a testament, depends on which sex prevails".

Similarly, in the 17th century, English jurist and judge, Edward Coke wrote in his *"Institute of the Lawes of England"* on laws of succession stating: *"Every heire is either a male, a female, or an hermaphrodite, that is both male and female. And an hermaphrodite (which is also called Androgynus) shall be heire, either as male or female, according to that kind of sexe which doth prevaile"*. However, until the mid-20th century, 'hermaphrodite' was used synonymously with intersex. Medical terminology shifted in the early 21st century, not only due to concerns about language, but also a shift to understandings based on genetics.

Societies have been long aware of intersex people except in Africa and one of the earliest evidence is found in the writings of the Greek historian, Diodorus Siculus in the first century BC when he wrote of the mythological Hermaphrodites "born with a physical body which is a combination of that of a man and that of a woman" and reputedly possessed supernatural properties. He also recounted the lives of Diophantus of Abae and Callon of Epidaurus. Ardhanarishvara, an androgynous composite form of masculine deity, Shiva and female deity, Parvati, originated in Kushan culture in the first century AD.

Hippocrates, Greek Physician, and Galen, Roman Physician, Surgeon and Philosopher, both viewed sex as a spectrum between masculinity and femininity with "many shades in between, including hermaphrodites, a perfect balance of male and female". Pliny the Elder, the Roman Naturalist described *"those who are both of both sexes, whom we call hermaphrodites, at one time androgyni" (from the Greek andr- "man" and gyn- "woman")*. Augustine, the Influential Catholic Theologian wrote in "The Literal Meaning of Genesis" that humans were created in two sexes, despite "as happens in some births, in the case of what we call androgynes".

Intersex people are those born with physical conditions that result in atypical internal or external reproductive anatomies or chromosomal anomaly. Although, surgeries are performed in correcting them, there is little evidence that they are effective and safe in the long-term; on the contrary, several recent studies have confirmed that early surgical treatment on genitals often results in psychological and sexual problems rather than better social adjustment.

The social power and authority of the medical establishment combined with fear and lack of awareness in general public allowed these surgeries to go on unquestioned, inflicting lifelong pain on those defined as intersex. Intersex issues are marginalized and need to be given more attention. This problem arises from the confusion surrounding intersexuality and its distinction from transsexual/transgender issues. Recent statistics indicate that almost 90% of cases were treated by some form of feminizing genitoplasticity. Even young boys rendered sexually ambiguous because of severe genital trauma were assigned female gender, as though the absence of genitalia was the sole determining factor in gender recognition.

Since the early 1950s, surgery and firm parental assurance in the chosen gender were believed to be sufficient to ensure the successful establishment of gender. Psychologists now realize that children develop preferred patterns of behavior before accepting a stable sexual identity and later, developing sexual orientation. The endocrine function of the sex-gland plays an important role in the development of secondary sex characteristics. Nature even proves the existence of intersexuality as evident in F.R. Lillies's recent analysis of the case of the free-martin. Amongst twin calves, cases of normal and female are very rare. If both are not of the same sex, in most cases a normal male is combined with an abnormal "hermaphroditic" female, the free-martin. It is now proven that this free-martin is a typical case of harmonic intersexuality.

In the male partner, the testis, with its intestinal tissue, develops first, when the ovary of the female has not yet reached the stage of endocrine function. Hence, the female comes under the influence of the male hormones, the ovary stops differentiation and all the sex-characters develop further in the male direction. The result is the free-martin, a calf with very much female external sex organs, almost male sexual ducts and a sex-gland containing sperm tubules without spermatogenesis.

Just as the differentiation of sexual characters is influenced by endocrine action, important characters of general organization are influenced by the hormones of thyroid, hypophysis, among others., like growth, correlation of organs, metamorphosis, nervous functions, metabolism and instincts. Therefore, heredity can be attributed to the condition of intersexuality, i.e. the fertilized egg furnishes in its protoplasm the chemical material and the physical substratum for the process of growth and differentiation. The chromosomes furnish the determinants for the specific direction of these processes which make the offspring similar to the parents: These factors are enzymes, which are not only characteristics in regard to their quality, but which are handed over to the sex-cell in the very exact quantities or concentrations.

As the reactions accelerated by these enzymes take place with a velocity in proportion to their concentration, a very subtle mechanism is given for the production of definite reactions with a different velocity, thus assuring the always returning rhythm of differentiation. Intersex is not a homogeneous singular classification and there are 40 different intersex variations known to science, as well as intersex people have many different kinds of bodies and different identities and lived experiences. Underlying traits of intersexuality may be determined prenatally, at birth, at puberty, or later in life.

Currently, there are confusions amongst society, the legal fraternity and the medical field when it comes to the issues of intersex and this is evident when Morgan Carpenter (2018) states:

"intersex bodies remain "normalized" or eliminated by medicine, while society and the law "others" intersex identities. That is, medicine constructs intersex bodies as either female or male, while law and society construct intersex identities as neither female nor male".

For this reason, there ought to be laws that seek to protect intersex from abuses of their fundamental rights as humans as well as there should be the promotion of the Yogyakarta principles since most intersex people are defined by their sex characteristics and not their gender identities. The 2017 Yogyakarta Principles clarify that sex characteristics are distinct from sex, sexual orientation and gender identity, and that these attributes are intersectional:

"understanding 'sex characteristics' as each person's physical features relating to sex, including genitalia and other sexual and reproductive anatomy, chromosomes, hormones, and secondary physical features emerging from puberty;.....Recognizing that the needs, characteristics and human rights situations of persons and populations of diverse sexual orientations, gender identities, gender expressions and sex characteristics are distinct from each other; noting that sexual orientation, gender identity, gender expression and sex characteristics are each distinct and intersectional grounds of discrimination, and that they may be, and commonly are, compounded by indiscrimination on other grounds including race, ethnicity, indigeneity, sex, gender, language, religion, belief, political or other opinion, nationality, national or social origin, birth, age, disability, health (including

HIV status), migration, marital or family status, being a human rights defender or other status".

CHAPTER VIII

DISEASES & SEXUALITY

"Once a disease has entered the body, all parts which are healthy must fight it: not one alone, but all. Because a disease might mean their common death. Nature knows this; and Nature attacks the disease with whatever help she can muster"—Paracelsus.

Diseases have been with humanity for ages and as humanity progresses in civilization, there are new diseases discovered. However, all discovered diseases can be categorized into four main groups: infectious diseases, deficiency diseases, hereditary diseases (including both genetic diseases and non-genetic hereditary diseases) and physiological diseases. The term, 'disease' broadly refers to any condition that impairs the normal body functioning, hence diseases are associated with the dysfunction of the body's normal homeostatic processes.

Most sexually transmitted infections and diseases are either chronic or congenital. A chronic disease is a condition that persists over time, often characterized as at least six months but may also include illnesses that are expected to last for the entirety of the natural life of a person; and a congenital disease is a medical condition that is present at birth or as a result of a vertically transmitted infection from a parent such as HIV/AIDS.

Sexually transmitted infections (STIs) and sexually transmitted diseases (STDs) are major public health concerns globally, which affect quality of life and cause serious morbidity and mortality. STIs and STDs have direct impacts on one's sexuality, reproductive and child health through infertility, cancers and pregnancy complications, and they have an indirect impact through their role in facilitating sexual transmission of human immunodeficiency virus (HIV) and therefore they also have an impact on national and individual economies. More than a million sexually transmitted infections are acquired daily.

The term 'sexually transmitted disease' (STD) is a condition which is passable from a person to another through coitus. Sexually transmitted disease is usually contracted by a person by having unsafe vaginal, anal or oral sex with an infected person. A sexually transmitted disease may be called a sexually transmitted infection (STI) or venereal disease (VD). However, a sexually transmitted disease does not necessarily mean having coitus, oral or anal sex only. It is also possible to contract a sexually transmitted disease asymptomatically.

In males, common symptoms include pain or discomfort during sex or urination; sores, bumps or rashes on or around the penis, testicles, anus, buttocks, thighs or mouth; unusual discharge or bleeding from the penis; painful or swollen testicles. In females, common symptoms of having contracted a sexually transmitted disease may include pains or discomfort during sex or urination; sores, bumps or rashes around or on the vagina, anus, buttocks, thighs or mouth; unusual discharge or bleeding from the vagina and itchiness in or around the vagina.

Currently, there are more than twenty types of sexually transmitted diseases and they are usually caused by bacteria, viruses and parasites; however, all viral diseases contracted sexually are not currently curable. Today, there are over one hundred million cases of sexually transmitted infections and diseases (STIs/STDs) recorded annually.

Chancroid is a sexually transmitted disease caused by Gram-negative bacterium, Haemophilus ducreyi and is characterized by necrotizing genital ulceration which may be accompanied by inguinal lymphadenitis or bubo formation. Genital ulceration as a syndrome has been associated with increased transmission of human immunodeficiency virus (HIV) infection in several cross sectional and longitudinal studies. Chancroid may also be spread to other anatomical sites by auto-inoculation, a clinical feature first demonstrated experimentally by Ducrey in 1889.

It is occasionally within the context of localized urban outbreaks which may be associated with commercial sex work. Genital ulceration has also been shown to be a major co-factor in the transmission of HIV-1; hence, effective diagnosis and treatment of chancroid may play an important role in slowing down the HIV-pandemic in places where both diseases are prevalent—Africa and South-East Asia.

Naturally occurring chancroid is usually more prevalent in men than women. This sex difference has also been observed experimentally in both humans and macaques. Lesions usually occur on the prepuce and frenulum in men and on the vulva, cervix, and perianal area in women. Complications include phimos in men and further phagedenic ulceration due to secondary bacterial infection. Painful, tender inguinal lymphadenitis usually occurs in up to 50% of cases and the lymph nodes may develop into buboes.

In treating this condition, ciprofloxacin and erythromycin have shown to be very effective in treating chancroid. Pregnant women should be treated with either erythromycin or ceftriaxone regimens. Undiagnosed coexisting HSV infection, particularly in immunosuppressed HIV seropositive patients, may also account for some of the observed cases where treatment has failed to cure chancroid. Plasmid mediated antimicrobial resistance has been documented for a number of agents including penicillin, tetracycline, chloramphenicol, sulfonamides, and aminoglycosides.

Chancroid is a major cause of genital ulcer disease in many resource poor countries of Africa, Asia, and Latin America, although it remains relatively uncommon in the United States and Western Europe. Genital ulcers may be caused by other sexually transmitted agents apart from H. ducreyi, including Treponema pallidum, chlamydia trachomatis serovars L1-L3, Calymmatobacterium granulomatis, and herpes simplex virus (HSV). Prospective and cross-sectional case-control studies in Africa have provided substantial evidence that chancroid is a risk factor for heterosexual spread of HIV.

The differentiation of genital ulcers dates to ancient times. Hippocrates recognized that certain genital ulcers were accompanied by buboes, and Celsius divided genital ulcers into "dry and clean" and "moist and purulent". Chancroid was first differentiated from syphilis (hard chancre) in 1852 by Bassereau in France when he demonstrated that only patients with chancre could be reinfected at another skin site by auto-inoculation of purulent material from the ulcer. In 1889, Ducrey published on the identification of the 'virus' of the soft chancre. Ducrey inoculated the skin of the forearm of three patients with purulent material from their own genital ulcers.

His observations were confirmed by Krefting in 1892 and also by Unna the same year. The proportion of patients treated for sexually transmitted diseases who have specific genital ulcers depends on various factors such as (i) the prevalence of other STDs; (ii) circumcision rates (iii) diagnostic and treatment facilities; and (iv) specific sexual practices. Patients with genital ulcer comprise 18 to 70% of STD patients seen in clinics in East and Southeast Asia, Africa and India. An intermediate proportion of patients seen in areas of South America and the Caribbean have genital ulcer disease. In Sweden, England and the United States, as few as 3 to 4% of patients in some STD clinics have ulcerative lesions of the genitalia.

Granuloma Inguinal (Donovanosis) is also a genital ulcerative disease caused by intracellular gram-negative bacterium, Klebsciella granulomatis. This disease is common in India, South Africa and South America, although it previously was endemic in Australia. The disease is characterized by painless, slowly progressive ulcerative lesions on the genitals or perineum without regional lymphadenopathy; pseudobuboes also might occur.

The lesions are beefy red in appearance and can bleed. Extragential infections can occur with infection extensions to the pelvis or it can disseminate to intra-abdominal organs, bones, or the mouth. The lesion also can develop secondary bacterial infection and can coexist with other sexually transmitted pathogens. By the late 20th century, donovanosis had disappeared from most parts of the developed world. Donovanosis is linked to HIV transmission hence it causes for concern. Its treatment formerly involved multiple daily doses of antibiotics for a prolonged period of time, but two studies demonstrated the value of azithromycin, which required only one daily dosing for a week or once weekly dosing for 4-6 weeks.

Donovanosis was first described by McLeod in Calcutta, India in 1882. The term 'donovanosis' originates from the description of the etiological agent of granuloma inguinal made in 1905 by Donovan when working in a hospital in Madras. Donovan detailed the presence of intracellular inclusions in macrophages after a morphological study with special stains of materials extracted from lesions of his patients, which he believed to be caused by a protozoan. This concept persisted for three decades, given the inability to culture the material in different types of culture media. These intracellular inclusions were later termed 'Donovan bodies'.

At the time, treatment with antimonial was suggested. Antimonials were already being used to treat kala-azar. Leishman described the intracellular bodies in liver and spleen cells in 1903, and a similar observation was later made by Donovan. This sequence of discoveries explains the term, 'Leishman-Donovan bodies'. Donovan bodies in granuloma inguinale were then considered protozoa, analogous to Leishman bodies and therefore, the same treatment was indicated.

In 1931, Monbreun and Goodpasture tried to inoculate material rich in Donovan bodies with success. They established however that the microorganism causing the disease was not a protozoan. They described a Gram-negative bacillus that grew in a chorioallantoic membrane filtrate of chicken embryo, in capsulated and non-capsulated forms. In 1939, Greenbalt and others reproduced the disease in four volunteers using material from pseudobuboes, but failed to grow any organism in the chorioallantoic membrane of chicken embryos.

In 1943, Anderson managed to isolate the microorganism in a yolk sac from embryonated eggs, demonstrating that it was a Gram-negative, immobile bacterium, found in encapsulated and non-encapsulated forms, which would be capable of producing antigen that resulted in positive reactions when injected intradermally in patients. Hence, Anderson proposed the creation of a new species: Donovania granulomatis. The term, 'donovanosis' was proposed in 1950 in honor of Donovan by Marmell and Santora which became acceptable to the scientific community.

Donovanosis is more prevalent in blacks and individuals with poor hygiene, and being endemic in tropical and subtropical countries such as Papua New Guinea, Brazil, South Africa, and Argentina. Donovanosis is more common in adults aged 20-40 years irrespective of gender predilection since at this stage, sexual activities are greater. Donovanosis in rare cases can be transmitted from mother to children especially if mother has an untreated cervical donovanosis during childbirth.

A person with donovanosis has a greater risk of contracting HIV— the infected has 4.7 times increased risk of contracting HIV. A person likely to contract donovanosis are those of higher incidence of greater sexual activity; lesions found in the internal genitalia, such as uterine cervix, without other manifestations; presence of anal lesions associated with the practice of anal sex; concomitant STIs; sexual contact with sex workers, and having numerous sexual partners.

Furthermore, it can be contracted when one comes into contact with feces of a patient with donovanosis. Contamination would occur through anal or vaginal intercourse when there is contamination with feces. Extragenital lesions occur in 6% in cases and clinical manifestations occur in the genital region between 80-100%. The incubation period can be at least two weeks and maximum sixty days. Genitals are affected in 90% of cases and the inguinal region in 10%.

In general, the regions most affected in men are the coronal groove, the balanoprepucial area, and the anus. In women, the areas commonly affected are the labia minora, vaginal furcular and sometimes the cervix and upper genital tract, where they can simulate carcinumas. In treating donovanosis, intravenous emetic tartar introduced by Aragón and Vianna in 1913 was the first effective drug in the treatment. However, currently the recommended first-line therapy is azithromycin, two tablets of 500mg a week for three weeks or until complete healing of the lesions.

Another, option is 100mg of doxycycline every twelve hours that can be used for a minimum of twenty-one days or complete healing. Ciprofloxacin (750mg every 12 hours) for 21 days or until complete healing is also effective. Sulfamethoxazoletrimethopim (400/800mg every 12 hours) can also be used for a period of not less than twenty-one days. If there is no response in the aspect of the lesion in the first days of treatment, it is recommended to add an intravenous aminoglycoside such as gentamicin 1mg/kg/day, three times a day for twenty-one; and most severe cases, the use of parenteral therapy with gentamicin or chloramphenicol 500mg orally four times a day.

Gonorrhea is another common sexually transmitted disease and it is a bacterial infection.

For example, in the United States alone in 2018, an estimated 1.6 million new infection cases were recorded; and an estimated 98 million new cases of gonorrhea occur annually, according to the World Health Organization estimates. The causative agent of gonorrhea is the bacterium, Neisseria gonorrhoeae, whose existence is suggested by texts from as early as Leviticus to the writings of Herodotus in the Fifth Century BCE. However, by the 1930s, a remedy was found to cure the infection through the use of penicillin and sulphonamides in the 1930s and 1940s. Nonetheless, the bacterium developed resistance to each antibiotic used against it.

Consequently, N. gonorrhoeae was listed in 2013 as one of the most urgent antibiotic-resistant threat in a CDC report and in 2018 as a priority pathogen by the World Health Organisation (WHO). Ceftriaxone is both the first-line treatment, as well as the last remaining single – drug option, and susceptibility is diminishing rapidly. Due to this, the treatment of gonorrhea is one of a dual nature by using ceftriaxone and azithromycin. However, there are causes for concern as the dual-antibiotic regime may not be effective in the long-term. In 2014, the worldwide first case of dual therapy failure was reported in the United Kingdom and in 2018, a similar case that also failed to respond to the last-resort therapy, spectinomycin. In 2017, over 44,000 cases of gonorrhea were diagnosed in England alone. In England, the incidence of gonorrhea is on the average of 12% per year since 2008. Gonorrhea tends to cause local outbreaks, spreading quickly when it becomes introduced into clustered sexual networks. Around half of all gonorrhea cases are diagnosed in Men who have Sex with Men (MSM).

The facility with which N. gonorrhoeae is able to alter its genome has contributed to the emergence and rapid dissemination of antimicrobial resistance. Gonococci are easily able to acquire genetic material from other lineages, and even other species, through both transformation (uptake from the environment) and conjugation (transfer for example of a plasmid between bacterial cells in direct contact). Penicillin was first used in treating gonorrhea in 1930 by microbiologist Cecil Paine, who used a crude extract of penicillin-producing fungus to cure a baby with an ophthalmic infection in Sheffield.

By 1943, penicillin was being used treat sulphonamides-resistant urethral gonorrhoeae and gradually became the primary treatment and by 1976, penicillin was no more used to treat gonorrhoeae due to disseminating chromosomal resistance and the identification of a plasmid-mediated ß-lactamase-producing strain in Liverpool. High-level chromosomally-mediated resistance emerged in the USA ten years later and quickly spread worldwide. Tetracyclines were discovered in 1945 and first prescribed to treat gonococcal infection in individuals allergic to penicillin. Chromosomally-mediated resistance of gonorrhoeae to tetracycline was documented as early as 1957.

Both penicillin and tetracycline resistance are more common among MSM (44%) compared to heterosexual men (16%) and women (9%). This is because of a cell wall that is resistant to hydrophobic molecules and is thus well adapted to the rectal environment. Ciprofloxacin was introduced in the early 1980s and was widely welcomed as a replacement for penicillin in the treatment of gonorrhea due to their minimal side effects, single-dose formulation and efficacy at all infection sites, including the pharynx.

However, in 1990, the first report of treatment failure was recorded in London and around 1994, Japan recorded treatment failure at an increased dosage of 500mg from 250mg. By 2002, ciprofloxacin resistance cut across all genders and sexualities: 7% of women, 12% of heterosexual men and 9% of MSM tested positive for resistance. Thus, ciprofloxacin was removed from the treatment guidelines in 2005. This led to the use of cefixime as a source of treatment yet by 2008, little resistance was detected and by 2010, the total level of resistance had passed the 5% threshold at which the WHO recommends that first-line treatment guidelines should be changed.

The majority of the resistance was concentrated in MSM population and this led to the abandonment of cefixime as a first-line treatment in May, 2011 and then came 500mg ceftriaxone and 1g azithromycin as a combination treatment for gonorrhea. Even though dual-therapy is now recommended in treating gonorrhea, the first reported case worldwide occurred in December, 2014 in a British man reporting heterosexual contact in Japan. Test of cure revealed that the treatment had been successful at clearing congenital infection, but unsuccessful against the pharyngeal infection.

In February, 2018, a similar case was reported of a British man having contracted gonorrhea in Southeast Asia. Gonorrhea is also known as "the clap". Gonorrhea when untreated may cause infertility and regular screening can help detect instances when an infection is present despite being asymptomatic. Gonorrhea is usually contracted by having unprotected vaginal, anal or oral sex and sometimes from mother to baby by pregnancy, labor or nursing. Symptoms include painful urination and abnormal discharge from the penis or vagina.

Men may experience testicular pain and women may experience pains in the lower stomach and some cases, be asymptomatic. Pains can occur during sexual intercourse or during urination and a person can experience fever, irregular menstruation, pus, sore throat or urinary urgency. The bacterium tends to target warm, moist areas of the body including the urethra, eyes, throat, vagina, anus, female reproductive tract (the fallopian tubes, cervix and uterus). Symptoms usually occur within 2 to 14 days after exposure.

A person with a penis may not develop noticeable symptoms for several weeks and some men may never develop symptoms. Gonorrhea infection in the rectum may cause bleeding, discharge, itching, pain during defecating and soreness. An untreated gonorrhea can cause serious and long-lasting problems, including increased chance of getting HIV infection in other parts of the body such as skin or joints.

HIV/AIDS remains a leading cause of illness and deaths especially in developing countries and currently about 38 million people globally live with HIV/AIDS including about 1.5 million children. HIV/AIDS patients are predominantly found in Africa and India. In the United States for instance, in 2004, an estimated 944,306 persons had received a diagnosis of AIDS and of these, 529,113 persons representing 56% had died. HIV is a virus that damages the immune system, and untreated HIV affects and kills CD4 cells which are a type of immune cells. Over time, as HIV kills more CD4 cells, the body is more likely to get various types of conditions and cancers. HIV is transmitted through bodily fluids such as blood, semen, breast milk, vaginal and rectal fluid. Without treatment, a person with HIV is likely to develop a serious conditions called Acquired Immunodeficiency Disease Syndrome (AIDS).

A person with AIDS experiences symptoms such as encephalitis and meningitis which affect the central nervous system; retinitis which affects the eyes; pneumocystis pneumonia, tuberculosis and tumors which affects the lungs, skin and gastrointestinal parts as well as esophagitis and chronic diarrhea. The main symptoms of HIV infections include fever, weight loss, malaise, headache, neuropathy, pharyngitis, sores and thrush around the mouth, sores around the esophagus, myalgia, liver and spleen enlargement, lymphadenopathy, nausea and vomiting.

The effects of HIV on the body are dire and enormous: skin sores, aches and pains, balance issues, dementia, fatigue, tongue trouble such as inflammation, lesion or white patches, cough which may be a sign of tuberculosis or other serious pulmonary infections, respiratory infections, hypertension, neuropathy, flu-like symptoms such as fever, chills and night sweats, anxiety and depression, seizures, mouth ulcers which could be the result of infections such as herpes, swollen glands, heart strain, eating problems, shingles, diarrhea, bumpy skin and itchiness.

With antiretroviral therapy (ART), HIV can be well-managed and life expectancy can be nearly the same as someone who has not contracted HIV. Healthy adults generally have a CD4 count of 500-1600 per cubic millimeter. A person with HIV whose CD4 count falls below 200 per cubic millimeter will be diagnosed of AIDS. A person living with AIDS is vulnerable to a wide range of illnesses including pneumonia, tuberculosis, oral thrush, cytomegalovirus, cryptococcal meningitis, toxoplasmosis, cryptosporidiosis and cancers. The most common route of transmission is through vaginal or anal sex as well as through exposure to the blood, semen, vaginal and rectal fluids and breast milks of a person living with HIV.

HIV is rare in oral sex but only if there are bleeding gums or open sores in the person's mouth; being bitten by a person with HIV only if the saliva is bloody or there are open sores in the person's mouth; contact between broken skin, wounds or mucous membranes and the blood of someone living with HIV. HIV is a variation of a virus that can be transmitted to African chimpanzees. Scientists suspect the simian immunodeficiency virus (SIV) jumped from chimps to humans when people consumed chimpanzee meat containing the virus.

Once inside the body of man, the virus mutated into what is known as HIV today and this likely occurred in the 1920s. HIV spread from person to person throughout Africa over the course of several decades. Eventually, the virus migrated to other parts of the world. Scientists first discovered HIV in human blood sample in 1959 from a man living in now Kinshasa, Democratic Republic of Congo and did not hit public consciousness until the 1980s. Kinshasa is known for having the most genetic diversity in HIV strain in the world and many of the first cases of AIDS were recorded there too.

In the 1960s, the 'B' subtype of HIV-1 (a subtype of strain M) had made its way to Haiti. At the time, many Haitian professionals who were working in the colonial Democratic Republic of Congo during the 1960s returned to Haiti. Initially, they were blamed for being responsible for the HIV epidemic, and suffered severe racism, stigma and discrimination as a result. HIV-1 subtype M is now the most geographically spread subtype of

HIV internationally. By 2014, this subtype had caused 75 million infections.

In the early 1980s, there were rare types of pneumonia, cancer, and other illnesses being reported to doctors making the world conscious to the existing of HIV/AIDS. In 1981, in the United States, reporting of unusually high rates of the rare forms of pneumonia and cancer in young gay men begin, therefore, initially naming the disease, Gay-Related Immune Deficiency (GRID) because it was thought to affect only gay men. In 1982, the disease was renamed AIDS. Canada reported its first case of AIDS in March of that year. It was at this point that, it was realized that the infection can be sexually transmitted and caused by HIV. During this period, there were reported cases of blood transfusion recipients getting the virus. Scientists realized the disease was also spreading among other populations such as haemophiliacs and heroin users.

However, in 1983, it was discovered that women can become infected with HIV/AIDS through heterosexual sex. The HIV virus was isolated and identified by researchers where it was originally called Lymphadenopathy-Associated Virus (LAV), the virus was confirmed as the cause of AIDS. This led to the first conference on AIDS in 1985 held in Georgia, USA, and then the next one was held in Montreal, Canada. In 1986, it was discovered that HIV can be passed from mother to child through breast-feeding; and fortunately for the world, in 1987, the U.S. Food & Drug Administration approved the first-antiretroviral drug, AZT. Fortunately for the world, in 1996, CANFAR-funded researcher, Dr. Mark Wainberg contributed to the development of 3TC, a drug being used to treat HIV. This combination of drug therapy brought an immediate decline of 60-80% in rates of AIDS-related deaths and hospitalization for patients.

In 1999, researchers found a strain of SIV (called SIVcpz) in a chimpanzee that was almost identical to HIV in humans. The researchers concluded that it proved chimpanzees were the source of HIV-1 through the hunting of chimps as meat. The same scientists conducted further research into how SIV could be developed in the chimps. They discovered that the chimps had hunted and eaten two smaller species of monkeys (red-capped mangabeys and greater spot-nosed monkeys). These smaller monkeys infected the chimps with two different strains of SIV. The two different SIV strains then joined together to form a third virus (SIVcpz) that could be passed on to other chimps and this is the strain that can also infect humans.

SIVcpz was transferred to the humans as a result of the chimps being killed and eaten, or their blood getting into cuts and wounds on people in the course of hunting. Normally, the hunter's body would have fought off SIV, but on a few occasions the virus adopted itself within its new human host and became HIV-1. There are four main groups of HIV strains, each with a slightly different genetic make-up. This supports the hunter theory because every time SIV passed from a chimp to a human, it would have developed in a slightly different way within the human body, and produced a slightly different strain than one strain of HIV-1. The most studied strain of HIV is HIV-1 Group M which is the strain that has spread throughout the world and is responsible for the vast majority of HIV infections today.

HIV can be diagnosed using antibody/antigen tests (the commonest used tests). They can show positive results especially within 18-45 days after someone initially contracts HIV. Antibody tests check the blood solely for antibodies. Between 23 and 90 days after transmission, most people will develop detectable HIV antibodies which can be found in the blood or saliva. These tests are done using blood tests or mouth swabs, and they include: OraQuick HIV Tests which provide results in as little as 20 minutes; Home Access HIV-1 Test system—the person pricks their fingers and send the blood sample to a licensed laboratory. They can remain anonymous and call for results the next business day; and Nucleic acid test (NAT) which is for people who have early symptoms of HIV or have a known risk factor. This test looks for the virus itself.

It takes 5 to 21 days for HIV virus to be detected in the blood. This test is usually accompanied or confirmed by an antibody test. In 1985 when HIV testing first became available, the main goal of such testing was to protect the blood supply. Since the 1980s, the demographics of HIV/AIDS have changed; increasing proportions of infected persons are aged less than 20 years; women, persons living outside metropolitan areas and heterosexual men and women who frequently are unaware that they are at risk for HIV.

The annual estimated number of new infections has been stable at approximately 1.5 million since 1998 when people who were newly infected with HIV were between 2.1 million and 4.2 million people in 1997 and since 2010, new HIV infections have declined by 31% from 2.1 million to 1.5 million as at 2020 and new infections among children have declined by 53% from 320,000 in 2010 to 150,000 in 2020. AIDS-related deaths have been reduced by 64% since the peak in 2004 and by 47% since 2010.

In 2020, around 680,000 people died from AIDS-related illness globally compared to 1.9 million people in 2004 and 1.3 million in 2010. AIDS-related mortality has declined by 53% among women and girls and by 41% among men and boys since 2010. In 2020, key populations (sex workers and their clients, gay men and other men who have sex with men, transgender people, and their sexual partners and people who inject drugs accounted for 65% of HIV infections globally with 93% of new HIV infections outside of sub-Saharan Africa; 39% of new HIV infections in sub-Saharan Africa.

The risk of acquiring HIV is 25 times higher among gay men and other men who have sex with men; 26 times higher for sex workers; 34 times higher for transgender women and 35 times higher for people who inject drugs. Every week, around 5000 young women aged 15-24 years become infected with HIV with 6 in 7 new HIV infections among adolescents aged 15-19 years being girls in sub-Saharan Africa. Young women aged 15-24 years are twice as likely to be living with HIV than men.

In sub-Saharan, women and girls account for more than 50% of all new HIV infections with about 35% of women globally having experienced physical and/or sexual violence—in some regions, women who have experienced physical or sexual violence are 1.5 times more likely to acquire HIV than women who have not experienced such violence. Men who are educated are at 2.7% risk and educated women are at 0.8% riskier at contracting HIV when the educational level is of at least college; and men are at 3.0% when the educational level is less than college with 5.6% for women.

With a first phase 3-placebo-controlled efficac study of a vaccine to prevent HIV-1 infection, 1.9% of women acquired HIV-1 infection as a result of heterosexual transmission of HIV and the rate for MSM was 7.2%. Despite producing neutralizing and CD4 blocking antibody responses in all vaccines assessed for immunogenicity, the vaccine was ineffective in preventing HIV-1 infection or in modifying postinfection markers of disease progression. Global prevalence among adults—the percent of people ages currently around 15-49 who are infected—has leveled since 2001 and is current around 0.7%; there is about 1 in 5 people with HIV (19%) who are still unaware they are infected.

HIV remains a leading cause of death worldwide amongst women of reproductive age. In most parts, the HIV prevalence rate is less than 1% but between 1-5% in West and Central Africa but greater than 10% in Southern and Eastern Africa. In Eastern and Southern Africa, an estimated 20.7 million people are living with HIV and two-thirds of children living with HIV found in this region; Western and Central Africa, an estimated 4.9 million people are living with HIV although new infections amongst adults declined by 25% between 2010 and 2019 with women and girls accounting 58% of the estimated 240,000 new HIV infections in the region. Most HIV infections are transmitted heterosexually and young people ages 15-24 years' account for approximately a third of new HIV infections.

Numerous preventive interventions exist to combat HIV and they include: behavioral change problem, condoms, HIV testing, blood supply safety, male circumcision, harm reduction efforts for injecting drug users. Additionally, research has shown that engagement in HIV treatment improves individual health outcomes and significantly reduces the risk of transmission. Those with undetectable viral loads have effectively no risk of transmitting HIV sexually. Pre-exposure prophylaxis (PrEP) has also shown to be an effective HIV preventive strategy in individuals at high risk for HIV infection.

In 2015, WHO recommended PrEP as a form of prevention for high risk individuals in combination with other prevention methods. Experts recommend that prevention be based on 'knowing one's epidemic' using a combination of preventive strategies, bringing programmes to scale, and sustaining efforts over time. HIV treatment include the use of combination antiretroviral therapy (ART) to attack the virus itself and medications to prevent and treat the many opportunistic infections that can occur when the immune system is compromised with HIV. Combination ART was first introduced in 1996 and it has led to dramatic reductions in morbidity and mortality and currently approximately 59% of all HIV people are virally suppressed which means they are likely healthier and less likely to transmit the virus.

PrEP is highly effective for HIV- negative people for preventing HIV when taken as prescribed and it reduces the risk of getting HIV from sex by about 99% and it reduces the risk of getting HIV from injection drug use by at least 74%. PrEP therefore is advisable for people who are in an ongoing sexual relationship with a partner living with HIV who does not have an undetectable viral load; if one is gay or bisexual and has multiple sexual partners and barely uses condoms; if one is gay or bisexual in a new sexual relationship but not yet aware of the partner's HIV status and doesn't always use condom; for someone who is not using condoms with partners of the opposite sex whose HIV status is unknown and who are at high risk of HIV infection (for example, those who inject drugs, have multiple partners or have bisexual male partners); those who have sex for money, or receive gifts for sex and for someone who has shared injecting equipment or has been in a treatment programme for injecting drug use.

A person taking PrEP should first test for HIV to ensure s/he doesn't have HIV already. A person who has HIV already then taking PrEP may increase the likelihood of developing drug resistance which makes HIV treatment less effective. Evidence of a second human immunodeficiency virus, HIV-2 was first demonstrated in a study of Senegalese women in 1985. HIV-2 was subsequently found to be highly prevalent in many countries in West Africa (especially Nigeria and Mauritania) and has been present in populations in that region as early as 1960s.

PrEP can be taken daily or on-demand. Daily PrEP involves taking 1 pill each day. With daily PrEP, a person can feel protected from HIV whenever they have sex or inject substances. It is for people who have possible exposure to HIV on a frequent basis or an unpredictable basis. On-demand PrEP is only for cis-gender men who have sex with men (MSM). On-demand PrEP involves taking 2 pills, 2-24 hours before a possible sexual exposure to HIV and then continuing to take 1 pill each day until 2 days after the last possible sexual exposure. A person using PrEP should have an HIV test every three months to ensure they have not acquired HIV. PrEP isn't meant for only MSM but it works for all manner of people as long as the drugs are taken before and after sex as directed. While PrEP can prevent HIV, it does not prevent other sexually transmitted infections or pregnancy.

Aside the tablet forms of the PrEP, it comes also in the form of vaginal rings. In July, 2020, European Medicine Agency (EMA) gave a positive opinion on the use of the vaginal ring containing the anti-HIV drug dapivirine as PrEP, and in January, 2021, WHO recommended it as an additional HIV prevention option. It is a ring made of silicone similar to a contraceptive, and it is inserted in the vagina and slowly releases dapivirine over the course of the month. After a month, one will need to replace it.

In a study done with couples in Africa, it emerged that PrEP reduced infections by 75% in heterosexual men and women. But some other studies had less impressive results, because too many of the people taking part did not take PrEP regularly. In studies, when PrEP appears not to have worked for a person, it showed that the person was actually not taking the medication. In people who were able to take PrEP regularly, only occasionally missing doses, PrEP appears to prevent almost 100% of infections.

In a study done with gay men in England, the use of daily PrEP reduced HIV infections by 86% and this same finding was found in a study with gay men in France, where PrEP taken before and after sex also reduced infections by 86%. In addition to PrEP tablets and vaginal rings, there are also other delivery methods under research such as injectables and implants. In a study, an injection of the anti-HIV drug, cabotegravir every 8 weeks was found more effective than PrEP in gay and bisexual men and transwomen.

Syphilis affects large number of people globally and people infected with syphilis have a high rate of contracting HIV due to genital ulcers. WHO estimates that approximately 450 million people are actively infected with a treatable sexually transmitted diseases with an estimated rate of syphilis of approximately 12 million active infections based on 1999 estimates; with almost two-thirds of these cases in sub-Saharan Africa and South/Southeast Asia. In sub-Saharan Africa, between 2 and 17% of women test positive for syphilis in antenatal clinics and rates of HIV co-infections are very high.

HIV and syphilis are common among all sexualities especially gay men because of a reduction in a safe sex practice especially unprotected oral sex; changes in risk behaviors including the use of the internet to meet partners and use of recreational drugs. A study by Blocker and colleagues reported an overall median seroprevalence for HIV of 15.7% (27.5% in males and 12.4% in females) in people with syphilis in the United States of America.

Furthermore, much higher rates for HIV co-infection were detected in relation to certain risk factors: intravenous drug use (22.5%-70.6%) and gay sex (68-90%). In one Spanish study of 1161 HIV positive patients followed-up for 38 months, the baseline syphilis seroprevalence was 13% and a further 4% acquired syphilis in follow-up. Syphilis through genital ulcer disease may increase the risk of HIV transmission. For example, one mathematical model has suggested that approximately 1000 additional cases of heterosexual HIV transmission occur annually in the United States as a result of syphilis.

Using syphilis and HIV co-infection data from black Americans in 2000, Chesson and colleagues have calculated that 545 cases in HIV transmission were facilitated by syphilis in couples discordant for HIV. The additional health cost of the 545 potentially preventable HIV infection was estimated at US $113 million. Syphilis occurs in three stages: primary, secondary and tertiary.

In an HIV-negative patient, primary syphilis generally develops after an incubation period of twenty-one days with a painless chancre at the site of inoculation and holds same for HIV-positive patients but primary disease is more likely to be asymptomatic and HIV-positive patients more often present with secondary or tertiary infections. Primary and secondary syphilis are on the raise due to the increased importance of oral sex in transmission and the primary lesion may not be in the genital area.

Skin lesions are a common manifestations of secondary syphilis (72%). The commonest type is a diffuse maculopapular rash which usually appears about six weeks after the primary lesions and signifies haematogenous spread of T. palladium. A generalized macular rash with palmar-plantar involvement may also occur, but other types may occur such as lichenoid, papular, papulosquamous, ulcerated, and urticarial lesion with hair loss varying from alopecia to involvement of the eyebrows and even total loss of body. Nodular and annular skin lesions over the face, back and limbs are reported as are large plaques on face, neck and upper extremities. Nodular skin lesions can be seen in secondary or tertiary syphilis. Vesiculobullous skin lesions may occur in congenital syphilis.

Musculoskeletal manifestations can be associated with congenital, secondary and tertiary syphilis and can mimic a wide range of rheumatic and systemic diseases with joint involvement. There are many causes of sexually transmitted arthritis and arthralgia, inflammatory arthritis, and neuropathic arthritis may occur during any stage of congenital or acquired syphilis. Arthritis can also be the initial presentation of syphilis with HIV infection and synovitis may occur in the presence of marked CD4+ lymphocytes depletion. A person with HIV and coinfection of syphilis has a risk of 23.5% of developing neurosyphilis if untreated.

Neurosyphilis may affect the brain, spinal cord or peripheral nerves. Neurosyphilis can be in the form of headache, hearing loss, spastic parapareiss secondary to syphilitic meningomyelitis, medullary syndromes, stroke, gait disturbances, and optic atrophy or pupillary changes. Personality changes are the commonest symptoms of late syphilis with HIV and are due to syphilitic vasculitis with lacunar infarcts. In treating syphilis, penicillin remain stay as mainstay of therapy for all stages and sites of syphilis and in all patient groups.

However, drugs such as doxycycline, amoxicillin, erythromycin, probenecid, azithromycin and ceftriaxone are all used in treating syphilis. However, the best way to prevent syphilis is to practice safe sex through the use of condoms during any type of sexual contact. In addition, it may be helpful to use a dental dam or condom during oral sex; avoid sharing sex toys and getting screened for STIs and talking to one's partner about their results. Syphilis can also be transmitted through shared needles; therefore, people must avoid sharing needles if using injected drugs.

Congenital syphilis is an ancient disease that continues to plague infants worldwide and it remains a major cause of fetal and neonatal mortality globally. The global burden of congenital syphilis is confounded further by the high prevalence of coinfection with HIV in adults, as syphilis is a known risk factor for acquisition of HIV. In the United States of America, between 1999 and 2013, there were 6383 cases of congenital syphilis reported from CDC with a neonatal mortality of 11.6/1000 births and a case fatality rate of 6.5%. of the 418 death, 82% were stillbirths.

Importantly, the majority of deaths occurred among infants born to mothers with untreated or inadequately treated syphilis and 59% occurred by 31 weeks of gestation. Since 2012, there has been a steady increase in cases of congenital syphilis reported to the CDC with 628 cases (15.7/1000) live births reported in 2016 that included 41 syphilitic stillbirths. Syphilis is transmitted to the fetus transplacentally following maternal spirochetemia, although transmission to the newborn could occur intrapartum by contact with maternal genital lesions. Intrauterine transmission is supported by the isolation of the organism from umbilical and blood and amniotic fluid by rabbit infectivity testing.

The isolation of T. pallidum from as many as 74% of amniotic fluids specimens obtained from women with early syphilis also suggests that the organism is capable of traversing the fetal membrane, gain access to the amniotic fluid and result in fetal infections. Intrauterine transmission is also supported by the finding of abnormalities consistent with congenital syphilis both in utero and at births, as well as by detection of specific IgM antibodies in T. pallidum infected serum obtained by cordocentesis and in neonatal serum obtained at birth.

In 1950, Ingraham reported that among 251 women with untreated syphilis of less than 4 years' duration, 41% of their infants were born alive, and had congenital syphilis, 25% were stillborn, 14% died in the neonatal period, 21% had low birth weight but no evidence of syphilis, and 18% were normal full term infants. Among mothers with late latent infection, only 2% of their infants had congenital syphilis. In 1952, Fiumara and colleagues reported that untreated maternal primary or secondary syphilis resulted in 50% of infants having congenital syphilis while other 50% were stillborn, premature or died in the neonatal period.

With early and late latent infections, 40% and 10% of infants respectively had congenital syphilis.

The first sign of syphilis is a small, painless sore. It can appear on the sexual organs, rectum, or inside the mouth. Syphilis can sometimes be asymptomatic and can cause major damage to important organs like the heart and brain. Syphilis is only spread through direct contact with syphilitic chancres. It cannot be transmitted by sharing a toilet with another person, wearing another person's clothing, or using another person's eating utensils. Syphilis is most infectious in the primary and secondary stages.

The primary stage of syphilis occurs 3 to 4 weeks after a person contracts the bacteria. It begins with a small, round sore which is painless but highly infectious. The sore may appear wherever the bacteria entered the body such as on or inside the mouth, genitals or rectum. At the secondary stage of syphilis, skin rashes and sore throat may develop. The rash wont itch and is usually found on the palms and soles, but it may occur anywhere on the body.

At the secondary stage, symptoms may include headaches, swollen lymph nodes, fatigue, fever, weight loss, hair loss and aching joints. These symptoms will go away whether or not treatment is received. Nonetheless, without treatment, the person still has syphilis. The third stage of the disease is the latent or hidden stage, where there aren't any noticeable symptoms yet the bacteria remains in the body. This stage could last for years before progressing to the tertiary syphilis.

Research suggests that 15-30% of people who don't receive treatment for syphilis will enter this stage. Tertiary syphilis can be very life-threatening. At this stage, the outcomes include blindness, deafness, mental illness, memory loss, destruction of soft tissues and bones, neurological disorders like stroke or meningitis, heart disease and neurosyphilis, which is an infection of the brain or spinal cord.

Congenital syphilis can be life-threatening for babies causing deformities, developmental delays, seizures, rashes, fever, swollen liver or spleen, anemia, jaundice or infectious sores. If a baby has congenital syphilis and it is not detected, the baby can develop late stage syphilis and this can cause damage to their bones, teeth, eyes, ears and brain.

Chlamydia trachomatis in the genital tract was first indirectly described when a nongonococcal or amicrobiana, ophthalmia was observed in newborns. C. trachomatis is the most common sexually transmitted bacterial infection with approximately 100 to 150 million new cases occurring each year, affecting 68 million females with most of the infections being asymptomatic. The prevalence of C. trachomatis is 3.8% and 2.7% for women and men respectively. However, it is estimated that five out of one thousand will develop tubal factor infertility. The long-term effects in female with PID include chronic abdominal pain, ectopic pregnancy, and infertility. In males, epididymitis is the most severe complication although it can cause infertility.

Chlamydial infections are usually common with young people between 15 and 24 years who account for 63% of all reported cases. Chlamydia is very common in women, and heterosexual men compared to Men who have Sex with men (MSM). Between 2005 and 2015, more than 16% of women, 9% of heterosexual men and 8% of MSM have tested positive for chlamydia. Chlamydia trachomatis, the bacterial causal agent of chlamydia causes cervicitis in women and urethritis in men, as well as extragenital infections, including rectal and oropharyngeal infections. Lymphogranuloma venereum (LGV) caused by a more invasive serovars of C. trachomatis is increasingly prevalent among Men who have Sex with Men (MSM) in some settings. Maternal infection is associated with serious adverse outcomes in neonates, such as preterm birth, low birth weight, conjunctivitis, nasopharyngeal infection and pneumonia.

Uncomplicated genital chlamydia can be treated using azithromycin of 1g orally as a single dose; doxycycline 100mg orally twice a day for seven days; tetracycline 500mg orally four times a day for seven days; erythromycin 500mg orally four times a day for seven days; ofloxacin 200-400mg orally twice a day for seven days. While anorectal chlamydial infection is treated with doxycycline 100mg orally twice a day for seven days over azithromycin 1g orally as a single dose; and genital chlamydial infection with pregnant women is treated with azithromycin over erythromycin; with azithromycin over amoxicillin; amoxicillin over erythromycin.

Lymphogranuloma venereum (LGV) is treated using doxycycline 100mg orally twice for twenty-one days over azithromycin 1g orally weekly for three weeks. However, if doxycycline is contraindicated, azithromycin should be provided. When neither treatment is available, erythromycin 500mg orally four times a day for twenty-one days as an alternative.

For all neonates, the WHO STI guideline recommends topical ocular prophylaxis for the prevention of gonococcal and chlamydial ophthalmia neonatorum. For ocular prophylaxis, the WHO STI guideline suggests one of the following options for topical application to both eyes immediately after birth: tetracycline hydrochloride 1% eye ointment; erythromycin 0.5% eye ointment; povide iodine 2.5% solution (NOT ALCOHOL-BASED POVIDONE IODINE SOLUTION), silver nitrate 1% solution and chloramphenicol 1% eye ointment. These recommendations apply to the prevention of both chlamydial and gonococcal ophthalmia neonatorum.

Symptoms of uncomplicated chlamydial infection in women include abnormal vaginal discharge, dysuria, and post-coital and intermenstrual bleeding. Symptomatic men usually present with urethral discharge and dysuria sometimes accompanied by testicular pains. Infections at non-genital sites are common. Rectal infection may manifest as a rectal discharge, rectal pain or blood in the stools, but is asymptomatic in most cases. Oropharyngeal infections can manifest as pharyngitis and mild sore throats but symptoms are rare. Lymphogranuloma venereum (LGV), caused by a more invasive serovars of C. trachomatis, affects the submucosal connective tissue and can spread to regional lymph nodes. It commonly presents as a unilateral, tender inguinal or femoral lymph node and a genital ulcer or papule. Anorectal exposure may result in proctitis, rectal discharge, pain, constipation or tenesmus. Left untreated, LGV can lead to rectal fistula or stricture. Apart from sexual transmission, transmission of C. trachomatis by artificial insemination has been demonstrated.

Chlamydia causes include sex without a condom and unprotected oral sex, which are the main ways a chlamydia infection can be transmitted. Also, penetration does not necessary have to occur to contract it. Touching genitals together may transmit the bacteria; and it can be contracted during anal sex. Also, chlamydia can be transmitted from mothers to newborn babies.

Human papillomavirus (HPV) is another sexually transmitted infection and it is the commonest sexually transmitted infection in the United States of America. Globally, more than 290 million women have HPV infection. It is a viral infection that normally causes skin or mucous membrane growth (warts). Some types of HPV can cause different types of cancers especially of the lower part of the uterus that connects to the cervix, cancers of the anus, penis, vagina, vulva and the back of the throat (oropharyngeal). HPV infections are usually transmitted sexually or through other skin-to-skin contact. 4.5% of all cancers worldwide (630,000 new cancer cases per year) are attributable to HPV: 8.6% in women and 0.8% in men.

In most cases, the body's immune system defeats an HPV infection before it creates warts. When warts do appear, they vary in appearance depending on which kind of human papillomavirus is involved. The common types of warts are genital warts—these appear as flat lesions, small cauliflower-like bumps or tiny stem-like protrusions. In women, genital warts appear mostly on the vulva but can also occur near the anus, on the cervix or in the vagina. In men, genital warts appear on the penis and scrotum or around the anus. Genital warts rarely cause discomfort or pain, though they may itch or feel tender; common warts—common warts appear as rough raised bumps and usually occur on the hands and fingers. In most cases, common warts are simply unsightly, but they can also be painful or susceptible to injury or bleeding; plantar warts— they are hard, grainy growths that usually appear on the heels or balls of the feet; and flat warts—they are flat-topped, slightly raised lesions. They can appear anywhere, but children usually get them on the face and men tend to get them in the beard areas with women tending to get them on the legs. Nearly all cervical cancers are caused by HPV infections.

HPV infections occur when the virus enters the body usually through a cut, abrasion or small tear in the skin. The virus is transferred primarily by skin-to-skin contact. Genital HPV infections are contracted through sexual intercourse, anal sex and other skin-to-skin contact in the genital areas. Some HPV infections that result in oral or upper respiratory lesions are contracted through oral sex.

Warts are contagious and they can spread through direct contact with a wart or when someone touches something that already touched a wart. The risk factors of HPV infection include the number of sexual partners (the more sexual partners, the riskier one could contract a genital HPV infection, and having sex with a partner who has had multiple sex partners also increases the risk); age (common warts occur mostly in children, and genital warts occur most often in adolescents and young adults); weakened immune systems, damaged skin (areas of skin that have been punctured or opened are more prone to developing common warts).

Genital warts can be reduced by using a latex condom, reducing the number of sexual partners and being in mutually monogamous sexual relationships. Ninety percent of HPV infections go away on their own within two years; however, because the virus is still in the body during this time, a person may unknowingly transmit HPV. When the virus doesn't go away on its own, it can cause serious health problems such as genital warts and recurrent respiratory papillomatosis. It is estimated that eighty percent of women will contract at least one type of HPV during their lifetime. Genital warts can be treated with prescription medication, burning with an electrical current, or freezing with liquid nitrogen.

Nonetheless, getting rid of the physical warts doesn't treat the virus itself and the warts may return. Cancers that develop from HPV may be treated by methods such as surgery, chemotherapy and/or radiation therapy or a combination of methods. Routine screening for HPV and cervical cancers are important for identifying, monitoring and treating health problems that may result from HPV infection. Gardasil-9 vaccine is also available for the prevention of genital warts and cancers caused by HPV.

It is estimated that ninety-five percent of anal cancers are caused by HPV infections and the commonest is by HPV-16 while HPV-16 and 18 account for at least seventy percent of cervical cancer cases. Cervical cancer is the fourth commonest cancer among women globally, with an estimated 570,000 new cases in 2018 and nearly ninety percent of the 311, 000 deaths globally in 2018 occurred in Low and Middle Income Countries (LMICs). Women living with HIV are six times more likely to get cervical cancer compared to women without HIV and an estimated five percent of all cervical cancer cases are attributable to HIV. HPV can be reduced through male circumcision, sex education tailored to age and culture, health information and warnings about tobacco use.

Other HPV-attributable anogenital cancers include 8,500 vulvae; 12,000 vaginas; 35,000 anuses (half occurring in men), and 13,000 penises. In the head and neck, HPV-attributable cancers represent 38,000 cases of which 21,000 are oropharyngeal cancers occurring in more developed countries. These cancers are caused by HPV 16/18 and HPV 6/11/18/31/33/45/52/58 of which the relative contributions are 73% and 90% relatively. HPV includes a family of DNA viruses that infect basal epithelial cells, causing benign and malignant lesions of the skin and mucosae of the anogenital and upper aero-digestive tract. Epidemiological studies and mechanistic evidence led to the classification of HPV types 16, 18, 31, 33, 35, 39, 45, 51, 52, 56, 58, and 59 as carcinogenic and HPV 68 as probably carcinogenic. These types are referred to as high risk types.

Amongst women with normal cervical cytology, earlier reports show 10.4% and 11.7% HPV prevalence in 2007 and 2010 respectively, adjusted to 9.9% in 2019. The highest HPV prevalence in these women was found in Oceania (30.9%) and Africa (21.1%) followed by Europe (14.2%), America (11.5%) and Asia (9.4%). In the general female population, 32.1% of 576, 281 gynecologically healthy and unhealthy women were HPV carriers in 2011 and Asia and Africa were found to have the highest prevalence rate of 45.5% and 29.6% respectively. HPV usually affect adolescent girls and women under 25 irrespective of the geographical location, although in Africa (East and West Africa) and America (Central and Southern Africa) regions, there are rebounds in HPV infections in adults above 45 years old.

In men, the global prevalence rate of genital HPV infection is almost similar to that in women; the transmission rates being quite similar as well. Indeed, in a recent study conducted in 2014, 9.0% of 4,065 healthy men from Africa, America, Asia, and Europe were found to be HPV carriers. Homosexuals and HIV infected men are at an increased risk, with higher incidence rates greater than 90% of HPV anal infection than those in heterosexual men, in whom the number of sexual partners determine the risk of HPV infection.

In addition, for all men, the HPV infection rate is as high among the youngest as it is among the oldest, and varies very little with age. In terms of geographical distribution, the incidence of HPV infection in men is higher in Africa, especially South African men (17.2% per year) and lower in Asia (3.2% per year). Low-and-middle income countries have a higher prevalence of all HPV genotypes compared with those in developed regions. It is well-known fact that poverty associated with idleness is the main cause of transmission of sexually transmitted infections including HPV in low-and-middle-income regions.

Furthermore, because majority of women in general start sexual intercourse early, this reason explains the very high prevalence rates of high-risk oncogenic genital HPVs observed in young women, especially in low-and-middle-income countries. Interestingly, early marriages followed by high divorce rates are crucial factors in increasing viral transmission; and the lack of access to screening and healthcare remains a challenge in developing countries especially in women when they marry very early (i.e. less than 21 years) leading to a lack of health empowerment.

CHAPTER IX

SEXUALLY STRANGED & ENLIGHTENMENT?

"Insist on yourself; never imitate. Your own gift can offer with the cumulative force of a whole life's cultivation, but of the adopted talent of another, you have only an extemporaneous, half possession"—Ralph Waldo Emerson.

The progress and civilization of the society can never be written without factoring the contributions of the numerous socially awkward and marginalized people. The socially-awkward enlightened are people who have contributed ideas that have helped improve God, reason, nature and humanity being synthesized into the worldwide view of acceptance. These sexual minorities yet brilliant people are celebrators of reason and promotors of power by which humans understand the universe and improve their own goals. They are the epitomes of knowledge, freedom and happiness. The chapter pays tributes to both past and present non-heterosexuals who have impacted graciously the civility and progress of humanity as a whole.

Alan Mathison Turing, Mathematician

Alan Mathison Turing, born June 23, 1912 in London, England and died June 7, 1954 was a British mathematician and logician who made major contributions to mathematics, cryptanalysis, logic, philosophy, and mathematical biology and also to the new areas later named computer science, cognitive science, artificial intelligence, and later life. He entered the University of Cambridge to study mathematics in 1931. After graduating in 1934, he was elected to a fellowship at King's College in recognition of his research in probability theory. In 1936, Turing's seminal paper, *"On Computable Numbers, with an Application to the Entscheidungsproblem [Decision Problem]"* was published and this paper had profound significance for the emerging science of computing.

In 1938, Turing graduated with a Ph.D. in mathematical logic from the Princeton University. While working on the Entscheidungsproblem, Turing invented the universal Turing machine, an abstract computing machine that encapsulates the fundamental logical principles of the digital computer. Having returned from the United States to England in 1938, he joined the Government Code and Cypher School, and at the outbreak of war with Germany in September, 1939, he moved to the organization's wartime headquarters at Bletchley Park, Buckinghamshire. During the autumn of 1939 and the spring of 1940, Turing and others designed a code-breaking machine known as the Bombe. For the rest of the war, Bombes supplied the Allies with large quantities of military intelligence. By the early 1942, the cryptanalysts at Bletchley Park were decoding about thirty-nine thousand intercepted messages each month, a figure that rose subsequently to eighty-four thousand per month.

In 1942, Turing also devised the first systematic method for breaking encrypted messages by the sophisticated German cipher machine that the British called "Tunny". At the end of the war, Turing was made an Officer of the Most Excellence Order of the British Empire (OBE) for his code-breaking work. His design for the Automatic Computing Engine (ACE) was the first complete specification of an electronic stored-program all-purpose digital computer. He also wrote the first-ever programming manual, and his programming system was used in the Ferranti

Mark I, the first marketable electronic digital computer in 1951.

Turing was a founding father of artificial intelligence and of modern cognitive science, and he was a leading early proponent of the hypothesis that the human brain is in large part of digital computing machine. Turing was elected a fellow of the Royal Society of London in March, 1951. In March, 1952 he was convicted of "gross indecency"—i.e. homosexuality, a crime in Britain at that time—and he was sentenced to 12 months of hormone 'therapy' and now with a criminal record, he would never again be able to work for Government Communication Headquarters (GCHQ), the British government's postwar code-breaking center. In 1952, he published "**The Chemical Basis of Morphogenesis**" describing aspects of his research on the development of form and patterns in living organisms.

In the midst of this groundbreaking work, Turing was discovered dead in his bed, poisoned by cyanide. In 1954, the motive of his death was established to be the hormone 'treatment' he received at the hands of the authorities following his trial for being gay. However, it was speculated that Turing was murdered by the secret services given that he, Turing knew so much about cryptanalysis at a time when homosexuals were regarded as threats to national security. One of his profound quotes is:

> "The isolated man does not develop any intellectual power. It is necessary for him to be immersed in an environment of other men, whose techniques he absorbs during the first twenty years of his life. He may then perhaps do a little research of his own and make a very few discoveries which are passed on to other men. From this point of view, the search for new techniques must be regarded as carried out by the human community as a whole, rather than by individuals".

Florence Nightingale, British Nurse, Statistician and Social Reformer

Florence Nightingale, born May 12, 1820, Florence Italy and died August, 13, 1910, London, England. She was a British nurse, statistician and a social reformer who was the foundational philosopher of modern nursing. She was put in-charge of nursing British and allied soldiers in Turkey during the Crimean War of 1853-1856 which was fought mainly on the Crimean Peninsula between the Russians and the British, the French, and Ottoman

Turkish with support from January, 1855 by the army of Sardinia-Piedmont. Her efforts to formalize nursing education led her to establish the first scientifically based nursing school—the Nightingale School of Nursing at St. Thomas' Hospital in London in 1860.

She was the first woman awarded the Order of Merit in 1907, and International Nurses Day observed annually on May 12 commemorates her birth and celebrates the important roles of nurses in health care. She was born to William Edward and Frances Nightingale. Florence was named after the city she was born in and she was a precocious child intellectually for which her father took particular interest in her education guiding her through history, philosophy, and literature. She excelled in mathematics and languages and was able to read and write French, German, Italian, Greek and Latin at an early age. Never satisfied with the traditional role of females—home management—she preferred to read the great philosophers and to engage in serious political and social discourse with her father.

Although, Florence wanted to be become a nurse at age 16, her attempts were thwarted by her family as an inappropriate activity for a woman of her stature especially since she came from an affluent home. Despite family reservations, Nightingale was eventually able to enroll at the Institution of Protestant Deaconesses at Kaiserwerth in Germany for two weeks of training in July, 1850 and again for three months in July, 1851. There she learned basic nursing skills, the importance of patient observation and the values of good hospital organization. In 1853, Nightingale became the superintendent of the Institution for Sick Gentlewomen (governesses) in Distressed Circumstances in London, where she successfully displayed her skills as an administrator by improving nursing care, working conditions, and efficiency of the hospital.

In October, 1853, the British troop base and hospitals for the care of the sick and wounded soldiers were primarily established in Scutari across the Bosporus from Constantinople (Istanbul). The status of the care of the wounded was reported to the London Times stating that soldiers were treated by an incompetent and ineffective medical establishment and that the most basic supplies were not available for care. The British public raised an outcry over the treatment of the soldiers and demanded that the solution be improved drastically. Sidney Herbert, then Secretary of State wrote to Nightingale requesting she lead a group of nurses to Scutari. On October, 21, 1854, Nightingale led a sanctioned party of thirty-eight women and arrived in Scutari at the Barrack Hospital on November,5. At the camp, she brought changes and established standards of care such as bathing, clean clothing and dressings, and adequate food.

Attention was also given to psychological needs through assistance in writing letters to relatives and through providing educational and recreational activities. She herself wandered the wards at night, thus earned her the title of **"Lady with the Lamp"**. Her accomplishments in providing care and reportedly reducing the mortality rate to about two percent brought her fame in England through the press and the letters of the soldiers. In September, 1856, she met with Queen Victoria and Prince Albert to discuss the need for reform of the British military establishment. Based on her meticulous record keeping regarding the running of the Barrack Hospital, causes of illnesses and death, the efficiency of the nursing and medical staffs, and difficulties in purveyance, a royal commission was established which based its findings on the statistical data and analysis provided by Nightingale.

In 1855, as a form of gratitude and respect, the Nightingale Fund was established and through private donations £45,000 was raised by 1859 as well as granted a prize of $250,000 from the British government, and was put at Nightingale's disposal which brought about the Nightingale School of Nursing in 1860. The school formalized secular nursing education, making nursing a viable and respectable option for women who desired employment outside of the home. The model was taken globally by matrons. Nightingale's statistical models such as the Coxcomb chart which she developed to assess mortality and her basic concepts regarding nursing remain applicable today.

Nightingale's role in improving the health of households was through her most famous publication, **"Notes on Nursing: What It Is and What It Is Not"** which provided direction on how to manage the sick has been in continuous publically worldwide since 1859. Later, additional reforms were financed through the Nightingale Fund, and a school for the education of midwives was established at King's College Hospital in 1862. Believing that the most important location for the care of the sick was in the home, she established training for district nursing, which was aimed at improving the health of the poor and vulnerable. Throughout the US Civil War, she was frequently consulted about how to best manage field hospitals. Nightingale also served as an authority on public sanitation issues in India for both the military and civilians, although she had never been to India herself. One of her quotes is: *"Wise and humane management of the patient is the best safeguard against infection"*. She was a lesbian even though many believe she was asexual. Nightingale was never married and rebuffed at least four marriage proposals including one from a man who reportedly pursued her for nine years. She is believed to be a lesbian because in some letters of hers she spoke of a female cousin saying *"I have never loved but one person with passion in my life, and that was her"*. More evidence that she had more than friendships with women comes from a line in a memoir which states, *"I have lived and slept in the same beds with English Countesses and Prussian farm women. No *woman has excited passions among women more than I have*".

Sophia Parnok, Russian Poet, Journalist and Translator.

Sophia Parnok was born on August 11, 1885 in Taganrog, Yekaterinoslav Governorate, Russian Empire and died on August 26, 1933 in Karinskoye, Odintsovsky District, Moscow Oblast, Soviet Union. She was a Russian poet, journalist and a translator. Beginning from age six, she wrote poetry in a style quite different from the predominant poets of her time, revealing her own sense of lesbianism, Jewish identity and Russianness. She worked as journalist under the pen name of Andrei Polianin and she has been referred to as "Russia's Sappho" as she wrote openly about her seven lesbian relationships. She was born into an affluent family of professional Jews outside the Pale of Settlement.

Completing her studies at the Mariinskaya Gymnasium, in 1905, she moved to Geneva and attempted to study music, but lacked any real drive and quickly returned to Russia. In 1906, she published her first book of poems under the pseudonym Sophia Parnok and married Vladmir

Volkenstein in 1907. However, two years into the marriage, the marriage failed and she began working as a journalist. From 1913, Parnok exclusively had amorous relationships with women and used those erotic relationships to fuel her creativity. Her muses propelled her to publish five collections of poetry and write several librettos for opera before dying in 1933. Barred from publications of her poetry after 1928, Parnok's works were mostly forgotten until after the Soviet Union and with increased scholarship since that time, resulted in the publication of her collected works for the first time in 1979.

She was born actually as Sonya Yakovlevna Parnokh to a physician mother, one of the first women doctors in the empire and a Jewish pharmacist father who was also the owner of an apothecary. In 1902, Parnokh spent the summer in the Crimea where she had her first real romance with Nadezhda "Nadya" Pavlovna Polyakova, her muse for the next five years. As she approached her graduation, Parnokh and her father's relationship became increasingly strained. His disapproval of her failure to apply herself seriously to her writing and to her lesbianism brought them into conflict. She graduated with the gold medal (equivalent to the western designation summa cum laude) in May, 1903. Shortly before the 1905 Revolution, she was baptized into the Russian Orthodox faith and her writings from this period reflect a new interest in religion and an exploration of Christianity.

In 1906, she returned to Russia, yet her father's refusal to welcome her and his reduction of her allowance pressed Parnokh to begin searching in earnest for a publisher. Using her contact with Volkenstein, her former husband as a leverage, she asked him to help her find a publisher and instructed him to have the work printed under the name of Sophia Parnok because "I detest the letter kh (Russian:x)". Her first published work, 'The Autumn Garden' was in November, 1906 in the Journal for Everyone, edited by Viktor Mirolyubov. To escape her father's influence and be independent, Parnok and Volkenstein married in September,1907 and moved to Saint Petersburg. Parnok enrolled in the Bestuzhev Courses to study law and continued publishing poems in various journals. She also began doing translation works, having been invited in 1908 by Liubov Gurevich to coedit French-Russian translation of Petits poèmes en prose by Charles Baudelaire.

Between 1910 and 1917, Parnok worked as a journalist under the pseudonym Andrei Polianin, specifically choosing to separate her literary works from her journalism. Her works include 'Poems' (1916) containing 60 poems; 'Roses of Pieria (1922)' contained 20 poems, 'The Vine' (1923) contained 23 poems which traced Parnok's life from her physical birth to her spiritual rebirth in Sudak; 'The Little Mermaid (libretto) (1923); 'Music' (1926) contained 33 poems; Half-Whispered (1927) contained 38 poems and was dedicated to Tsuberiller; and Prologue (1928), Those Unfading Dyas (1983). In early, 1921, she was arrested and sent to a prison in Sudak where she contracted a severe case of tuberculosis. She also suffered from both bronchitis and stomach problems caused by her Graves' disease. In all, she wrote two hundred and sixty-one poems during her ailing period.

Ben A. Barres, American Neurobiologist

Ben A. Barres born on September 13, 1954 and died on December 27, 2017 was an American neurobiologist at Stanford University. His research focused on the interaction between neurons and glial cells in the nervous system. Beginning in 2008, he was Chair of the Neurobiology Department at the Stanford University of Science of Medicine. He transitioned to male in 1997, and became the first openly transgender scientist in the National Academy of Science in 2013. Barres was born on September 13, 1954 in West Orange, New Jersey, assigned female as Barbara A. Barres.

As a child, his salesman father and homemaker mother saw him as a tomboy. He later recalled: "Internally I felt strongly that I was a boy. This was evident in everything about my behavior". At age 17, he learned that he had been born with Müllerian agenesis, for which he received surgical alteration. He obtained a Bachelor of Science in Biology from Massachusetts Institute of Technology in 1976 and a medical degree from Dartmouth Medical School in 1979 and a residency in neurology at Weill Cornell Medicine. In studying pathology reports, he noticed a correlation between neural degeneration and irregular patterns of glial cells in the brain and intrigued, resigned his residency to pursue research in neuroscience at Harvard Medical School.

He completed his PhD in neurobiology in 1990 and did postdoctoral training at University College, London. He joined the faculty of Neurobiology at the Stanford School of Medicine in 1993 and transitioned to male in 1997. During his time at Stanford, Barres discovered the importance of glial cells in the formation, development, maturation, and regeneration of neurons. His lab also discovered and developed methods for the purification and culturing of retinal ganglion cells and the glial cells with which they interact, including the oligodendrocytes and astrocytes of the optic nerve. He transitioned into male due to gender discrimination.

For example, he was denied at schools from science and mathematics courses, which he liked. A more serious event happened to his academics in MIT. After solving a difficult math problem that stumped many male students, his professor charged that it was solved for her (him) by a boyfriend. He was the top student in the class, but found it hard to get a willing supervisor for research. He lost a scholarship to a man who had only one publication, while he already had six. After transitioning, he noticed that people who were not aware of his transgender status treated him with respect much more than when he was presented as a woman. He died of pancreatic cancer at his home in Palo Alto, California.

He won severally awards including the teaching awards of the Kaiser Award for Excellence in Teaching, and the Kaiser Award for Innovative and Outstanding Contributions to Medical Education. He was a cofounder of Annexon Biosciences, Inc., a company making drugs to block neurodegeneration in Alzheimer's and other neurobiological diseases. He coauthored about seventeen publications and he is the author of *"Critical Role of Glia in Brain Development"* (2018) and *"The Autobiography of Transgender Scientist"* (2018).

Sally Kristen Ride, American Astronaut

Sally Ride was born on May 26, 1951 in Encino, California and died on July 23, 2012, La Jolla, California. She is the first American woman to travel into outer space. Ride showed great early promise as a tennis player, but eventually gave up her plans to play professionally and attended Stanford University where she earned her bachelor's degree in English and Physics in 1973. In 1978, as a doctoral candidate and teaching assistant in laser physics at Stanford, she was selected by the National Aeronautics and Space Administration

(NASA) as one of the six women astronaut candidates. She received her Ph.D. in astrophysics and began her training and evaluation courses that same year.

In August, 1979 she completed her NASA training, obtained a pilot's license and became eligible for assignment as a US space shuttle mission specialist. On June 18, 1983, she became the first American woman in space while rocketing into orbit abroad the shuttle orbiter Challenger. Sally Ride married fellow astronaut Steven Hawley in 1982 and they divorced five years later. She resigned from NASA in 1987 and in 1989 she became a professor of physics at the University of California, San Diego, and director of its California Space Institute until 1996.

From the 1990s, Sally Ride initiated or headed a number of programmes and organizations devoted to fostering science in education, particularly to providing support for schoolgirls interested in science, mathematics or technology. In 2013, she was posthumously awarded the Presidential Medal of Freedom. Ride remains the youngest American astronaut to have travelled to space having done so at the age of 32. She died of pancreatic cancer on

July 23, 2012. Her father had been a political science professor at Santa Monica College. She attended Portola Junior High (now Portola Middle School) and then Birmingham High School before graduating from the private Westlake School for Girls in Los Angeles on a scholarship.

She was the president and CEO of Sally Ride Science, a company she cofounded in 2001 that creates entertaining science programmes and publications for upper elementary and middle school students, with a particular focus on girls. Ride wrote and co-wrote seven books on space aimed at children, with the goal of encouraging children to study science. After her divorce with the husband, she and Tam O'Shaughnessy, a professor emerita of school psychology for twenty-seven years married. She received numerous awards such as the National Space Society's von Braun Award, and the NCAA's Theodore Roosevelt Award. She was inducted into the National Women's Hall of Fame and the Astronaut Hall of Fame.

On December 6, 2006, California Governor Arnold Schwarzenegger and First Lady, Maria Shriver inducted Ride into the California Hall of Fame at the California Museum for History, Women and the Arts. In April 2013, the US Navy announced that a research ship would be named in honor of Ride. This was done in 2014 with the christening of the oceanographic research vessel, RV Sally Ride (AGOR-28). She was awarded the Presidential Medal of Freedom, the highest civilian award in the United States posthumously.

Alan Lucil Hart, American Radiologist & Physician

Alan Hart born on October 4, 1890 and died on July 1, 1962, was assigned female at birth with the name Alberta Lucille Hart. In 1891, Hart's father, a successful merchant in Halls Summit, died in a typhoid fever epidemic, forcing Hart's mother to return to her native Oregon to raise her child. While a student at Albany, Hart carried on a number of love affairs with women; delighted in all masculine pursuits, including driving automobiles; and was an accomplished debater and writer for the school newspaper and yearbook.

Hart was an accomplished writer and published many works under his male pseudonym Robert Allen Bamford. Hart started medical school at University of Oregon in 1912 where he became the first female to win the Saylor medal. Although Hart had been going by his chosen name Robert and dressing masculine, it was not until 1917 that Hart underwent a hysterectomy and legally changed his name. Hart attended Stanford University before graduating top in his class from the University of Oregon Medical College.

This made Alan Hart, the first transgender man to undergo sex reassignment surgery in the United States. In 1918, he married Inez Stark, using the name, Robert Bamford. Eventually recognized by a classmate from medical school, the couple began a recurring pattern of relocations and job changes. This stress of continual secrecy led to their divorce. In 1925, Alan remarried and from 1935-1942, wrote four novels, including 'Doctor Mallory' and 'In the Lives of Men' set in the Pacific Northwest dealing with social issues within the medical field.

Hart earned a master's degree in radiology from the University of Pennsylvania in 1930 and another in Public Health in 1948. He took a job as Director of Radiology at Tacoma General Hospital in 1928. While working in radiology department of Tacoma General Hospital, Alan Hart recognized that although patients who had obvious tuberculosis

(TB) infections were being treated, none was getting ahead of the disease to manage the spread from asymptomatic patients. Hart began pioneering efforts to use x-rays machines to detect early TB infections, and was one of the first to document the spread of the disease. The images taken using x-rays allowed doctors to see any abnormalities or damage to the lung tissue caused by the bacteria.

Although x-rays had been utilized previously to locate gunshots and bone fractures during World War I, it was relatively novel at the time to use x-rays as a critical tool to screen for TB infection, allowing patients to be treated sooner, which often saved their lives. Early detection also meant that patients could be isolated earlier, lessening the spread of tuberculosis is overall and minimizing outbreaks. In 1937, Hart was named Idaho's Tuberculosis Control Officer. Hart established Idaho's first in-place and mobile TB screening clinics to spearhead the state's war against tuberculosis. Hart named his clinics 'chest clinics' to allow patients to discreetly get the help that they needed.

Due to his own story experiencing discrimination as a transgender man, Hart could empathize with patients who struggled with stigmatization. In 1948, Hart was appointed Director of Hospitalization and Rehabilitation for the Connecticut State Tuberculosis Commission. He was the author of Doctor Mallory (1935); The Undaunted (1936); In the Lives of Men (1937) and Doctor Finlay Sees It Through (1942). Hart earned a doctor of medicine degree from the University of Oregon Medical Department in 1917. Hart was married to Inez Start from 1918-1924, and to Edna Ruddick from 1924 until his death in 1962. His development of an x-ray process tool for early TB diagnosis helped bring the state's death toll rate to one-fifth of what it was, saving thousands of lives. There is the Alan L. and Edna Ruddick Hart Fund created for leukemia research.

Ellen DeGeneres, American Comedian & Television Host

Ellen Lee DeGeneres, born on January 25, 1958 in Metairie, Louisiana, United States to Elizabeth Jane, a speech therapist and Elliott Everett DeGeneres, an insurance agent. She graduated from Atlanta High School in May, 1976 after completing her first years of high school at Grace King High School before attending the University of New Orleans where she majored in communication briefly. Dissatisfied with university life, DeGeneres left to work in a law firm and later was involved in various jobs such as waitress, bartender, house painter and oyster shucker.

She began her comedian career in the late 1970s when she first performed in a local coffeehouse. With time, her comedies caught the attention of ShowTime and the cable network named her *Funniest Person of the Year, 1982*. Fortunes smiled on her when in 1986 she was invited to perform on The Tonight Show Starring Johnny Carson. Aside appearing on television in stand-up comedy routines, DeGeneres featured in television shows such as *One Night Stand* (1989), *Open House* (1989-90) and *Laurie Hill* (1992) as well as starring in *These Friends of Mine* in 1994. In 1997, Ellen DeGeneres revealed that she was gay and became the first prime-time show to feature an openly gay lead character; and in 2003, Ellen eventually launched her own syndicated talk show, *The Ellen*

DeGeneres Show. The show earned more than 20 Daytime Emmy Awards in its first five seasons.

In addition to her television work, DeGeneres appeared in films such as *Coneheads* (1993), *Mr. Wrong* (1996), comedy *EdTV* (1999), *Finding Nemo* (2003) and *Finding Dory* (2016). In 2012, DeGeneres received the Kennedy Center's Mark Twain Prize for American Humor and in 2016, she was awarded the Presidential Medal of Freedom. She is the author of several books including *My Point ... and I Do Have One* (1995), *Seriously ... I'm Kidding* (2011) and *Home* (2015). She is also an executive producer of several television shows including *Bethenny* (2012-2014), *Repeat After Me* (2015) and *Little Big Shots* (2015). She was first dated actress Anne Heche from 1998 and broke up in August, 2000 before her marriage to Portia de Rossi in 2008.

Elton John, English Singer-Songwriter

Sir Elton Hercules John, original name Reginald Kenneth Dwight, born on March 25, 1947 in Pinner, Middlesex, England is a British singer, composer and pianist. As a child prodigy on the piano, John was awarded a scholarship to the Royal Academy of Music at age 11. His first British recording success was with *'Lady Samantha'* in 1968 and his first American album, **Elton John** was released in 1970 and immediately established him as a major international star. His recordings were among the first to homogenize electric guitar and acoustic piano with synthesized instrumentation.

By 1973, Elton John was one of the world's best-selling pop performers. In the 1990s, John was the first male pop star to declare his homosexuality, suffering no noticeable career damage. He wrote songs for the film, *The Lion King* (1994) and *'Can You Feel the Love Tonight'* which won the Academy Award for best original song; the movie was adapted into a Broadway musical in 1997. Same year, a new version of his 1973 song *'Candle in the Wind"* revised by Taupin to mourn the death of Diana, Princess of Wales, became the most successful pop single in history selling more than 30 million copies. John composed the score for Billy Elliot, a stage adaptation of the popular film, and that musical premiered in London's West End in 2005 and made its Broadway debut in 2008 and won 10 Tony Awards including best musical in 2009. His songs included *Wonderful Crazy Night* (2016), *Peachtree Road* (2004).

He also contributed sound tracks to the animated movies 'The Road to El Dorado' (2000), *Gnomeo & Juliet* (2011). John was inducted into the Rock and Roll Hall of Fame in 1994 and he was knighted in 1998 by Queen Elizabeth II. Elton John has sold more than 300 million records during his music career. John had a difficult relationship with his father, Stanley Dwight, a member of the Royal Air Force. His parents divorced when he was a teenager, and he and his father clashed over his future. He dropped out of school at 17 to follow his dream. He started playing with a group called Bluesology, and he cobbled together his stage moniker from the names of two members of the group. John got his first break as a singer with his 1969 album **Empty Sky**, featuring songs by John and Taupin.

In 1990, after years of battling substance abuse issues, particularly cocaine, which may have triggered severe epileptic seizures, John went into rehabilitation. Established in the United States in 1992, the Elton John AIDS Foundation has brought in more than $400 million to support HIV/AIDS programmes around the world. In March, 2020, John hosted the iHeart Living Room Concert for America to raise funds for coronavirus relief efforts. John met his longtime partner, David Furnish at a dinner in 1993. The pair got married in a civil ceremony on December 21, 2005—the same day the Civil Partnership Act 2004 went into effect.

Michael Kors, American Designer

Michael Kors born as Karl Anderson Jr on Long Island, New York, on August 9, 1959. As a toddler, Kors worked as a model, appearing in national campaigns for products such as toilet paper and Lucky Charms cereal. Due to the divorce of his parents, Kors got his new name at age 5 when his mother married businessman, Bill Kors. He moved to New York in the 1970s to attend the Fashion Institute of Technology. However, he loved the city more than the school and dropped out after two semesters. In 1978, Kors went to work at the French boutique, Lothar's, which allowed him to design and merchandise his first fashion collection.

The well-received collection generated enough interest that Kors was able to start his own fashion line. He is the honorary chairman and chief creative officer of his brand. Michael Kors, which sells men's and women's ready-to-wear, accessories, watches, jewelry, footwear, and fragrance. Kors was the first women's ready-to-wear designer for the French house, Celine from 1997 to 2003. He was awarded CFDA Award for women's wear designer in 1999 and in 2003, he was awarded the CFDA Award for men's wear designer of the year. He graduated from John F. Kennedy High School in Bellmore, New York. Kors married his partner, Lance Le Pere on August 16, 2011 in Southampton, New York in The Hamptons.

As a teen, Kors began designing clothes and selling them out of his parents' basement, which he renamed *The Iron Butterfly*. Kors also took acting lessons when he was young, but stopped when he was 14 when he decided to focus on becoming a fashion designer. Kors has over 770 Lifestyle stores around the world. In January 2014, Forbes reported that Kors reached a personal fortune in excess of $1 billion. In 2010, Kors became the youngest recipient ever of the Geoffrey Beene Lifetime Achievement Award from the Council of Fashion Designers of America and received the Fragrance Foundation's FiFi Award for Lifetime Achievement, and received the Oliver R. Grace Award for Distinguished Service in Advancing Cancer Research, an annual honor bestowed by the Cancer Research Institute, a US nonprofit organization dedicated to advancing immune system-based treatments for cancer.

He was honored with the Golden Heart Lifetime Achievement Award by God's Love We Deliver, a non-profit organization that distributes fresh meals to people living with HIV/AIDS and other diagnoses, which he has been involved with for over 20 years. In 2015, Kors was named the Global Ambassador Against Hunger by the United Nation's World Food Program.

Stefano Gabbana & Domenico Dolce, Italian Fashion Designers

Stefano Gabbana, born in Milan, Italy on November 14, 1962 to a father who worked in a printing factory and a mother who worked for a laundry service. He graduated from the Istituto Superiore per le Industrie Artistiche, a design institute in Rome. He is the cofounder of the Dolce & Gabbana luxury fashion house. In 1980, Gabbana met Sicilian Domenico Dolce through Dolce's employer, designer Giorgio Correggiari. In 1983, Gabbana and Dolce left Correggiari to work on their own and two years later, they launched *Dolce & Gabbana S.P.A. (D&G)*.

In October 1985, the Dolce & Gabbana brand made its fashion show debut at Milano Collezioni's Nuovi Talenti. In March, 1986, D&G released its first collection and held its own show, 'Real Women'. A year later, the first D&G store was opened in Milan and in 1988, D&G established a partnership with Dolce's father, Saverio, who owned the manufacturing company, Dolce Saverio in Legnano, near Milan. In July, 1989, the company released its first lingerie and beachwear and its first menswear line in January, 1990. In October, 1992, D&G released its first fragrance, Dolce & Gabbana Parfum. The company, D&G line include ties, belts, handbags, sunglasses, watches and footwear. By 2003, the company sold more products in Italy than Armani, Gucci, Prada, and Versace and by 2009, the company had 113 stores and 21 factory outlets with a staff of 3,500 and an annual turnover of more than €1 billion. Gabbana appeared in the 2013 documentary, *Scatter My Ashes at Bergdorf's*, made about the fashion industry.

Domenico Mario Assunto Dolce, born on August 13, 1958 in Polizzi Generosa, Sicily. His father was a tailor and his mother sold fabrics and apparel. He moved to Milan to attend the fashion design school, Istituto Marangoni, but dropped out before graduating; confident he knew enough to work in the industry. His dream was to work for Armani. Gabbana and Dolce have received numerous honors for their fashion and cultural contributions with their first award, the International Woolmark Prize in 1991 and in 1993, their Dolce & Gabbana Parfum was named the Best Fragrance of the Year. Dolce and Gabbana were an open couple for many years until they ended their long-time relationship in 2003, but the duo still works together at D&G.

Tim Cook, American Chief Executive

Tim Cook born as Timothy Donald Cook in Robertsdale, Alabama on November 1, 1960 to Donald, a shipyard worker and Geraldine, a homemaker. Cook attended Robertsdale High School and graduated second in his class in 1978 and enrolled at Auburn University in Alabama graduating in 1982 with a bachelor's degree in industrial engineering, and earning a Master of Business Administration degree from Duke University's Fuqua School of Business in 1988. Cook was awarded the title of Fuqua Scholar—an honor given only to students at the business school who graduate in the top 10 percent of their class. Fresh out of the graduate school, Cook embarked on a career in the field of computer technology and he was hired by IBM, where he moved up the ranks to become the corporation's North American fulfillment director, managing manufacturing and distribution functions for IBM's Personal Computer Company in both North and Latin America.

Following a 12-year career at IBM, Cook in 1994 became the chief operating officer of the Reseller Division at Intelligent Electronics. After three years, he joined the Compaq Computer Corporation as vice president of corporate materials, charged with procuring and managing product inventory. His time there was short-lived, however: After a six-month stint at Compaq, Cook left for a position at Apple. Cook began working with Apple in early 1998, before the company had developed the iMac, iPod, iPhone or iPad, and when it was seeing declining profits instead of profit growth. However, things quickly changed after Cook came on board as a vice president.

Less than a year after his Apple debut, the corporation was reporting profits, an extraordinary shift from a recent report that showed a net loss of $1billion from the previous fiscal year. As Cook rose to executive vice president, he took responsibility for managing worldwide sales and operations, along with leading the Macintosh division and continued development of reseller/supplier relationships. In August, 2011, Cook was named Apple's new CEO and under his leadership in May, 2014, Apple announced its biggest acquisition to date when it bought Beats Music and Beats Electronics for $3 billion.

Following this, in June, 2014 Cook announced the latest version of the Apple operating system for desktop and mobile, OSX Yosemite and in September of the same year, Cook unveiled the iPhone 6 and iPhone 6 Plus and announced the first new product under his leadership, a wearable device to track fitness and health, the "Apple Watch". Under the watch of Cook as Apple CEO, Apple unveiled the iPhone X, which generated buzz in the tech world for its facial recognition system in 2017; introduced the Apple News app to give users access to articles from a wide range of sources. Under the leadership of Tim Cook, Apple became the first American public company to reach a value of $1 trillion as against a company market value of $348 billion.

In October, 2014, Cook was inducted by the Alabama Academy of Honor, the highest honor Alabama gives its citizens when he spoke about his home state's record of LGBT rights. Cook was misdiagnosed with multiple sclerosis in 1996 and he has since taken part in charity fundraising, such as cycle races to raise money for the disease. In 2017, Cook was awarded Honorary Doctor of Science from University of Glasgow, Scotland and awarded the Courage Against Hate Award from Anti-Defamation League in 2018.

Jon Stryker, American Architect

Jon Stryker born in 1958 is an American architect, philanthropist and activist for social and environmental causes. He is the heir to the Stryker Corporation medical supply company fortune. He is the founder and president of Arcus Foundation, a private international philanthropic organization primarily supporting great ape conservation efforts and LGBT causes. Stryker was born in Kalamazoo, Michigan. He earned a Bachelor of Arts degree in biology from Kalamazoo College in 1982 and a Master of Architecture degree from the University of California at Berkeley. Stryker is the president of Depot Landmark LLC, a development company specializing in the rehabilitation of historic buildings; and a founding board member of Greenleaf Trust, a privately owned bank in Kalamazoo, Michigan.

Stryker was named one of the Top 50 donors in US by the Chronicle of Philanthropy from 2006 to 2012 and in 2014. He was also named to Forbes' list of America's Top 50 Givers in 2018. He received the 2014 Global Vision Award from Immigration Equality, a US-based nonprofit organization that provides legal representation to LBGT and HIV-positive asylum seekers, detainees and binational couples. He is married to his longtime partner, Slobodan Randjelovic and has two children from his previous marriage. He was a public advocate for the passage of the Affordable Care Act, better known as Obamacare, and gave $2million to Priorities USA Action during the legislative battle over the Obamacare. Stryker gave $20 million to Kalamazoo College to establish the Jon L. Stryker Future Leaders Scholarship Program, a scholarship program aimed at helping students with financial needs and to increase diversity on campus; while the Arcus Foundation gave $25 million to establish the Arcus Centre for Social Justice Leadership at the college.

Jennifer Pritzker, American Investor and Philanthropist

Jennifer Natalya Pritzker born August 13, 1950 is an American investor, philanthropist and a member of the Pritzker family. Pritzker retired as a lieutenant colonel from the Illinois Army National Guard (ILARNG) in 2001 and was later made an honorary Illinois colonel. She is the founder of the Tawani Foundation in 1995, Tawani Enterprises in 1996 and the Pritzker Military Library in 2003. She is the first transgender billionaire. Born James Nicholas Pritzker to Robert Pritzker and Audrey Pritzker in Chicago, Illinois as a Jew. Her parents divorced in 1979 and has two half-siblings from the remarriage of her father, Robert, to Irene Dryburgh in 1980. Pritzker enlisted in the US Army on February 8, 1974 and served with the HQ Troop, and with the B Troop, 1st Squadron, 17th Calvary Regiment, 82nd Airborne Division based at Fort Bragg, North Carolina, rising to the rank of Sergeant.

After completing military service in February, 1977, Pritzker enrolled at Loyola University of Chicago, majoring in history and entered its Army Reserve Officers' Training Corps program. Pritzker graduated with BA in History in May, 1979 and received commission as an Army officer that same month. After 16 years in the Army Reserves and Illinois Army National Guard, Pritzker retired from the Army National Guard as a lieutenant colonel, in 2001. Interests of the company include significant Chicago real estate holdings. In 2016, Jennifer Pritzker was presented the Bonham Centre Award from The Mark S. Bonham Centre for Sexuality Diversity Studies, University of Toronto, for her contributions to the advancement and education of issues around sexual identification. In 2013, the Tawani Foundation donated $25 million to Norwich University, in Northfield, Vermont, the school credited with developing and establishing the first Naval Reserve Officers' Training Corp (ROTC) program in the country; and in 2016, through her Foundation, Pritzker gave $2 million donation to create the world's first endowed academic chair of transgender studies, at the University of Victoria in British Columbia. Pritzker has three children: a daughter and two sons.

Peter Thiel, German-American Entrepreneur & Venture Capitalist

Peter Andreas Thiel, born October 11, 1967 is the cofounder of PayPal, Palantir Technologies, and Founders Fund. He is the first outside investor in Facebook. Peter was born in Frankfurt, Germany to Susanne and Klaus Friedrich Thiel and he moved with his family to the United States as an infant. His father worked as a chemical engineer for various mining companies, creating an itinerant upbringing for Thiel and his brother. He spent a portion of his upbringing in Southern Africa before the family settled in California in 1977. He studied philosophy at Stanford University graduating with a Bachelor of Arts in 1989, during which time he founded *The Stanford Review*, a newspaper that was critical of political correctness.

He then earned a law degree from Stanford Law School in 1992, and shortly after graduating, he published *The Diversity Myth* (co-written with David Sacks) about alleged political intolerance at the university. After graduation, he worked as a judicial law clerk of the US Court of Appeals for the Eleventh Circuit, as a securities lawyer for Sullivan & Cromwell, as a speechwriter for former-US Secretary of Education, William Bennett and as a derivatives trader at Credit Suisse. He founded Thiel Capital Management in 1996 and he cofounded PayPal with Max Levchin and Luke Nosek in 1998 serving as chief executive officer until its sale to eBay in 2002. In 1998, Thiel and several others cofounded Confinity, which was designed to handle payments between Palm Pilots. The following year it merged with Elon Musk's X.com, and PayPal was created. After PayPal, he founded Clarium Capital and in 2004, he launched Palantir Technologies, a big data analysis company and served as its chairman. In 2005, he launched Founders Fund with PayPal partners, Ken Howery and Like Nosek. It invested in such companies as Airbnb, Lyft and Musk's SpaceX.

He acquired a 10.2% stake of Facebook in August, 2004 and sold the majority of his shares in Facebook for over $1 billion in 2012; cofounded Mithril Capital, serving as investment committee chair in 2012 and served as a part-time partner at Y Combinator from 2015-2017. The Thiel Foundation and Thiel Fellowship fund nonprofit research into artificial intelligence, life extension and sea steading. Thiel excelled in mathematics, and scored first in a California-wide mathematics competition while attending Bowditch Middle School in Foster City. At San Mateo High School, he read Ayn Rand, admired the optimism and anti-communism of then-President Ronald Reagan, and became valedictorian of his graduating class in 1985.

The Thiel Foundation is a supporter of the Committee to Protect Journalists (CPJ), which promotes the rights of journalists to report the news freely without fear of reprisal, and a supporter of the Human Rights Foundation, which organizes the Oslo Freedom Forum. He has received numerous awards and honors including Herman Lay Award for Entrepreneurship (2006); honored as a Young Global Leader by the World Economic Forum as one of the 250 most distinguishable leaders age 40 and under in 2007; awarded an honorary degree from Universidad Francisco Marroquin in 2009 and a TechCrunch Crunchie Award for Venture Capitalist of the Year in 2013. He is also the author of 'The Diversity Myth' in 1995 and 'Zero to One' in 2014. Thiel married his long-time partner, Matt Danzeisen in October, 2017 in Vienna, Austria. Danzeisen works as a portfolio manager at Thiel Capital and they have a baby daughter.

James Baldwin, American Writer & Playwright

James Baldwin, born on August 12, 1924 in Harlem, New York. He was one of the 20th century's greatest writers. Baldwin broke new literary ground with the exploration of racial and social issues in his many works. He was especially known for his essays on the Black experience in America. In 1953, Baldwin published the novel, 'Go Tell It on the Mountain' receiving acclaim for his insights on race, spirituality and humanity.

Baldwin was born to a single mother, Emma Jones and never knew the name of his biological father. His mother, Jones married a Baptist Minister named David Baldwin when he, James was about three years. James and his step-father, David had strained relationship, yet he followed in the footsteps of his step-father during his early teen years. He served as a youth minister in a Harlem Pentecostal church from the ages 14 to 16.

Baldwin developed a passion for reading at an early age and demonstrated a gift for writing during his school years. He schooled at the DeWitt Clinton High School in the Bronx, where he worked on the school's magazine with future famous photographer, Richard Avedon. Baldwin published numerous poems, short stories and plays in the magazine, and his early work showed an understanding for sophisticated literary devices in a writer of such a young age.

After graduating from high school in 1942, he had to put his plans for college on hold to help support his family, which included seven younger children. He took whatever work he could find, including laying railroad tracks for the US Army in New Jersey. During this time, Baldwin encountered discrimination frequently, being turned away from restaurants, bars and other establishments because he was African American. After being fired from the New Jersey job, Baldwin sought other works to make ends meet.

In July, 1943, Baldwin lost his father. He soon moved to Greenwich village, a New York City neighborhood popular with artists and writers. Devoting himself to novel, he took odd jobs to support himself. He befriended writer, Richard Wright, and through Wright, he was able to land a fellowship in 1945 to cover his expenses. Baldwin started getting essays and short shorts published in such national periodicals as *The Nation, Partisan Review and Commentary.* Three years on, he made a dramatic change in his life and moved to Paris on another fellowship.

The shift in location freed Baldwin to write more about his personal and racial background. The move marked the genesis of life as a 'transatlantic commuter' dividing his time between France and the United States. Baldwin had his first novel, 'Go Tell It on the Mountain', published in 1953. The loosely autobiographical tale focused on the life of a young man growing up in Harlem grappling with father issues and his religion.

In 1954, Baldwin received a Guggenheim Fellowship. He published his next novel, *Giovanni's Room* in 1955. The work told the story of an American living in Paris and broke new ground for its complex depiction of homosexuality, a then-taboo subject. Love between men was also explored in a later Baldwin novel, 'Just Above My Head' (1978). Baldwin was open about his homosexuality and relationship with both men and women.

Yet he believed that the focus on rigid categories was just a way of limiting freedom and that human sexuality is more fluid and less binary than often expressed in the US. Baldwin explored writing for the stage as well. He wrote 'The Amen Corner' which looked at the phenomenon of storefront Pentecostal religion. The play was produced at

Howard University in 1955 and later on Broadway in the mid-1960s. He is the author of *Notes of a Native Son* (1955) *and Nobody Knows My Name: More Notes of a Native Son* (1961), and *The Fire Next Time* (1963) which offered white readers a view of themselves through the eyes of the African American community.

In the work of 'The Fire Next Time', Baldwin offered a brutally realistic picture of race relations, but he remained hopeful about possible improvements. In the same year of 1963, Baldwin was featured on the cover of Time magazine. Baldwin wrote another play, *'Blues for Mister Charlie'*, which debuted on Broadway in 1964. The drama was loosely based on the 1955 racially motivated murder of a young African American boy named, Emmett Till. In that same year, his book with friend, Avedon entitled *'Nothing Personal'* hit the shelves of bookstore. The work was a tribute to slain civil rights movement leader, Medgar Evers.

In his 1968 novel, *'Tell Me How Long the Train's Been Gone,* Baldwin returned to popular themes—sexuality, family and the Black experience. Some critics panned the novel, calling it a polemic rather than a novel. By the early 1970s, Baldwin seemed to despair over the racial situation. He had witnessed so much violence in the previous decade—especially the assassination of Evers, Malcolm X, and Martin Luther King Jr.—caused by racial hatred. He also worked on a screenplay around this time, trying to adapt, 'The Autobiography of Malcolm X' by Alex Haley for the big screen. He also published a collection of poems, *Jimmy's Blues: Selected Poems*, in 1983 as well as the 1987 novel *Harlem Quartet*.

One of his novels, '*If Beale Street Could Talk*' was adapted into the Academy Award-winning film of the same name in 2018 and produced by Barry Jenkins. He received several honors and awards and they include Commandeur de la Légion d'honneur of 1986, Foreign Drama Critics Award, George Polk Memorial Award of 1963 and MacDowell Fellowships of 1954, 1958 and 1960. He has over 6 novels spanning between from 1953 and 1979; and several essays and short stories including '*Stranger in the Village*' of 1953; *Guide as Husband and Homosexual* of 1954; *Princes and Powers* of 1957 and *Letter from a Region of My Mind* of 1962.

David Geffen, Entertainment Producer

David Geffen born on February 21, 1943 in New York City. He became a millionaire by the age of 25 years. With Steven Spielberg and Jeffrey Katzenberg, he cofounded DreamWorks. He was born to Jewish parents, Abraham Geffen and Batya Volovskaya. Geffen's mother owned a clothing store in Borough Park called *Chic Corsets by Geffen*. Both parents were Jewish immigrants who met in British Mandatory Palestine and then moved to the United States. Geffen graduated from Brooklyn's New Utrecht High School in 1960. He attended the University of Texas at Austin before again dropping out. He then moved to Los Angeles, California to find his way in the entertainment business.

He attended Santa Monica College but soon left and he attributed his challenges in school to dyslexia. After a brief appearance as an extra in the 1961 film, *The Explosive Generation*, Geffen began his entertainment career at the William Morris Agency (WMA) where he became a talent agent through the interception of a letter from University of California (UCLA) to WMA and modifying the letter to show that he had attended and graduated from the university since he was to prove he was a college graduate to be employed. He was a mailroom clerk from 1964-1968. In 1968, he was a talent agent for Ashley Famous Agency and the Executive Vice President and Talent Agent for Creative Management Associates in 1969.

In 1971, Geffen cofounded Asylum Records in 1971 with Elliot Roberts and became a generator of the Southern California folk-rock sound and signed artists such as the Eagles, Tom Waits, Linda Ronstadt and J.D. Souther. Later in the 1970s, Geffen left the Asylum which was later acquired by Atlantic's parent company, Warner Communications and merged with Elektra Records where Geffen remained in charge until December, 1975 when he went to work as vice chairman of Warner Bros. film studios and retired in 1977 due to an erroneous diagnosis of cancer which emerged in 1980. In 1980, he founded Geffen Records and first signed Donna Summer and shortly released her 'The Wanderer' album, the lead single of which reached #3 on the Billboard Hot 100, and the album certified gold.

Geffen Records over the years has released according by artists including Elton John, Neil

Young, the Stone Roses, XTC and Olivia Newton-John. Through the Geffen Film Company, Geffen produced *Little Shop of Horrors* (1986), *Risky Business* (1983) and *Beetlejuice* (1988). In 1994, Geffen cofounded the DreamWorks SKG studio with Steven Spielberg and Jeffrey Katzenberg. Geffen has donated over $300 million to UCLA School of Medicine as well as funding the full cost of attendance for up to 30 students per year since 2017 Class; and in June 2021, Geffen gave $150 million to the Yale School of Drama to allow the drama school eliminate tuition for all students enrolled in masters, doctoral, and certificate programs, and in September, 2021 before the coming of this book, Columbia Business School dean announced that Geffen had made a landmark gift of $75 million to support the School's new facilities. He was named one of the 2010 recipients of Ahmet Ertegun Award from the Rock and Roll Hall of Fame and awarded with the President's Merit Award for 'indelible contributions to the music industry" in 2011.

Giorgio Armani, Italian Fashion Designer

Giorgio Armani born July 11, 1934 in the northern Italian town of Piacenza where he was raised by Maria Raimondi and Ugo Armani (an accountant for a transport company). He attended secondary school at the Liceo Scientifico Leonardo da Vinci in Milan and was inspired by the writings of A. J. Cronin's *The Citadel* to have a career in medicine. He enrolled in the University of Milan and after three years, he quit and joined the army. Due to his medical background, he was assigned to the Military Hospital in Verona. After his stint in the armed forces, Armani found a job as a window dresser at La Rinascente in 1957 and he went on to become a seller for the menswear department where he gained valuable experience in the marketing aspect of the fashion industry.

In the 1960s, Armani found himself in the Nino Cerruti Company, where he designed menswear. He polished his skills and for the next decades while still working at Cerrutti, Armani also freelanced, contributing designs to as many as ten manufacturers at a time. In 1973 with the persuasion of his friend and partner, Sergio Galeotti, Armani opened a design officer in Milan and engaged in extensive collaborations for a number of fashion houses including Allegri, Bagutta, Hilton and Tendresse. With an exposure by the international press during the runway shows at the Sala Bianca in the Pitti Palace in Florence,

Italy, he founded his own label on July 24, 1975 with his friend, Galeotti, Giorgio Armani S.p.A. in Milan and in October of the same year, he launched his first collection of men's ready-to-wear for Spring and Summer, 1976 under his own name.

In 1978, Armani signed an agreement with Gruppo Finanzario Tessile (GFT) which made it possible to produce luxury ready-to-wear in a manufacturing environment under the attentive supervision of the company's designer. In 1979, after founding the Giorgio Armani Corporation, he began producing for the United States and introduced the Main line for men and women. In the early 1980s, the company signed an agreement with L'Oréal to create perfumes and introduced the Armani Junior, Armani Jeans, and Emporio Armani lines and in 1982, the introduction of Emporio Underwear, Swimwear, and Accessories. Armani designed costumes for more than 100 films including *The Untouchables* of 1987 and designed the costumes for *American Gigolo* (1980) which grew his reputation.

As at 2009, Armani was spread in 37 different countries with over 60 retail networks with an annual turnover of $1.6 billion. Armani is credited with pioneering red-carpet fashion and was the first designer to ban models with a body mass index (BMI) under 18, after model Ana Carolina Reston starved herself to death due to anorexia nervosa. Armani operates seven luxury hotels and three vacation resorts under the Giorgio Armani name. He is the president of the Olimpia Milano basketball team. He is a bisexual.

Alexander The Great, King of Macedonia

The sexuality of Alexander the Great isn't clear but his sexual advances tips him towards being a bisexual. Alexander the Great also known as Alexander III or Alexander of Macedonia born 356 BCE, Pella, Macedonia [northwest of Thessaloniki, Greece and died June 13, 323 BCE, Babylon [near Al-Hillah, Iraq] who overthrow the Persian empire, carried Macedonian armies to India, and laid the foundations for the Hellenistic world of territorial kingdoms. He was the son of Philip II and Olympias. From age 13 to 16, he was taught by Aristotle who inspired him with an interest in philosophy, medicine and scientific investigation.

Left in-charge of Macedonia in 340 BCE during Philip's attack on Byzantium, Alexander defeated the Maedi, a Thracian people. Two years later, he commanded the left wing at the Battle of Chaeronea. A year after the victory, Philip divorced Olympias and after a quarrel at a feast, Alexander and his mother fled to Epirus and Alexander later went to Illyria. In 336, Philip was assassinated and Alexander acclaimed by the army succeeded without opposition. He then marched recovering a wavering Thessaly. Returning to Macedonia by way of Delphi, he advanced into Thrace in spring 335 and after forcing the Shipka Pass and crushing the Triballi, crossed the Danube to disperse the Getae; turning west, he then defeated and shattered a coalition of Illyrians who have invaded Macedonia.

In 14 days, Alexander marched 240 miles from Pelion in Illyria to Thebes. When the Thebans refused to surrender, he made an entry and razed their city to the ground, sparing only temples and Pindar's house; 6,000 were killed and all survivors sold into slavery. During most of years of ruling, he conducted lengthy military campaign throughout Western Asia and Northeastern Africa. By the age of 30, he had created one of the largest empires in history, stretching from Greece to northwestern India. He was undefeated in battle and is widely considered to be one of history's greatest and most successful military commanders.

Following his conquest of Asia Minor (present-day Turkey), Alexander broke the power of Persia in a series of decisive battles including those at Issus and Gaugamela and subsequently overthrew King Darius III and conquered the Achaemenid Empire in its entirety. Alexander endeavored to reach the 'ends of the world and the Great Outer Sea' and invaded India in 326 BC, achieving an important victory over King Porus at the Battle of the Hydaspes. Alexander's legacy includes the cultural diffusion and syncretism which his conquests engendered such as Greco-Buddhism and Hellenistic Judaism. He founded more than twenty cities that bore his name, most notably Alexandria in Egypt.

Alexander's spread of Greek culture resulted in Hellenistic civilization which developed through the Roman Empire into modern western culture. The Greek language became the lingua franca of the region and the predominant language of the Byzantine Empire up until its end in the mid-15th century AD. Military academies globally teach his tactics still and he is often ranked among the most influential people in human history.

King James, I, King of England & Scotland

James I, born June 19, 1566 in Edinburgh Castle, Edinburgh, Scotland and died March 27, 1625, Theobalds, Hertfordshire, England was king of Scotland as James VI from 1567 to 1627 and the first Stuart king of England from 1603 to 1625. James was a strong advocate of royal absolutism. James was the only son of Queen Mary of Scotland and her second husband, Henry Stewart, Lord Darnley. James lost his father when he was only 8 months old. James, a year old became the king of Scotland on July 24, 1567 and his mother, Queen Mary left the kingdom on May 16, 1568 and never saw her son again. The young James was kept fairly isolated but was given a good education until the age of 14.

He studied Greek, French and Latin and made good use of a library of classical and religious writings. James' education aroused in him literary ambitions rarely found in princes but which also tended to make him a pedant. James was kidnapped by William Ruthven, 1st Earl of Gowrie in 1582 and in 1583, James escaped and began to pursue his own policies as king. In 1589 James was married to Anne, the daughter of Fredrick II of Denmark, who in 1594 gave birth to their first son, Prince Henry. In 1584, he secured a series of acts that made him the head of the Presbyterian church in Scotland, with the power to appoint the church bishops. James became king of England when Elizabeth I died on March 24, 1603.

The opening years of his kingship was a time of material prosperity for both England and Scotland. He established peace by speedily ending England's war with Spain in 1604. James left a body of writings which include *'The Essayes of a Prentise in the Divine Art of Poesie"* (1584), two political treatises, *'The True Lawe of Free Monarchies'* (1598) and *'Basilikon Doron'* (1599), in which he expounded his own views on the divine right of kings; *'An Apologie for the Oath of Allegiance'* (1698), *'A Premonition to All Most Mightie Monarches*, (1609) and *Daemonologie* (1597). The 1616 edition of The Political Works of James was edited by Charles Howard McIlwain (1918). James famously oversaw a new authorized English translation of the Bible published in 1611 which became known as the King James Version.

He was a major advocate of a single parliament for England and Scotland. In his reign, the Plantation of Ulster and English colonization of the Americas began. Under James, the 'Golden Age' of Elizabethan literature and drama continued with writers such as William Shakespeare, John Donne, Ben Jonson and Sir Francis Bacon. Throughout his life, James had close relationships with male courtiers, which has caused debate amongst historians about his nature. James had a long relationship with George Villiers, 1st Duke of Buckingham as lovers. Sir John Oglander observed that he "*never yet saw any fond husband make so much or so great dalliance over his beautiful spouse as I have seen King James over his favourites, especially the Duke of Buckingham*" whom the king would, recalled Sir Edward Peyton, "*tumble and kiss as a mistress*". In his later years, James suffered increasingly from arthritis, gout and kidney stones. King James had seven children with Anne of Denmark of whom three reached adulthoods.

Socrates, Greek Philosopher

Socrates born to Sophroniscus, an Athenian sculptor and his mother, Phaenarete, midwife. He had three sons and was married to Xanthippe. He was unattractive by conventional standards due to his snub nose and bulging eyes. He served as a hoplite (a heavily armed soldier) in the Athenian army and fought bravely in several crucial battles. Socrates was physically attracted to beautiful young men. He was remarkable for the absolute command he maintained over his emotions and his apparent indifference to physical hardships.

Corresponding to these personal qualities was his commitment to the doctrine that reason, properly cultivated, can and ought to be the all-controlling factor in human life. To him, fear can only be dispelled by intellectual clarity and that if one believes upon the fear, upon reflection, that one should act in a particular way, then, necessarily, one's feelings about the act in question will accommodate themselves to one's belief. In 399 BCE, Socrates was tried soon after Athens's defeat at the hands of Sparta in the Peloponnesian War of 431-404 BCE leading to his death. He was born 470 BCE in Athens, Greece and his way of life, character, and thoughts exerted a profound influence on Western philosophy. He was a widely recognized and controversial figure in Athens so much that he was frequently mocked in plays of comic dramatists; and the best-known example is *The Clouds of Aristophanes* produced in 423 BCE.

At age 70, he was brought to trial on a charge of impiety and sentenced to death by poisoning by a jury of his fellow citizens. Socrates proposed elaborate answers to issues on justice and defended his views of the ideal society, the condition of the human soul, the nature of reality, and the power of art, among many other topics. To Socrates, a human doesn't need inquire into natural phenomena but s/he must devote one's life to one question only: how can he and others become good human beings or as good as possible. Since he was coming from a noble family, he received basic Greek education and learned his father's craft at a young age. He worked as a mason before he devoted his life to philosophy. He participated in three military campaigns during the Peloponnesian War, at Delium, Amphipolis and Potidaea, where he saved the life of Alcibiades, an Athenian General.

Socrates always emphasized the importance of the mind over the relative unimportance of the human body. This credo inspired Plato's philosophy of dividing reality into two separate realms: the world of the senses and the world of ideas, declaring that the latter was the only important one. Socrates believed that philosophy should achieve practical results for the greater well-being of the society. He attempted to establish an ethical system based on human reason rather than theological doctrine. Socrates pointed out that the human choice was motivated by the desire for happiness and that ultimate wisdom comes from knowing oneself. During Socrates' life, Athens was going through a dramatic transition from hegemony in the classical world to its decline after a humiliating defeat by the Spartans in the Peloponnesian War. Athens entered a period of instability and doubt about their identity and place in the world. As a result, they clung to past glories, notions of wealth and a fixation on physical beauty.

Socrates attacked these values with his insistent emphasis on the greater importance of the mind. While many Athenians admired Socrates' challenge to Greek conventional wisdom and the humorous way he went about it, an equal number grew angry and felt he threatened their way of life and uncertain future. In 399 BCE, he was accused of corrupting the youth of Athens and of impiety, or heresy. He chose to defend himself in court rather to exile himself. Rather than present himself as wrongly accused, Socrates declared he fulfilled an important duty of providing an important service to his community by continually questioning and challenging the status quo and its defenders. The jury was not swayed by Socrates' defenses and convicted him by a vote of 280 to 221. Athenian law allowed a convicted citizen to propose an alternative punishment to the one called for by the prosecution and the jury would decide.

Instead of proposing he be exiled, he suggested he be honored by the city for his contribution to their enlightenment and be paid for his services. The jury was not amused and sentenced him to death by drinking a mixture of poison hemlock. Before his execution, friends offered to bribe the guards and rescue him so he could flee into exile. He declined stating that he wasn't afraid of death, felt he would be no better off if in exile and he was still a loyal citizen of Athens, willing to abide by its laws, even the ones that condemned him to death. Socrates' impact was immense in philosophy after his death. Almost all philosophical currents after Socrates traced their roots to him; he was considered as the man who moved philosophy from a study of the natural world to a study of humanity.

The stoics relied heavily on Socrates and applied the Socratic method as a tool to avoid inconsistencies. Their moral doctrines focused on how to live a smooth life through wisdom and virtue, giving a crucial role to virtue for happiness and the relation between goodness and ethical excellence. Socratic thoughts found its way to the Islamic Middle East alongside that of Aristotle and the Stoics. For Muslim scholars, Socrates was hailed and admired for combing ethics with his lifestyle and his doctrines were altered to match Islamic faith such as his arguments for monotheism, for a caring god in particular and for the temporality of this world and rewards in the next world. In medieval time, little of Socrates thoughts survived in the Christian world as a world yet censored parts especially those which appeared to promote homosexuality or any possibility of pederasty. In modern times, Socrates thoughts marked the turning point of the principles of free subjectivity or self-determination.

CHAPTER X

BREAKING DOWN THE WALLS

"Pause and remember—When you fight reality, you will lose every time. Once you accept the situation for what it truly is, not what you want it to be, you are then free to move forward"—Jennifer Young.

"Life is a series of natural and spontaneous changes. Don't resist them; that only creates sorrow. Let things flow naturally forward in whatever way they like". — Laozi.

The harmonious living of all persons devoid of sexuality and tolerance of sexuality can only be achieved through the promotion of a comprehensive sexuality education. The significance of a sexuality education is to promote health and wellbeing, respect for human rights and gender equality, as well as empowers children and young people to lead healthy, safe and productive lives. With the promotion of comprehensive sexuality education especially in schools and the larger community, people would be taught, educated on the cognitive, emotional, physical and social aspects of sexuality.

This would in the long-term equip children and young people with knowledge, skills, attitudes and values that will empower them to realize their health, wellbeing and dignity; develop respectful social and sexual relationships; consider how their choices affect their own wellbeing and that of others; and understand and ensure the protection of their rights throughout their lives. There is the need for this comprehensive sexuality education because too many at times, people especially young and the illiterates receive confusing and conflicting information about relationships and sex, as they transition from one stage of life to another.

When comprehensive sexuality education is delivered effectively and efficiently, it empowers people to make informed decisions about relationships and sexuality and navigate a world where gender-based violence, gender inequality, early and unintended pregnancies, HIV and other sexually transmitted infections still pose serious risks to their health and wellbeing. In the same breadth, a lack of high-quality-age and developmentally-appropriate sexuality and relationship education may leave children and young people vulnerable to harmful sexual behaviors and sexual exploitation.

Diversity should be considered the very patchwork of our society. It is through diversity that the many gifts and talents we possess enrich and touch our lives. As we look around our communities and within our own families, it is not difficult to discover diversity. Accepting and respecting this diversity helps build a more comprehensive understanding of the human experience and a better society. In an effort to develop lessons that facilitated acceptance and respect for diversity, Contextual Teaching and Learning approach that infuses tolerance and diversity education along with Social Personal Individual Education Plan (IEP) goals and objectives should be encouraged.

Contextual Teaching and Learning (CTL) is based on the premise that people will learn better and remember more when they are able to find meaning in educative lessons. Inherent in this is the belief that people seek to make sense of new information in the context of their existing knowledge and experiences. The concept and guiding principles of CTL are rooted in brain research and the notion that when presented with information, the brain seeks patterns to link new information with familiar knowledge.

As a tenet of CTL is learning will come alive when new information is presented in a systematic manner that takes into consideration the existing schema of the learner; the goal of using CTL is to connect educative content with the social, cultural, physical and psychological experiences of the individuals. In doing so, the meaning for learning is discovered. This meaning then provides motivation and reason for learning. The CTL system emphasizes learning by doing. It is a holistic approach consisting of the following components: (a) making meaningful connections, (b) doing significant work (projects service learning activities, etc.), (c) self-regulating learning, (c) collaborating, (e) critical and creative thinking, (f) nurturing the individual, (g) reaching high standards, and (h) using authentic assessment.

When most people think about the words "diversity," "racism," and/or "tolerance," it is unlikely an image of a school classroom immediately comes to mind. However, this is the very place where educators must ensure that such issues are explored. Through tolerance and diversity education, teachers provide ALL with a solid foundation on which to build. A well-developed tolerance and diversity education program can enhance and promote acceptance and respect of differences while it encourages acculturation and multiculturalism. In turn, this mutual acceptance and interaction serves to sustain and validate the importance of respect for all humanity.

Breaking down the stereotyping of a given culture, disability, race, gender, religion, age, medical conditions, or sexual orientation should be at the foundation of tolerance and diversity education. This process helps ALL understand the role of values and how they help shape character. The process also provides a forum to introduce relationships that exist between history and social change. Tolerance and respect for people with individual differences requires continuous attention if we are to promote respect for diversity and remove barriers faced in communities.

Unfortunately, sexuality discrimination and intolerance towards diversity still exists in our society. Lack of knowledge and education in this area can contribute to intolerance and violence towards members of society. For instance, sometimes the sexuality-related comments heard warrant discussions and can be a source for lesson plans that incorporate Social Personal Skills. When these episodes occur, people need to know that such issues are real and visible within our communities. As educators of sexual inclusion and diversity, willingly or unwillingly, we play an important role in this process. An individual who acts in a socially responsible manner to triumph in spite of personal differences can make a positive contribution to our very diverse society.

One strategy to accomplish this and simultaneously contest prejudices is to use a multicultural instructional approach that fosters tolerance and respect for diversity. Such an approach benefits ALL. We must strive to encourage ALL to be tolerant and respectful of differences. This requires educators, parents, community leaders, state governments to help individuals realize that intolerance and negative attitudes towards others, merely due to their diversity, is detrimental not only to the person in question, but also to oneself. Stereotypical knowledge and beliefs about sexuality and gender limit the perspective people have available.

The state must provide accurate timely information in order to assist citizens in their formation of attitudes towards tolerance, respect, and acceptance of diversity. The information and education should include positive effective instruction on how to get along with others who may be different. Citizens must be able to work together in order to solve the many problems that they will encounter throughout their lives. Additionally, they will need to take a closer look at how values can be used as building blocks when confronted with barriers and social problems that occur in our diverse society.

The first step involves the self-examination of personal beliefs and biases. The acknowledgement that people tend to act on their beliefs is important for in many respects, we are what we do. It is undeniable that what we do as individuals is influenced by our values and biases. The second step requires an assessment of the personal beliefs and behaviors of the individuals. It is important to take inventory of where persons are in order to determine a course of action. Knowing the cultural background and underlying beliefs of a person provides the opportunity to develop lessons and activities from a multicultural framework. This information is used in the third step to incorporate newly created activities within plans that also infuses Social Personal IEP goals and objectives. Teaching the lessons is the fourth step. Since the goal is to change behavior and promote acceptance and respect for diversity.

The first step begins with the self-examination of personal biases towards tolerance and diversity. Before attempting to understand the diversity and the uniqueness of others, there should be the analysis of their personal preferences and tendencies. *"Knowledge is within the meanings people make of it; knowledge is gained through people talking about their meanings; knowledge is laced with personal biases and values; knowledge is written in a personal, up-close way; and knowledge evolves, emerges, and is inextricably tied to the context in which it is studied"*. The premise for this first step is that individuals must be mindful of their own cultural self-awareness in order to recognize the cultural underpinnings of their professional practice.

Conducting an honest self-inventory to identify personal beliefs and biases is critical. It is crucial that responses to the questions be truthful and candid. Taken seriously, this process helps identify cultural values embedded in interpretations of a people's difficulty. The discussions provide the opportunity to examine and identify biases and potential misconceptions in an informative and thorough manner. This assessment and awareness process results in clarifying respective personal values as well as those of the community and society at-large. As people engage in the values clarification process, it is vital that no one set of values or bias dominates the discussion. The process brings about a conscience effort to understand and respect tolerance and diversity.

The underlying assumption for this step is that the better individuals understand their personal and peers value systems, the more likely they would be to resist making unfounded and rash judgments about others. Furthermore, dialogue would allow ALL to openly acknowledge and recognize difference identified amongst them. The goal is to establish a foundation for respect of one another's cultural, sexual and racial differences.

The goals at the third stage are to: (a) create an inclusive and accepting environment for all the diverse learners present; (b) develop meaningful lessons and activities that present new knowledge in context of the peoples' existing frame of reference; and (c) infuse targeted Social Personal

IEP goals and objectives. Since one of the original reasons for adopting the CTL approach is to reduce problem behaviors and increase respectful behaviors, the notion that acting in the role of a bystander who does nothing can be as hurtful and distressing as committing an injustice or callous act, serving as a guiding tenet for the lessons and activities developed.

The concrete and often hands-on lessons that evolve help individuals and groups in three specific ways. First, they became aware of views outside their original box of beliefs. Second, the activities serve to increase exposure and a knowledge base for grasping the content. Finally, the activities provide them with knowledge and strategies for use in our ever-increasing diverse world. Designing the units and specific lessons require a thorough understanding of the traditional values and norms, then identifying which current events, groups and individuals' interests, and specific Social Personal objectives to infuse, teach, and/or reinforce.

To accomplish this, a pool of activities should be developed that infuse specific Social Personal Curriculum objectives. Alignment of the activities to the content involve thinking through and linking current issues and interests with historical events. It is important to begin teaching the concept of diversity with concrete examples. Keeping the initial lessons concrete and focused on the diversity within the society allows ALL individuals to become familiar with the respective culture each person brings. This provides an opportunity to discover common ground for communication among ALL individuals in the society. The initial lessons on diversity and tolerance should start with showing a selection of a sampled individual family. The rich discussions should center on the subjects of character, sexuality, gender, intelligence, integrity, citizenship, discrimination, and resiliency. The sexual and gender differences within the family provides the visual representation needed to bring home the importance of tolerance and acceptance of diversity, especially in this ever changing world filled with nontraditional families.

Many of the most divisive issues in our culture fall into the sexual domain. Consider one that many communities struggle with: the issue of sexual orientation. There are seven points issues examined—matters of truth and fairness—that can guide communities and societies in implementing an approach to tolerance and diversity education that is respectful of diverse conscience concerning the complex issue of sexual orientation.

Communities must teach members to respect all people and should not tolerate violence or harassment toward any member for any reason. All persons, regardless of sexual orientation, deserve to be treated with justice and respect. Currently they are not; people are constantly calling each other 'fags.' Or they say, 'You're so gay. ' Slurs such as these and other demeaning language or harassment based on sexual orientation should not be permitted in the larger environment any more than we permit ethnic, racial, or religious denigration.

A 'zero tolerance' policy for disrespectful behavior, however, is not enough. Comprehensive character education, integrated into every phase of life—from the parent's example to the handling of rules and discipline to the extracurricular program—is needed to develop an inner attitude of respect for all persons and to establish respect as normative within the broader social culture. Citizens should be made aware of the harassment some citizens have suffered because of their sexual orientation. State governments, traditional authorities and civil society organizations, which are in the best position to influence the peer culture, should be assigned a leadership role in creating an environment that is safe and respectful for all.

While teaching tolerance as respect for persons, societies must also teach respect for diversity of moral and religious conscience concerning sexual behavior. If societies treat the issue of sexual orientation, they must in truth teach that while some people consider homosexual and bisexual sex morally acceptable, others do not. Parents, educators and the civil society should make it clear that to have conscience-based objections to certain sexual behaviors does not make a person 'prejudiced'.

People should learn what a prejudice is: a judgment that someone is inferior as a person because he or she is a member of a certain race, gender, or other group. By contrast, moral judgments concerning homosexual sex, bisexual sex, or premarital heterosexual sex are judgments about the rightness of certain sexual behaviors, not judgments about the worth or dignity of persons. One can affirm persons without affirming their sexual behavior. To help people understand the difference between a prejudice and a conscience-based belief about sex, one needs to explain the larger vision of sexuality that might lead a person to disapprove of certain sexual behaviors.

For example, orthodox Catholic and Protestant Christians, Muslims, and orthodox Jews believe (though individual members of these faith traditions sometimes dissent from their religion's historical teaching) that sexual intimacy is reserved by God for a husband and wife in marriage. In this view, the two purposes of sex—the expression of faithful, committed love in a complementary union and the procreation of new life issuing from that union—can be fulfilled only in heterosexual marriage. By this standard, all forms of sex outside heterosexual marriage are considered wrong. Homosexual persons, like single heterosexuals, may enjoy intellectual, emotional, and spiritual intimacy with other persons but are called to refrain from sexual intimacy and to live chastely with the help of God's grace.

These are truth claims, rooted in a world view. Others are certainly free to disagree with this vision. But it is not reasonable, respectful, or just—either to individuals or their families—to denigrate a conscience-based objection to sex outside heterosexual marriage by labeling it ‚homophobic‘ or ‚heterosexist‘ and then treating it as if it were the moral equivalent of racism, sexism, and gender inequalities. The message of tolerance and diversity education should not be, '*Abandon your moral and religious beliefs*', but rather, '**Treat all persons with respect, no matter how strongly you may disagree with them**'.

If we wish to foster this ethic of respect, we will be careful to use a language of respect. Terms like ‚homophobia" may not meet that standard. If 'homophobia' were used only to mean "fear or hatred of homosexuals", all persons of character would agree we should reject such irrational attitudes. But "homophobia" is often either not defined or used in a broad-brush way to refer disparagingly to any disapproving judgment of homosexuality. 'Homophobia' is an ambiguous term at best, insulting at worst, and not likely to contribute to the mutual respect needed for ethical discourse about this sensitive issue.

The state can create a safe, caring, and welcoming community for all citizens without affirming all the lifestyle choices and sexual identities that may be present in its communities. Proposals to affirm 'sexual minorities' through discussions of gay families or through curricular integration of 'famous gay people' may be well-meaning, inspired by the wish to help all students feel recognized and validated. But this approach does not work if the basis for validation is morally controversial. Societies can and should affirm all members of their communities by treating everyone with warmth and respect, nurturing the gifts of all, and inviting all to contribute actively to the life of the state.

The state cannot, however, legitimately treat a controversial sexual behavior as a "cultural category" comparable to race, ethnicity, or religion and then affirm that sexual category in the name of having an "anti-bias curriculum." For the state to affirm homosexual sexual activity in this way is to abuse its moral authority by giving officials approval to a behavior that many people, as a matter of conscience, believe to be morally wrong.

The origins of sexual orientation are uncertain. Many think there is a "gene" that "causes" a person to have a particular sexual orientation while amongst others, it is the agenda and tool of the 'devil' to destroy God's chosen ones and nations. Societies can correct this misconception by teaching the scientific truth: Research reveals no consensus on the factors influencing sexual orientation. There is no certainty of evidence at present to substantiate a biological theory, just as there is no evidence to support any single psychological explanation'.

Health education should promote abstinence for all youth regardless of sexual orientation. In deciding how to approach the issue of sexual orientation, societies must decide what to say in health education. The stakes are high. All should learn that sexual intimacy outside a monogamous commitment is high-risk behavior regardless of who your partner is. They should know that, condoms provide less than complete protection against HIV, the AIDS virus (87% protection if used correctly 100% of the time); some protection against gonorrhea for men; but no reliably proven protection against other STDs, including herpes, chlamydia, syphilis, and human papilloma virus (the cause of virtually all cervical cancer).

Societies should know that HIV can be transmitted to both heterosexual and homosexual males and females through oral sex, which is now on the rise as early as middle school. Human papilloma virus can also be transmitted through oral sex. Condoms are more likely to tear and fail during anal sex (compared to vaginal intercourse). And—what is at least as important—there is no condom for the heart.

Providing help for people who believe they are homosexual or bisexual or are unsure of their orientation must be done in a way that does not put them at greater risk. In a study by Remafedi (1991) of 34,707 Minnesota teens, 25.9% of 12-year-olds said they were uncertain whether they were heterosexual or homosexual. By adulthood, approximately 2% of the population self-identifies as homosexual according to the 1990 report of the University of Chicago's National Opinion Research Center. Another study by Remafedi (1991) found, as have other researchers, a significantly higher risk of attempted suicide among teens who identify themselves as homosexual or bisexual. However, the data showed that for each year's delay in bisexual or homosexual self-labeling, the odds of a suicide attempt significantly diminished.

People who are struggling with issues of sexual orientation clearly need appropriate counseling and the experiences of belonging (having friends, feeling a sense of community in the family, participating in extra-curricular activities, etc.) that all need. But some families and communities, perhaps with the best of intentions, have taken further steps such as forming 'gay/straight alliances' (that often encourage individuals to 'come out' and ‚live the truth about themselves'), establishing gay clubs, and connecting individuals to gay community organizations.

In the light of the above data, it is reasonable to ask whether such actions may in fact put individuals at greater risk—by leading them to prematurely (and perhaps erroneously) identify themselves as homosexual or bisexual. In their 1995 Handbook of Child and Adolescent Sexual Problems, psychiatrists Michael Lundy and George Rekers point to another danger: Once an adolescent male identifies himself as gay, he is likely to initiate homosexual sexual activity that involves life-threatening health risks. Epidemiologists estimate that 30% of all 20-year-old sexually active homosexual males will be HIV-positive by the time they are 30. According to the Austin-based Medical Institute for Sexual Health, homosexually active males are also at significantly increased risk for other STDs, including hepatitis, gonorrhea, anal cancer, and gastrointestinal infections.

Finally, tolerance and diversity education should teach individuals that persons of conscience often disagree about public policies concerning sexual behavior, especially in cases where rights conflict. A person's sexual choices, whether heterosexual or homosexual, may collide with other people's rights and legitimate interests. Reasonable persons may differ as to how such conflicts should be resolved, but respect for conscience must always be taken into account. For example, in California the state Supreme Court ruled in favor of a couple who, on grounds of religious conscience, refused to rent to an unmarried heterosexual couple that was cohabiting. The courts ruled that New York City could not compel a church to hire child-care workers who professed a sexual lifestyle that violated the church's teachings. Similarly, most religious denominations do not admit practicing homosexuals to the ordained ministry, just as those faiths that permit clergy to marry would not ordain a heterosexual who is sexually active outside marriage—for the reason that such individuals would not be able to serve as role models for the faith's teachings regarding sexual morality.

Consider a parallel case: the continuing, often acrimonious debate about the Boy Scouts' policy disqualifying professed homosexuals from leadership or membership. A woman in wrote a letter to an editor criticizing local schools and churches for 'supporting bigotry against homosexuals' by permitting Scouts to meet on their property. Is this a fair accusation? The Scouts' policy, like the above-mentioned restrictions on religious ordination, is based on what the organization sees as a relevant moral standard. Others may disagree, but does it make sense to say, 'I reserve the right to approve of homosexuality, and I insist you do, too, even if it violates your conscience to do so'?

Historically, respect for moral and religious conscience has been one of the distinguishing virtues of democratic societies. Totalitarian societies have no respect for conscience; their jails, as any Amnesty International report will document, are full of prisoners of conscience. And yet, in our discourse about diversity, the language of conscience is conspicuously absent. Perhaps this is because to confront matters of moral and religious conscience is to bring our deepest differences to the fore. The sociologist James Hunter, observes: *'For all the talk of multiculturalism and celebrating difference, ours is a society that is scared to death of difference'*.

In the quest for inclusiveness, Hunter says, we seek a 'safe' morality and end up with a standard of tolerance and diversity that is, ironically, intolerant of the judgments of conscience. What, then, are the moral imperatives facing tolerance and diversity education? At least two: First, to take every possible step to create an environment that assures safety and respect for every person. Second, to take equal measures to foster respect for moral and religious conscience. For tolerance that does not respect conscience is not tolerance at all, and there can be no authentic diversity unless we honor the integrity of personal conscience.

BIBLIOGRAPHY

Balsam, R. H. (2009). Sexuality and Shame: SENSUALITY AND SEXUALITY ACROSS THE DIVIDE OF SHAME. By Joseph Lichtenberg. Psychoanalytic Inquiry Book Series, Volume 25. New York: The Analytic Press, 2008, 160 pp., $34.95. SHAME AND SEXUALITY: PSYCHOANALYSIS AND VISUAL CULTURE. Edited by Claire Pajaczkowska and Ivan Ward. London: Routledge, 2008, 242 pp., £19.99. Journal of the American Psychoanalytic Association, 57(3), 723-739.

Balthazart, J. (2011). Minireview: Hormones and human sexual orientation. Endocrinology, 152(8), 2937-2947.

Bamforth, N. (1995). Sexuality and Law in the New Europe.

Bamforth, N. (2012). Sexuality and citizenship in contemporary constitutional argument. International journal of constitutional law, 10(2), 477-492.

Bateman, P. W., & Bennett, N. C. (2006). The biology of human sexuality: evolution, ecology and physiology. Verbum et Ecclesia, 27(1), 245-264.

Bates, T. (1996). Decades ago, an Oregon Doctor Tried to Redefine Gender. *The Oregonian, Section B, pp. 1-5.*

Becker, M. E. (1996). Discrimination Helps Companies Trade on Women's Sexuality. ABA Journal, 82, 40.

Belda Junior, W. (2020). Donovanose. Anais Brasileiros de Dermatologia, 95(6), 675-683.

Birksted-Breen, D. (2016). The work of psychoanalysis: Sexuality, time and the psychoanalytic mind. Routledge.

Blackburn, J. A., & Dulmus, C. N. (Eds.). (2007). Handbook of gerontology: Evidence-based approaches to theory, practice, and policy. John Wiley & Sons.

Blackmer, C. E. (1995). The Veils of the Law: Race and Sexuality in Nella Larsen's Passing. College Literature, 22(3), 50-67.

Blechner, M. J. (2016). Psychoanalysis and sexual issues. Contemporary Psychoanalysis, 52(4), 502-546.

Bowden, F. J. (2005). Donovanosis in Australia: going, going.... Sexually transmitted infections, 81(5), 365-366.

Branson, B. M., Handsfield, H. H., Lampe, M. A., Janssen, R. S., Taylor, A. W., Lyss, S. B., & Clark, J. E. (2006). Revised recommendations for HIV testing of adults, adolescents, and pregnant women in health-care settings. Morbidity and Mortality Weekly Report: Recommendations and Reports, 55(14), 1-CE.

Buss, D. M., & Schmitt, D. P. (1993). Sexual strategies theory: an evolutionary perspective on human mating. Psychological review, 100(2), 204.

Carpenter, L. M. (2010). Gendered sexuality over the life course: A conceptual framework. Sociological Perspectives, 53(2), 155-177.

Cooper, J. M., & Sánchez, P. J. (2018, April). Congenital syphilis. In Seminars in perinatology (Vol. 42, No. 3, pp. 176-184). WB Saunders.

Daniluk, J. C. (1999). When biology isn't destiny: Implications for the sexuality of women without children. Canadian Journal of Counselling and Psychotherapy, 33(2).

de la Maza, L. M., Zhong, G., & Brunham, R. C. (2017). Update on Chlamydia trachomatis vaccinology. Clinical and Vaccine Immunology, 24(4), e00543-16.

Delphy, C. (1993, January). Rethinking sex and gender. In Women's Studies International Forum (Vol. 16, No. 1, pp. 1-9). Pergamon.

Dialmy, A. (2010). Sexuality and Islam. The European Journal of Contraception & Reproductive Health Care, 15(3), 160-168.

Dimen, M. (2005). Sexuality and suffering, or the eew! Factor. Studies in Gender and Sexuality, 6(1), 1-18.

Dimijian, G. G. (2005, July). Evolution of sexuality: biology and behavior. In Baylor University Medical Center Proceedings (Vol. 18, No. 3, pp. 244-258). Taylor & Francis.

Dixson, A. F. (1998). Primate sexuality: comparative studies of the prosimians, monkeys, apes, and human beings. Oxford University Press, USA.

Dixson, A. F. (2009). The evolutionary biology of human female sexuality.

Domes, K., Norton, R. A., Maraun, M., & Scheu, S. (2007). Reevolution of sexuality breaks Dollo's law. Proceedings of the National Academy of Sciences, 104(17), 7139-7144.

Dowell, D., & Kirkcaldy, R. D. (2012). Effectiveness of gentamicin for gonorrhoea treatment: systematic review and meta-analysis. Sexually transmitted infections, 88(8), 589-594.

Eisenberg, M. E., Madsen, N., Oliphant, J. A., Sieving, R. E., & Resnick, M. (2010). "Am I qualified? How do I Know?" A qualitative study of sexuality educators' training experiences. American Journal of Health Education, 41(6), 337-344.

Estellon, V., & Mouras, H. (2012). Sexual addiction: Insights from psychoanalysis and functional neuroimaging. Socioaffective Neuroscience & Psychology, 2(1), 11814.

Fellmeth, A. X. (2008). State regulation of sexuality in international human rights law and theory. Wm. & Mary L. Rev., 50, 797.

Finnis, J. M. (1993). Law, morality, and sexual orientation. Notre Dame L. Rev., 69, 1049.

Ford, A. T., Fernandes, T. F., Rider, S. A., Read, P. A., Robinson, C. D., & Davies, I. M. (2004). Endocrine disruption in a marine amphipod? Field observations of intersexuality and de-masculinisation. Marine environmental research, 58(2-5), 169-173.

Fortenberry, J. D., McFarlane, M. M., Hennessy, M., Bull, S. S., Grimley, D. M., St Lawrence, J., ...

& VanDevanter, N. (2001). Relation of health literacy to gonorrhoea related care. Sexually transmitted infections, 77(3), 206-211.

Gamson, J., & Moon, D. (2004). The sociology of sexualities: Queer and beyond. Annu. Rev. Sociol., 30, 47-64.

Ganesh, S. (2008). Assimilation, sexuality and the contours of relational care in Academe. Women's Studies in Communication, 31(2), 268-275.

Giffney, N., & Watson, E. (2017). Clinical encounters in sexuality: Psychoanalytic practice and queer theory (p. 494). Punctum books.

Giugliano, J. R. (2003). A psychoanalytic overview of excessive sexual behavior and addiction. Sexual Addiction & Compulsivity, 10(4), 275-290.

Glynos, J. (2000). Sexual identity, identification and difference: a psychoanalytic contribution to discourse theory. Philosophy & Social Criticism, 26(6), 85-108.

Goh, B. T. (2005). Syphilis in adults. Sexually transmitted infections, 81(6), 448-452.

Goldschmidt, R. (1917). Intersexuality and the endocrine aspect of sex. Endocrinology, 1(4), 433-456.

Gutiérrez, R. A. (2012). Islam and sexuality. Social Identities, 18(2), 155-159.

Haggerty, C. L., Gottlieb, S. L., Taylor, B. D., Low, N., Xu, F., & Ness, R. B. (2010). Risk of sequelae after Chlamydia trachomatis genital infection in women. The Journal of infectious diseases, 201(Supplement_2), S134-S155.

Hardy, S. A., & Raffaelli, M. (2003). Adolescent religiosity and sexuality: An investigation of reciprocal influences. Journal of adolescence, 26(6), 731-739.

Heinze, E. (2000). Sexual orientation and international law: A study in the manufacture of cross-cultural sensitivity. Mich. J. Int'l L., 22, 283.

Holmberg, S. D., Moorman, A. C., Williamson, J. M., Tong, T. C., Ward, D. J., Wood, K. C., ... & HIV Outpatient Study (HOPS) Investigators. (2002). Protease inhibitors and cardiovascular outcomes in patients with HIV-1. The Lancet, 360(9347), 1747-1748.

Holtgrave, D. R., & Crosby, R. A. (2003). Social capital, poverty, and income inequality as predictors of gonorrhoea, syphilis, chlamydia and AIDS case rates in the United States. Sexually transmitted infections, 79(1), 62-64.

Jackson, S., & Scott, S. (2007). Faking like a woman? Towards an interpretive theorization of sexual pleasure. Body & Society, 13(2), 95-116.

Jackson, S., & Scott, S. (2010). Rehabilitating interactionism for a feminist sociology of sexuality. Sociology, 44(5), 811-826.

Jenzen, O., & Munt, S. R. (2016). Queer theory, sexuality and religion. The Ashgate research companion to contemporary religion and sexuality, 61-74.

Kaufmann, G. R., Perrin, L., Pantaleo, G., Opravil, M., Furrer, H., Telenti, A., ... & Swiss HIV Cohort Study Group. (2003). CD4 T-lymphocyte recovery in individuals with advanced HIV-1 infection receiving potent antiretroviral therapy for 4 years: The Swiss HIV Cohort Study. Archives of internal medicine, 163(18), 2187-2195.

Kernberg, O. F. (2011). The sexual couple: A psychoanalytic exploration. The Psychoanalytic Review, 98(2), 217-245.

Kitzinger, C. (1999). Intersexuality: Deconstructing the sex/gender binary. Feminism & Psychology, 9(4), 493-498.

Korenromp, E. L., Sudaryo, M. K., de Vlas, S. J., Gray, R. H., Sewankambo, N. K., Serwadda, D., ... & Habbema, J. D. F. (2002). What proportion of episodes of gonorrhoea and chlamydia becomes symptomatic? International journal of STD & AIDS, 13(2), 91-101.

LaFond, R. E., & Lukehart, S. A. (2006). Biological basis for syphilis. Clinical microbiology reviews, 19(1), 29-49.

Lanjouw, E. (2017). Chlamydia trachomatis: Clinical, bacterial, and host aspects of a silent love bug.

Lewis, D. A. (2000). Diagnostic tests for chancroid. Sexually transmitted infections, 76(2), 137-141.

Lewis, D. A. (2003). Chancroid: clinical manifestations, diagnosis, and management. Sexually transmitted infections, 79(1), 68-71.

Lickona, T. (2016). Tolerance, diversity, and respect for conscience: The neglected issue. State University of New York at Cortland.

Lingiardi, V., & Capozzi, P. (2004). Psychoanalytic attitudes towards homosexuality: An empirical research. The International Journal of Psychoanalysis, 85(1), 137-157.

Lucal, B. (1999). What it means to be gendered me: Life on the boundaries of a dichotomous gender system. Gender & Society, 13(6), 781-797.

Lynn, W. A., & Lightman, S. (2004). Syphilis and HIV: a dangerous combination. The Lancet infectious diseases, 4(7), 456-466.

Marlink, R., Kanki, P., Thior, I., Travers, K., Eisen, G., Siby, T., ... & Gueye, E. H. (1994). Reduced rate of disease development after HIV-2 infection as compared to HIV-1. Science, 265(5178), 1587-1590.

Martin, P. Y. (2004). Gender as social institution. Social forces, 82(4), 1249-1273.

McClelland, S. I., & Frost, D. M. (2014). Sexuality and social policy. In APA handbook of sexuality and psychology, Vol. 2: Contextual approaches. (pp. 311-337). American Psychological Association.

Miller, K. J., & Sessions, M. M. (2005). Infusing Tolerance, Diversity, and Social Personal Curriculum into Inclusive Social Studies Classes Using Family Portraits and Contextual Teaching and Learning. Teaching Exceptional Children Plus, 1(3), n3.

Mir-Hosseini, Z. (1800). Sexuality, Rights, and Islam: Competing Gender Discourses in Postrevolutionary Iran. Na.

Morse, S. A. (1989). Chancroid and Haemophilus ducreyi. Clinical Microbiology Reviews, 2(2), 137-157.

Moss, K. (2005). From sworn virgins to transvestite prostitutes: performing gender and sexuality in two films from Yugoslavia. Sexuality and gender in postcommunist Eastern Europe and Russia, 79-94.

Nagel, J. (2003). Race, ethnicity, and sexuality: Intimate intersections, forbidden frontiers (Vol. 2). New York: Oxford University Press.

Nichols, M. (1990). Lesbian relationships: Implications for the study of sexuality and gender. Homosexuality/heterosexuality: Concepts of sexual orientation, 350-364.

O'Farrell, N., & Moi, H. (2010). European guideline for the management of donovanosis, 2010. International journal of STD & AIDS, 21(9), 609-610.

Ojo, M. A. (2005, June). Religion and sexuality: Individuality, choice and sexual rights in Nigerian Christianity. In Understanding Human Sexuality Seminar Series (Vol. 4, pp. 1-15).

Paavonen, J., & Eggert-Kruse, W. (1999). Chlamydia trachomatis: impact on human reproduction. Human reproduction update, 5(5), 433-447.

Patil, V. (2013). From patriarchy to intersectionality: A transnational feminist assessment of how far we've really come. Signs: Journal of Women in Culture and Society, 38(4), 847-867.

Pickett, B. L. (2004). Natural Law and the Regulation of Sexuality: A Critique. Rich. JL & Pub. Int., 8, 39.

Preves, S. E. (2002). Sexing the intersexed: an analysis of sociocultural responses to intersexuality. Signs: Journal of women in Culture and Society, 27(2), 523-556.

Reed, G. M., Drescher, J., Krueger, R. B., Atalla, E., Cochran, S. D., First, M. B., ... & Saxena, S. (2016). Disorders related to sexuality and gender identity in the ICD-11: revising the ICD-10 classification based on current scientific evidence, best clinical practices, and human rights considerations. World Psychiatry, 15(3), 205-221.

rgp120 HIV Vaccine Study Group. (2005). Placebo-controlled phase 3 trial of a recombinant glycoprotein 120 vaccine to prevent HIV-1 infection. The Journal of infectious diseases, 191(5), 654-665.

Richardson, D. (1998). Sexuality and citizenship. Sociology, 32(1), 83-100.

Richardson, D. (2007). Patterned fluidities⊗Re) imagining the relationship between gender and sexuality. Sociology, 41(3), 457-474.

Risley, C. L., Ward, H., Choudhury, B., Bishop, C. J., Fenton, K. A., Spratt, B. G., ... & Ghani, A. C. (2007). Geographical and demographic clustering of gonorrhoea in London. Sexually transmitted infections, 83(6), 481-487.

Rutter, V., & Schwartz, P. (2011). The gender of sexuality: Exploring sexual possibilities. Rowman & Littlefield Publishers.

Sanjakdar, F. (2018). Can difference make a difference? A critical theory discussion of religion in sexuality education. Discourse: Studies in the Cultural Politics of Education, 39(3), 393-407.

Schmidt, R. A., & Voss, B. L. (2005). Archaeologies of sexuality. Routledge.

Schober, J. M. (1999). Long-term outcomes and changing attitudes to intersexuality. BJU international, 83(s 3), 39-50.

Smith, G. P. (1983). Sexuality, Privacy and the New Biology. Marq. L. Rev., 67, 263.

Spinola, S. M., Bauer, M. E., & Munson Jr, R. S. (2002). Immunopathogenesis of Haemophilus ducreyi infection (chancroid). Infection and immunity, 70(4), 1667-1676.

Stein, A. (2004). From gender to sexuality and back again: Notes on the politics of sexual knowledge. GLQ: A Journal of Lesbian and Gay Studies, 10(2), 254-257.

Sullivan, N. (2009). The somatechnics of intersexuality.

Symons, D. (1980). Précis of The evolution of human sexuality. Behavioral and Brain Sciences, 3(2), 171-181.

Tomsen, S., & Mason, G. (2001). Engendering homophobia: Violence, sexuality and gender conformity. Journal of Sociology, 37(3), 257-273.

Trees, D. L., & Morse, S. A. (1995). Chancroid and Haemophilus ducreyi: an update. Clinical Microbiology Reviews, 8(3), 357-375.

Uzzell, D., & Horne, N. (2006). The influence of biological sex, sexuality and gender role on interpersonal distance. British Journal of Social Psychology, 45(3), 579-597.

Wake, N. (2008). Sexuality, intimacy and subjectivity in social psychoanalytic thought of the 1920s and 1930s. Journal of community & applied social psychology, 18(2), 119-130.

Wake, N. (2008). Sexuality, intimacy and subjectivity in social psychoanalytic thought of the 1920s and 1930s. Journal of community & applied social psychology, 18(2), 119-130.

Warnke, G. (2001). Intersexuality and the Categories of Sex. Hypatia, 16(3), 126-137.

Whittles, L. K., White, P. J., Paul, J., & Didelot, X. (2018). Epidemiological trends of antibiotic resistant gonorrhoea in the United Kingdom. Antibiotics, 7(3), 60.

Wiley, D., & Bortz, W. M. (1996). Sexuality and aging—usual and successful. The Journals of Gerontology Series A: Biological Sciences and Medical Sciences, 51(3), M142-M146.

Wolkomir, M. (2009). Making heteronormative reconciliations: The story of romantic love, sexuality, and gender in mixed-orientation marriages. Gender & Society, 23(4), 494-519.

World Health Organization. (2015). Sexual health, human rights and the law. World Health Organization.

World Health Organization. (2016). WHO guidelines for the treatment of Chlamydia trachomatis.

Young, P. D., Shipley, H., & Trothen, T. J. (Eds.). (2015). Religion and sexuality: Diversity and the limits of tolerance. Ubc Press.

Yusuf, B. (2005). Sexuality and the marriage institution in Islam: An appraisal. Afr. Regional Sexuality Res. Center.

www.ingramcontent.com/pod-product-compliance
Lightning Source LLC
Chambersburg PA
CBHW070747230426
43665CB00017B/2276